Thoreau Amongst Friends

Thoreau

AMONGST FRIENDS
AND PHILISTINES
AND OTHER
THOREAUVIANA

BY
Dr. Samuel Arthur Jones

EDITED BY
George Hendrick

OHIO UNIVERSITY PRESS
ATHENS, OHIO, LONDON

Preface & Introduction © Copyright 1982 by George Hendrick "Thoreau: An
Appreciation," "Thoreau Amongst Friends and Philistines" © Copyright
Ohio University Press

Library of Congress Cataloging in Publication Data

Jones, Samuel Arthur, 1834-1912.
Thoreau amongst friends and Philistines, and other Thoreauviana.

Includes bibliographical references.
1. Thoreau, Henry David, 1817-1862—Addresses, essays, lectures.
2. Authors, American—19th century—Biography—Addresses, essays, lectures. I. Hendrick, George. II. Title.

PS3053.J617 1983   818'.309   82-6444
                                    AACR2
ISBN 0-8214-0675-2

Contents

Preface

NOT many years after the death of the homeopathic physician and Thoreauvian scholar Dr. Samuel Arthur Jones (1834–1919), his son, Professor P. V. B. Jones of the Department of History of the University of Illinois, moved his father's papers and many of his books to Urbana, Illinois. Professor Jones carefully preserved his father's collection, but he did not, for whatever reasons, let American-literature scholars know of its existence.

During the summer of 1974, when I was an associate member of the University of Illinois Center for Advanced Study, I was engaged in writing a book on Henry S. Salt, Thoreau's English biographer and one of Dr. Jones's friends. I knew of the long correspondence between Salt and Dr. Jones and had searched without success for it when, serendipitously, through a chance remark overheard by my friend Clark Spence, I learned that at least one Salt letter was extant—and in Urbana. In fact, I found the Salt part of the correspondence in Professor Jones's house, located only a few hundred feet away from the Center for Advanced Study, where I had been working daily for several months. Professor Jones had been dead for some years, but his widow allowed me to search the house for more of Dr. Jones's papers. In a trunk in a bedroom, in a secret compartment in a desk, in the library, and in boxes in the attic, I found Dr. Jones's professional and scholarly papers, and his correspondence both with leading Thoreau enthusiasts and scholars and with peo-

ple who had known the
Thoreaus. I also found
letters by Thoreau, Long-
fellow, Dr. Holmes, Mrs.
Stowe, and other writers.
The University of Illinois
has now acquired the Jones
Collection, including many
of the rare books Dr. Jones
had collected; his Thoreau
first editions, his immense
Carlyle collection, and his
medical books had been sold
not long after his death to
meet some immediate pressing financial needs of his
family, but the remainder of
the collection was intact.

Copies of many of Dr.
Jones's Thoreau articles
were in the collection, and I
found mention of others in
his correspondence and in
Thoreau bibliographies.
After reading the ones
available to me, I became
convinced that a volume of
the Thoreau essays should
be published. The Univer-
sity of Michigan Library
furnished me with a set of
Dr. Jones's articles in the
Inlander, a journal published on that campus, and
has given me permission to
publish the essays. Brown

University gave me per-
mission to print an unpublished article by Dr. Jones
from the Albert E. Lownes
Thoreau Collection, Brown
University Library. I found
"Thoreau amongst Friends
and Philistines," Dr. Jones's
last extended Thoreau work,
in a secret compartment of
a desk in the Jones home. It
is being published for the
first time in this volume;
permission to publish was
granted by the Rare Book
Room of the University
of Illinois.

The Concord Free Public
Library has allowed me to
publish Dr. Jones's letters to
Fred Hosmer. I am grateful
to librarians at the University of Illinois and the
Concord Free Public Library
for their assistance. I am
also indebted to the late
Mrs. P. V. B. Jones and the
late Miss Mary Cooley, Dr.
Jones's granddaughter for
their help. I owe a special
debt of gratitude to Sylvia
Arnstein, who, while
staying with Mrs. P. V. B.
Jones, found a letter of
Henry Salt to Dr. Jones
and mentioned that fact to

Clark Spence of the University of Illinois history department. He knew I was searching for the letters and therefore called me immediately. Miss Arnstein helped me with the search for Thoreauviana in the following weeks. Had it not been for Miss Arnstein and Professor Spence, the Jones Collection would not have been discovered and this volume, and several others, would not have been possible. My work has been aided also by Fritz Oehlschlaeger; by Dr. Jones's grandchildren, Paul Haller Jones, Samuel N. Jones, and Agnes Kay; and by Dean Emeritus Robert W. Rogers and Director Daniel Alpert of the University of Illinois. My work has also benefited from conversations over a long period with my colleagues Nina Baym and Jack Stillinger. Finally, I wish to thank the Research Board of the university for its continued and generous support.

George Hendrick

University of Illinois at Urbana-Champaign

Introduction

DR. SAMUEL ARTHUR JONES (1834–1912) was one of the important Thoreauvian scholars of the nineteenth century, but his essays and studies are exceedingly difficult to locate. Some appeared in the *Inlander* magazine published by the University of Michigan, his books on Thoreau were published in limited editions of from ninety to two hundred copies each, and some of his most significant writing was not published at all but remained unread in a son's home for over fifty years. This is not to say that Dr. Jones has been completely ignored; two of our major modern Thoreau scholars saw to it that his contributions to Thoreau scholarship were not forgotten: Professor Raymond Adams, a dean of our tribe, wrote in the *Thoreau Society Bulletin* of July 1951 that Dr. Jones and his friends A. W. Hosmer and Henry S. Salt laid "the foundations for Thoreau's modern reputation," and Walter Harding, another of our deans, in *A Thoreau Handbook* and in *The New Thoreau Handbook* (with Michael Meyer), also praised the good doctor's writings. More recently, after I discovered the Jones Collection in 1974, I edited Horace Hosmer's letters to Dr. Jones in a volume entitled *Recollections of Concord and the Thoreaus*; and Fritz Oehlschlaeger and I have published many of Dr. Jones's Thoreauvian letters in *Toward the Making of Thoreau's Modern Reputation*.[1] My edition of Dr. Jones's published and unpublished Thoreau essays makes it possible, for the first time, to assess his scholarly achievement.

At the time Dr. Jones began his Thoreau scholarship, the most influential critics of Thoreau were Emerson, Lowell, Channing, and Sanborn. Emerson in his edition of Thoreau's letters had presented his friend as a stoic, and he suppressed evidence to the contrary. Lowell had fostered the belief that Thoreau was a mere imitator of Emerson, that he "had not a healthy mind" and that he "had no humor." Channing overemphasized Thoreau's eccentricities, and F. B. Sanborn's biography, with its tedious digressions and its shoddy scholarship, was detrimental to Thoreau's reputation. Walter Harding in *A Thoreau Handbook* and in *The New Thoreau Handbook* (with Michael Meyer) and Oehlschlager and Hendrick in *Toward The Making of Thoreau's Modern Reputation* have traced the permutations of these misinterpretations of Thoreau, and these findings need not be repeated here. It is, however, against the backdrop of

critical misperceptions of Thoreau that we should read Dr. Jones's essays.

Just who was Dr. Jones? He was born in Manchester, England, of Welsh parents and was brought to the United States in 1842. He attended the Free Academy in Utica, New York, before reading medicine with a Dr. Watson. Samuel Arthur Jones then enrolled in the Pennsylvania Homoeopathic Medical College in Philadelphia and should have received his M.D. degree from that institution in 1860, but he and two other students expressed doubts about the competence of two of their professors, and as a result the young men were "blackballed." The three students then published in 1860 an account of the controversy in *Who, Which, What and Wherefore: or, A Few Facts for the Homoeopathic Profession.* In this pamphlet, the three charged, among other things, that the professor of surgery was "ignorant of Anatomy" and that even his minor surgical operations were unsuccessful. The bill of complaints ended with this impassioned paragragraph, probably written by Jones:

It is a well-known fact that we as Homoeopaths are taunted with knowing little of Surgery; and in the face of the humiliating truths, we here express regarding the chair of Surgery, we do appeal to the Guardians of our *Alma Mater* that this disgraceful state of things be remedied. Let us, for the sake of Homoeopathia, in this the first fortress, from which she did battle with the time-worshipped systems of Alloeopathy, let us, we pray, have such men in the chairs of Surgery, and of Practice, as shall do honor to our cause, and enable us to cope more successfully with our enemies.[2]

The charges made by the three students were seemingly true; those faculty members were incompetent and the accusers were excellent students. Dr. Charles J. Hempel, a prominent homeopathic physician and educator, wrote almost two decades later, *"It was admitted by all their classmates, that they* [the three dissidents] *were the brightest and best qualified members of the graduating class of that year."*[3] The controversy was to bring about major changes in the faculty of the college, but meanwhile S. A. Jones was without the medical degree he had been seeking. He soon found a more congenial faculty in St. Louis, and the Missouri Homoeopathic Medical College awarded him an M.D. degree in 1860. After the reorganization of the medical faculty in Philadelphia, the three students were reexamined there in 1861. The board of examiners this time found "that these young gentlemen were *better entitled to a diploma than any students they had ever had before,"* and the college awarded Dr. Jones his second M.D. degree.[4]

This incident is a characteristic one in Dr. Jones's life; he never allowed his own personal well-being to stand in the way of what he considered the necessity to speak the truth as he understood it. He relished public controversy and used all the rhetorical strategies at his command to make his points.

The twice-doctored Jones began practice in Englewood, New Jersey, where he remained until the Civil War began. He then served as an assistant surgeon in the Union Army until inflammatory rheumatism caused him to be invalided home. He returned to private practice, then married, and eventually fathered nine children.

Dr. Jones had begun to collect books as early as 1856, and though he was far from wealthy and had a family to support, he continued to amass large numbers of medical and literary works for most of his life. Before the turn of the century his collection included over four thousand medical books as well as collections of the works of Carlyle and the New England Transcendentalists (to name just two of his literary interests), a personal library that can properly be called impressive. Before the late 1880s, however, his chief interest was medicine, specifically homeopathic medicine.

Although homeopathy is now largely forgotten in the United States, it was widely practiced in Western Europe and in America in the nineteenth century. Homeopathy was developed by the German physician Samuel Hahnemann (1757–1834), who, dissatisfied with the medical practice of his time, put forth his own theory: Let likes be cured by likes. He was suggesting that patients should be treated with "drugs which produce in a healthy person the symptoms found in those who were ill."[5] Hahnemann and most of his followers believed in infinitesimal doses of drugs; that is, "the smaller the dose the more effective [it is] in stimulating the vital force."[6] The prescribing of minute doses was in direct opposition to the beliefs and practices of many regular—or what Hahnemann called "Allopathic"—physicians, who often prescribed massive doses of purgatives and frequently bled their patients.

It is almost miraculous that patients survived treatment by regular physicians. Many, of course, did not. For example, when William Ticknor, Hawthorne's friend and publisher, became ill with pneumonia in 1864 while the two were on a trip together, the allopathic doctor, according to Hawthorne, "belabored with pills and powders, and then proceeded to cup, and poultice, and blister, according to the ancient rule of that tribe of savages."[7] The patient died.

The "regular" physicians in nineteenth-century America were strongly opposed to Hahnemann's theories, and the struggles, verbal and otherwise, between homeopaths and allopaths were often fierce. Dr. Jones relished the struggles,

and the homeopathic journals frequently published his attacks on the "enemy." Not surprisingly, he turned to medical education as another way to advance the cause, and along with his general practice he held the Chair of Histology and Pathology in the New York Homoeopathic Medical College, where he was able to propagate his views of medicine.

In 1875 Dr. Jones was called to the deanship of the College of Homoeopathic Medicine then being established at the University of Michigan in Ann Arbor, a city in which he was to spend the rest of his life. This position was to require all of his skills, for the legislature had dictated the establishment of the college over the strong opposition of the medical faculty at the university. He did attract students to the college, however, and he developed a teaching faculty, established "a laboratory of experimental pathogenesy," and proved himself a stimulating teacher; but his rela-

tionships with the allo-
pathic doctors, some of
his own colleagues, and
with the administration
of the university were
stormy. One faculty member
charged that Dr. Jones, in
his lectures, used improper
language and took God's
name in vain and that he
called the president of the
university a "Jelly Bag."[8]
Another charge was that
while members of the
homeopathic faculty were
walking down the street, Dr.
Jones saw two ladies and
"began prancing and neigh-
ing in imitation of a stallion
sighting a mare, to the
disgrace of the entire faculty."[9] The regular medical
men were constantly work-
ing to disband or discredit
the homeopathic medical
college, which they con-
sidered unsound and quack
ridden. Undoubtedly Dr.
Jones used extreme lan-
guage in his struggles. He
probably did call the president a "Jelly Bag." It is
known that he told Presi-
dent Angell, "You don't
have enough calcium in
that backbone of yours to
whitewash the bald spot on
the top of your head."[10] Dr.
Jones's sharp language was
also employed when he
set out to combat those he
considered Thoreau's
enemies.

Within five years, Dr.
Jones could no longer keep
up the struggle at the university; he resigned from
the faculty (he had left the
deanship in 1878) and es-
tablished a private practice
in Ann Arbor. For a few
years he continued his almost superhuman work
schedule—combining a
large practice with the editorship of a section of the
*American Homoeopathic
Observer* while continuing
to produce massive numbers
of articles on medical subjects for publication in the
professional journals of
homeopathic medicine. During the latter part of the
1880s, however, he began
to turn more and more from
medical to literary subjects
in his scholarly investiga-
tions. In addition to his
interest in collecting
Carlyle, he became engross-
ed in the New England

Transcendentalists, specifically Thoreau.

Dr. Jones had many qualities that made him a distinguished Thoreau scholar. Both as a physician and as a scholar he was an outsider. He did not accept the medical theories of allopathic physicians; neither did he accept the interpretations of Thoreau's life and work presented by Emerson, Sanborn, or Lowell. A skilled diagnostician, he wanted to know the facts and he wanted to know what they meant. In medicine, he took elaborate personal histories, and if the facts led him to believe that belladonna was the correct drug to use for an illness, he would single-mindedly follow that treatment; if the facts led him to believe that Emerson, Sanborn, and Lowell were wrong in their interpretations of Thoreau, then he would write "the truth" as he saw it, even though that meant disagreeing with the "masters." He wanted to know the facts about the characters of the elder Mr.

and Mrs. Thoreau, about Thoreau's night in jail, about Walden as an underground railway stop, about when and where Thoreau published his books and articles, and where the critics published their articles and books on Thoreau. As medical scientist, he tested drugs in his search for better treatments for his patients; as scholar he sought out letters and documents by and about Thoreau. An "irregular" medical man, Dr. Jones felt great kinship with Thoreau, that questioner of everything conventional.

By all accounts, Dr. Jones was a man of great personal integrity, with stern moral views; both qualities were useful in understanding Thoreau, who also possessed these characteristics. Dr. Jones, after extended homeopathic-allopathic quarrels, was disputatious, but this very quality allowed him to attempt to demolish what he felt were erroneous criticisms of Thoreau. In addition, as Martin Kaufman and

Joseph Kett in their excellent studies of homeopathy have shown, there was a strong affinity between transcendentalism and homeopathy. Both philosophies opposed rationalism and emphasized mysticism. Both philosophies were predicated on a belief in the unity of the universe and both emphasized the correspondence theory. Many leading transcendentalists were believers in homeopathy and many homeopathic physicians espoused transcendentalism

Dr. Jones began first to collect Thoreau first editions, then to write about the Concordian. His first essay was "Thoreau: A Glimpse," read before the Unity Club of Ann Arbor on 2 December 1889 and printed in the *Unitarian* of January, February, and March 1890. The essay, which showed that Thoreau was not a mere imitator of Emerson, is a judicious one, written by an outsider far removed from the New England literary establishment. Not only did Dr.

Jones attack the misinterpretations of Lowell but he also presented Thoreau as a man of principle, praised his antislavery writings and his noncompliance with a government whose policies concerning slavery he did not accept, and justified Thoreau's defense of John Brown. This essay brought Dr. Jones to the attention of the leading Thoreauvians of the day. The pioneering bibliography he had appended to the printed version of his lecture was used by H. G. O. Blake, Thoreau's friend and literary executor, as an addition to *Thoreau's Thoughts* (1890). Jones also began a correspondence with Thoreau's friend Daniel Ricketson. More importantly, he began corresponding with Henry S. Salt, the Englishman whose 1890 biography of Thoreau was the first study to give a full, unbiased view of the Concordian. During his 1890 visit to Concord, Jones met A. W. (Fred) Hosmer, an untiring friend of Thoreauvians, and Hosmer's distant relative,

Horace Hosmer, who had been a student in the school conducted by the Thoreau brothers. Fred Hosmer and Dr. Jones were convinced that Lowell, F. B. Sanborn, Emerson, and several others were presenting a biased picture of Thoreau, and together the two set out to set the record straight. They were particularly helpful in supplying information to Salt for his 1896 revised edition of the Thoreau biography. The letters of these three Thoreauvians have recently been published in *Toward the Making of Thoreau's Modern Reputation.*

After his auspicious beginning as a Thoreau scholar, Dr. Jones in his subsequent Thoreau studies produced work that can be divided into three distinct categories: bibliographies, essays on Thoreau's life, and essays on Thoreau's biographers, editors, and critics. His two strictly bibliographic studies are not represented in this collection since that part of his work is now out of date.

Dr. Jones's first bibliog-

raphy was followed in 1894 by the more extensive *Bibliography of Henry David Thoreau*, published by the Rowfant Club of Cleveland. Only ninety copies were printed. The work was then of great importance because, for the first time, scholars and students had a competent bibliography upon which they could base their work. My collection of Dr. Jones's Thoreau studies concentrates on the last two categories of his work, but his bibliographic essay, "An Afternoon in the University Library," a history of the 1862 edition of *A Week on the Concord and Merrimack Rivers*, charmingly written in the Landor manner, is included in the appendix at the end of this volume.

The essays in the first section of this volume all concern themselves with Thoreau's life, and they are arranged chronologically. "Thoreau: A Glimpse" is followed by the previously unpublished "Thoreau: An Appreciation," a wide-ranging essay remarkably free of the common nineteenth-century misinterpretations of Thoreau. The next study, "Thoreau's Inheritance," was written specifically to correct what Dr. Jones thought was Sanborn's misrepresentations of the characters of Henry Thoreau's parents. Dr. Jones's studies led him to locate the letters of Thoreau to Calvin Greene, and this important find is detailed in the Prefatory Note to *Some Unpublished Letters of Henry D. and Sophia E. Thoreau.* "Thoreau's Incarceration" is one of Dr. Jones's greatest achievements as a researcher, for he sought out Sam Staples, the Concord jailer, and then went to commendable efforts to sift fiction, fact, and fancy concerning Thoreau's night in jail. This section ends with Dr. Jones's reprint of Emerson's obituary of Thoreau, which appeared in the Boston *Daily Advertiser,* and Dr. Jones's note concerning the obituary.

The second section of this anthology contains Dr. Jones's essays on Thoreau's biographers, editors, and critics. Once again the studies are arranged in chronological order. His "Thoreau and His Biographers" is a shrewd, valid assessment of biographical works by William Ellery Channing, H. A. Page, F. B. Sanborn, and Henry Salt. The article is a model of clarity and of sound literary judgment. The next essay, "Thoreau and His Works," is a review of the ten-volume Houghton Mifflin edition of *The Writings of Henry David Thoreau,* which concludes with Jones's strongly held view: "Thoreau must be regarded neither as a naturalist, nor as an author, but simply as one who 'did not wish to live what was not life.' " "Vox Clamantis in Deserto" is concerned with the meaning of *Walden* and with the specific misinterpretations of Lowell and of Bradford Torrey, the editor of the 1897 edition of Thoreau's classic work. Over the years Dr. Jones had collected many difficult-to-locate early essays and reviews concerning Thoreau, and he republished them in a volume called *Pertaining to Thoreau*. His introduction to that immensely useful volume is reprinted here. "Thoreau as a Skulker" was unpublished until 1976 when Walter Harding printed it in the *Thoreau Society Bulletin*; it is another of Dr. Jones's spirited defenses of Thoreau, in this instance against the views of Robert Louis Stevenson. His "Notable New Book" is a review of Sanborn's edition of *The Service*, and it contains severe comments on Margaret Fuller and disguised barbs aimed at Sanborn.

Section three is a logical extension of the essays in the previous section. Dr. Jones consistently quarreled with the critics who misinterpreted Thoreau, and he praised the Thoreau studies of Henry S. Salt. In his last Thoreau project, unpublished until now, Dr. Jones reprinted ten English reviews of Salt's Thoreau studies and five "American estimations of Thoreau,"

interweaving his own flavorful comments into the text. "Thoreau amongst Friends and Philistines" is a fitting conclusion for this collection of essays since it contains a wide range of critical opinion on Thoreau in late-Victorian England and America plus Dr. Jones's own trenchant observations.

Dr. Jones carried out his literary studies under great handicaps. Sanborn and H. G. O. Blake controlled most of the primary materials on Thoreau, and Dr. Jones quarreled with both. Dr. Jones believed Sanborn morally reprehensible for not seeing active service in the Civil War. Jones's willingness to quarrel with Sanborn and others whose interpretations of Thoreau he disputed alienated him from the gentle Blake. As a result of these disagreements with Sanborn and Blake, Dr. Jones did not have access to Thoreau collections. In addition, he had too little time to devote to his Thoreau studies.

His practice was a demanding one. He wrote Fred Hosmer on 18 October 1891:

> For though it is Sunday, I have got to make a country ride of twenty-four miles. Fred, if you ever have a boy and he says a word about being a doctor, just take a hickory shingle and whale the seat off him then and there; it'll hurt for the time, but . . . he'll bless you for it when he gets his senses. I'll be hanged if my life, year out and year in, isn't like a dog chasing his own tail—an eternal round and round, and round. "Doctor, *are* you comin?" "You bet!!"[11]

Four years later, on 17 February 1895, Dr. Jones described to Fred Hosmer the hazards inherent in making winter visits in Michigan: "A typical New England winter with its impassable drifts and blinding storms and bitter winds and journeyings through fields and the devil to pay generally! Four hours in getting six miles, and having GOT, the serious question IF it was possible to get back. And the poor man died yesterday morning, after all." In this same letter, he mentioned another activity that reduced the time he could devote to literary work: "Moreover, the old school doctors who have fought Homoeopathy in the university for the last twenty years are making one supreme effort to have the college that I founded ABOLISHED. To frustrate their machinations has kept my typewriter HOT in such moments as I could get from the drudgery of practice." His efforts to preserve and spread homeopathy were untiring, even after he had severed his ties to the University of Michigan.

A further hindrance to his literary scholarship was his lack of formal training in literature. He was well read, but he was self-taught and rather defensive about it. On 28 May 1893, he wrote Fred Hosmer, "I am NOT a literary man, . . . but I must stick to my trade and leave this Thoreau matter henceforth to purely literary men like Mr. Salt—IT is THEIR trade." He did not, of course, do so, but he clearly had to spend much time learning the writing trade. Not surprisingly, at times he made factual errors. Far from the Harvard and Concord libraries, he did not always have the primary source materials he needed; he incorrectly referred to Storrow Higginson as "Storms Higginson"; he thought that Ripley wrote the *Tribune* review of 1849 of *A Week on the Concord and Merrimack Rivers*; he thought that "Sympathy" was addressed to John Thoreau, Jr. Given his accomplishments, however, his mistakes are relatively minor.

Finally, badly overworked, he had what he called a "collapse" during the summer of 1897 and had to be taken to a Michigan summer cottage for a rest. For years, after his daily medical rounds he had stayed up late reading and writing, then could not get to sleep; finally, his tireless exertions proved "too much for an old fool past sixty," as he wrote Fred Hosmer on 28 August 1897.

He recovered from his "collapse" and returned to his old schedule. On the fifth of July 1899, he was contemplating "reprinting all my papers on Thoreau, which will make a volume by themselves. When this is done I shall sweep up my shop floor and dry up. This Thoreau business has been going on now for ten years and I am emptied of all I have found regarding it." For some reason, he did not reprint his Thoreau essays, but he was not done with Thoreau; he published *Pertaining to Thoreau*, that excellent collection of early reviews and articles, and finished (but did not publish) "Thoreau amongst Friends and Philistines."

This latter collection was completed (except for one set of annotations) after the death of Carroll, his favorite son, in 1901. He wrote Fred Hosmer on 21 September 1901 that he would get interested in his writing, then think of his dead son, "and with it the question, 'What's the use, all is vanity.' Then, Fred, the 'sassy' book hides its diminished head, and I sink into the idleness of despair." "Thoreau amongst Friends and Philistines" was to be his last sustained Thoreau effort, for his health failed completely and he could not go on with literary studies.

Dr. Jones was unduly modest in his judgments about his Thoreau work. Writing to Fred Hosmer on 20 March 1896 about the revised, much improved 1896 edition of Salt's biography of Thoreau, he took some credit for that excellent life: "Just think how all this [the revised biography] has been brought about; I visit Concord; you show me around and take me to see Horace Hosmer. Then we write interminably about Thoreau matters and and you probe them out, and the result is that Sanborn's misrepresentations are at last corrected."

In his last letter to Fred Hosmer, written 30 April 1903, just a week before Hosmer's death, Dr. Jones tried again to summarize his and Hosmer's place in Thoreau scholarship:

Has it ever occurred to you that the "Glimpse" is really the beginning of the Thoreau revival? It was the "Glimpse" that got me the acquaintance with Miss Eliza Hosmer; through her I got to know you; a desire to see Concord took me there; and from that day you and I have done our duty to Thoreau's memory —far the smaller part being mine. Then came the Rowfant Club's "Bibliography", which, by the way, fetches $25.00 readily now. The Rowfanters got Horace E. Scudder to read a paper before the Club— paying him handsomely therefor. When he saw what the Rowfant Club is, he suddenly woke up to the fact that Thoreau might be a far bigger pumpkin than any in the pile,—and, lo! "The Riverside Edition of Thoreau's COLLECTED WORKS" appeared! This is history, and my dear Fred, we had a hand in it.

Dr. Jones could be fanciful when he wrote history, but fancy aside, Salt, Hosmer, and Jones did play a significant role in reappraising Thoreau's work. Dr. Jones was born in the age of Victoria, and some of his language is perhaps too florid for modern taste, but at his best, his prose is simple and direct. He may seem, at first glance, unduly argumentative, but Thoreau *was* misunderstood. His views about Thoreau and Thoreau's friends, enemies, and critics are strongly, often amusingly, stated. He undeniably could have done more scholarly work[12] had he had more free time and had he had access to other primary Thoreau materials held by Blake and Sanborn, but what he accomplished was important and deserves to be made more easily accessible to readers. He did, after all, play a major role in the making of Thoreau's modern reputation.

1. See Raymond Adams, "Fred Hosmer, The 'Lerned Clerk,' " *Thoreau Society Bulletin,* no. 36 (July 1951): 1-2; Walter Harding, *A Thoreau Handbook* (New York: New York University Press, 1971), pp. 35, 39, 90, 128, 206, 210; George Hendrick, ed. *Remembrances of Concord and the Thoreaus* (Urbana: University of Illinois Press, 1977); and Fritz Oehlschlaeger and George Hendrick, eds., *Toward the Making of Thoreau's Modern Reputation* (Urbana: University of Illinois Press, 1979).

2. "Dr. Samuel Arthur Jones," *Medical Century* 19 (April 1912), and *Who, Which, What and Wherefore: or, A Few Facts for the Homoeopathic Profession* (Philadelphia: n.p., 1860), pp. 1-8. Xerox copies of both of these items were furnished by the Hahnemann Medical College Library in Philadelphia.

3. "Prof. Jones Vindicated." This otherwise unidentified clipping was furnished by the Hahnemann Medical College Library.

4. Ibid.

5. Martin Kaufman, *Homeopathy in America: The Rise and Fall of a Medical Heresy* (Baltimore and London: Johns Hopkins Press, 1971), p. 25. For other discussions of homeopathy, see also Joseph Kett, *The Forma-*

tion of the American Medical Profession (New Haven: Yale University Press, 1968), and Harris Coulter, Divided Legacy (Washington, D.C.: McGrath Pub. Co., 1973-77), 3 vols.

6. Kaufman, p. 26.

7. Randall Stewart, Nathaniel Hawthorne (New Haven: Yale University Press, 1948), p. 236.

8. "Correspondence relating to the charges made against Professor Samuel A. Jones, 1880," records of the Homoeopathic Medical School, Michigan Historical Collections, Bentley Historical Library, University of Michigan.

9. Ibid.

10. Quoted in Walter Harding, ed., "More Excerpts from the Alfred Hosmer Letter Files,"

Thoreau Society Bulletin 123 (Spring 1973): 6.

11. The letters of Dr. Jones to A. W. Hosmer which follow are published courtesy of the Concord Free Public Library.

12. In addition to the Thoreau bibliographies not reprinted here, I have not used two of Dr. Jones's unpublished essays on Thoreau (delivered on 19 January 1981 and 23 January 1898) since he used much of the information in them in his published work. The essay delivered in February of 1891—"Thoreau: An Appreciation"—is used. Copies of these three essays are in the Concord Free Public Library and the Rare Book Room of the University of Illinois Library.

A Note on Editorial Method

My headnotes to Dr. Jones's articles are italicized. All footnotes in Dr. Jones's articles have also been italicized and inserted into his texts. The following materials are as Dr. Jones wrote or transcribed them, and only obvious typographical mistakes have been corrected.

Section One

Dr. Jones on Thoreau's Life

Thoreau: A Glimpse

"Thoreau: A Glimpse" originally appeared in the Unitarian, *vol. 5 (February, March, and April 1891); a revised version appeared in Dr. Jones's collection* Thoreau: A Glimpse *(Concord: Albert Lane: Erudite Press, 1903). Dr. Jones was collecting Carlyleana when, as he wrote, he "came upon Thoreau's impassioned 'Plea for Captain John Brown,' wounded and in prison. The spark found the tinder ready, and the fire then kindled is burning yet." The text reproduced here is the revised version, embodying the factual corrections suggested by Alfred W. Hosmer after the original appearance of the article.*

HIS best biographer says that "on the spot where Thoreau lived at Walden there is now a cairn of stones, yearly visited by hundreds, and growing in height as each friend of his muse adds a stone from the shore of the fair water he loved so well." There is another monument, also growing in height, the initial contribution by Emerson, the very latest from the hand of John Burroughs. Emerson's is a votive offering—cypress and rosemary—lovingly laid on Thoreau's grave more than a quarter of a century ago; and yet today as fresh as if the chaplet had been plucked in Paradise from the Tree of Life.

Running down the long and growing list of contributors, we find those who had known Thoreau in the flesh and they who have studied him in his books. If from all these sketches it were possible to make a photographic "composite," I much doubt if the Recording Angel could recognize the man by the picture.

The most subtle "Critical Essay" gives only the measure of its writer—he betrays his own limitations—and, at its best, the most searching study of a dead author's "Life, Character, and Opinions" is only a post-mortem examination. The spirit eludes; the felicitous last word is still to be said. It is this expectancy that gives to the proper study of an author's life its special charm of "lastingness." By "proper study" I mean such a breadth of research as includes all collateral reading, so that, at last, you shall have rambled along the many rivulets which united make the resulting river of fact. But no author, living or dead, is ever known to his contemporaries. On the thirteenth of this month "gruff Sam Johnson" will have been dead one hundred and five years, yet we know absolutely more of him than was possible even to Boswell: thanks to Croker, Napier, and Dr. Birkbeck Hill.

If, however, you are a proper student the discrepancies and contradictions of criticism will send you from the critics to the author himself; and that result I take to be about the happiest outcome of all criticism—it certainly will be in Thoreau's case.

Another observable feature of the critical function is the endeavor to account for an author by means of such factors as heredity, environment, and the "Zeitgeist"—a certain "Spirit of the Age" that somehow manages to mould a Luther and manufacture a Tetzel by the same twist of the wrist; as if Nature threw dice and loaded them on occasion! In Thoreau's instance I feel obliged to eliminate largely the influence of heredity. Considering his ancestry, Thoreau is quite a psychological surprise. A maternal grandfather turned from expounding the laws of God to confounding those of the Commonwealth—dropped Theology and took up Law. A maternal uncle was a "character"—a free-and-easy, unstarched rambler who, with little "property," no family, an utter indifference to "public opinion," took life as easily as his famous nephew did earnestly. There was too much of him for a "loafer" and not enough for a philosopher. Thoreau's father was "a small and unobtrusive man, grave and silent, but inwardly cheerful and social, and noted for 'minding his own business'." Thoreau's mother, according to a credible witness,

> "Was one of the most unceasing talkers in Concord. Her gift of speech was proverbial, and wherever she was, the conversation fell largely to her share.
>
> "She was also subject to sharp and sudden flashes of gossip and malice, which never quite amounted to ill-nature, but greatly provoked the prim and commonplace that she so often came in contact with."

If her "flashes" ever took the shape of "sheet-lightning," we can but hope that Thoreau pére was a non-conductor!

So much for heredity; but it were unjust to leave the Thoreau family in the shadow of such a picture. Says one who had lived with them:

> "The atmosphere of earnest purpose which pervaded the great movement for the emancipation of the slaves, gave to the Thoreau family an elevation of character which was ever afterwards perceptible, and imparted an air of dignity to the trivial details of life. The children of the house, there were four of them, as they grew up all became school-teachers, and each displayed peculiar gifts in that profession. But they were all something more than teachers, and becoming enlisted early in the anti-slavery cause or in that broader service of humanity which 'plain living and high thinking' imply, they gradually withdrew from that occupation,—declining the opportunities by which other young persons, situated as they were, rise to worldly success, and devoting themselves, within limits somewhat narrow to the pursuit of lofty ideals. . . . To meet one of the Thoreaus was not the same as to encounter any other person who might happen to cross your path. Life to them was something

more than a parade of pretensions, a conflict of ambition, or an incessant scramble for the common objects of desire. . . . Without wealth, or power, or social prominence, they still held a rank of their own, in scrupulous independence, and with qualities that put condescension out of the question."

That "great movement for the emancipation of the slaves" was somewhat extensive. In the year 1835 there were in the United States not less than two thousand Anti-Slavery Societies, and you can imagine what a membership that implies! How many families, think you, did "the atmosphere of earnest purpose" thus transfigure? We are to remember that this very "atmosphere" could put nothing into the Thoreau family; it could only develop that which was already there. It did not "give them" an elevation of character,—it simply supplied the conditions that revealed their moral altitude. There were not a few in those days—and all too many of them clergymen— whom that very "movement", despite the "atmosphere of earnest purpose," sank lower than the common sewers. It was an asphyxiating atmosphere to Things; it was fatal to all two-legged invertebrates: it was respirable only by true manhood; and those Thoreaus throve in it, shot up towards Heaven, and their altitude "was ever afterwards perceptible."

Thoreau's immediate environment was severely "Transcendental", as he was born, lived, and died in Concord; and there of course Emerson was the "deus ex machina"—quite an addition to any environment. Thoreau enjoyed an unusual intimacy with Emerson, having lived for quite a while in his family; and this I presume gave Mr. Lowell the opportunity to call Thoreau "a pistillate plant kindled to fruitage by the Emersonian pollen." It seems to me as if Lowell gets on all fours whenever he mentions Emerson; he always writes of him as if all the gods of Olympus had put on clean linen when Emerson was moulded—an admiration that dwindles into adulation.

It was fortunate for Lydia Maria Childs that she did not live in Concord, or some of her own ideas would have been ascribed to "Emersonian pollen" floating around to the detriment of other people's originality. You remember the famous couplet,—

> "And, striving to be man, the worm
> Mounts through all the spires of form."

It is the keystone of Conway's claim that Emerson, not Darwin, first broached the idea of evolution. Well, this couplet first appears in the second edition of Emerson's "Nature", published in 1849. If you should read Mrs. Child's "Letters from New York, First Series"—a somewhat notable book in its day—possibly you may find in Letter XXVI, written in September, 1842 and published in 1843, the pollen that "kindled to fruitage" the Emersonian idea. Emerson's son has nobly said,—"The charge of imitating Emerson, too often made against Thoreau, is idle and untenable, though unfortunately it has received some degree of sanction in high quarters. . . . Thoreau was incapable of conscious imitation. His faults, if any, lay in exactly the other direction." A pronouncement which speaks volumes for the sagacity and critical insight of Dr. Edward Waldo Emerson.

The same well-qualified authority also gives us this statement, namely: "The history of Mr. Emerson's first acquaintance with Mr. Thoreau is this: When the former was delivering a new lecture in Concord, Miss Helen Thoreau said to Mrs. Brown, Mrs. Emerson's sister, 'There is a thought almost identical with that in Henry's journal,' which she soon after brought to Mrs. Brown. The latter carried it to Mr. Emerson, who was interested, and asked her to bring this youth to see him. She did, and thus began a relation that lasted all their lives of strong respect and even affection, but of a Roman character."

So far as concerns environment, if Thoreau got a stimulus from it he was also a stimulus in it. As diamond cuts diamond, so the attrition of mind against mind brings out the facets of character, and the process that shaped Thoreau also gave shape to others.

How far was Thoreau influenced by the "Zeitgeist?" It was indeed a potent "Geist." Emerson writes of it to Carlyle,—

"We are all a little wild here with numberless projects of social reform. Not a reading man but has a draft of a new Community in his waistcoat pocket. I am gently mad myself, and am resolved to live cleanly."

It is believed that Carlyle's "Sartor Resartus" had a hand in the raising of that Geist; and it was a spirit that would not be laid by bell and candle. Kant's "Critique of Pure Reason" put a new leaven into the minds of men, and the fermenting process was called "Transcendentalism." Germany had it, France had it, and New England had it in the superlative degree. O. B. Frothingham, its best historian says,— "New England furnished the only plot of ground on the planet, where the transcendental philosophy had a chance to show what it was and what it proposed." The Yankee, as usual, outdid "all creation!"

A dozen years ago a semi-clerical mountebank said in a public lecture: "What is Transcendentalism? You will not suspect me of possessing the mood of that acute teacher, who, on the deck of a Mississippi steamer, was asked this question, and replied, 'See the holes made in the bank yonder by the swallows. Take away the bank and leave the holes, and this is Transcendentalism'." This is just the kitchen wit of a Cook. The very tornado that prostrates the lordly oak also fills the air with flying straws and the refuse of the roadside; just so this storm of transcendental thought caught up both strong men and weak, and thus it got both a sublime aspect and a ludicrous. From one point of view you can discover such whimsical antics as would make an angel weep; and from another you can see some of the noblest of our race striving to scale Heaven by the very ladder that Jacob saw in his dream. That they could not take the whole world with them is the

chief failure of Transcendentalism—and only a sodden fool
can laugh at that.

In the Communities to which the Transcendental thought
gave rise—and these bankrupted the generous souls who gave
their all to found them—one thing is noticeable, namely, they
banded themselves together to help one another to that higher
life for which they yearned.

Thoreau could easily have joined Ripley's Community at
Brook Farm or Alcott's at Fruitlands. He did neither. He built
his shanty at Walden and went there ALONE. Here was the
sanity of genius recognizing the divine behest,—"Work Out
Your Own Salvation!"

Lowell is pleased to regard this Walden episode as a
pastoral masquerade, a "Transcendentalist" theatricality, a
sham. Dr. Garnett thinks Lowell's critical essay "half reveals
a suspicion that the apostle of Nature may have been something of a charlatan." Lowell had arraigned the dead-and-
buried Thoreau in this wise:

> "His shanty-life was a mere impossibility, so far as his
> own conception of it goes, as an entire independency of
> mankind. The tub of Diogenes had a sounder bottom. Tho-
> reau's experiment actually presupposes all that compli-
> cated civilization which it theoretically abjured. He squats
> on another man's land; he borrows an axe; his boards, his
> nails, his bricks, his mortar, his books, his lamp, his fish-
> hooks, his plough, his hoe, all turn state's evidence against
> him as an accomplice in the sin of that artificial civiliza-
> tion which rendered it possible that such a person as Henry
> D. Thoreau should exist at all."

This is perhaps the most explicit indictment that has been
filed against Thoreau. It is a misconception: it has in it traces
of even a malignant misconception,—the wish being father to
the thought. I seriously question if any literature contains a
more pitiful ineptitude. Emerson says, "we descend to meet." I
think it would hold good if Thoreau had an appointment with

his critic. In depicting Thoreau, Lowell looked down and saw the shadow of him in a mud-puddle: he should have looked up at the man and had the azure heavens for a background.

Thoreau had proved himself a man of principles and of convictions, a man who had found some things on which he not only could stand, but MUST: and all this before he had borrowed Alcott's axe to cut the sills of his Walden shanty. Lowell should have remembered this; for while he could sing his stinging stanzas in the slave's behalf, Thoreau had spoken the words that blistered where they touched. Hear him on the conduct of certain newspapers, when slavery stained the sunlight that fell on the monument at Concord Bridge:

"Could slavery suggest a more complete servility than some of these journals exhibit? Is there any dust which their conduct does not lick and make still fouler with its slime? I do not know whether the Boston Herald is still in existence, but I remember to have seen it about the streets when Simms was carried off. Did it not act its part well— serve its master faithfully? How could it have gone lower on its belly? . . . When I have taken up this paper with my cuffs turned up, I have heard the gurgling of the common sewer in its every column."

He also said in the same address,

"I would remind my countrymen that they are to be men first, and Americans only at a late and convenient hour. No matter how valuable the law may be to protect property, even to keep soul and body together, if it do not keep you and humanity together."

One other instance, still from the same address. A slave, Anthony Burns, had been apprehended in Massachusetts and the most intense excitement prevailed. The Commissioner, Mr. Edward G. Loring, was called by the State to examine the law and decide if the slave must be given up. Thoreau said,

"Massachusetts sat waiting Mr. Loring's decision, as if that could in any way affect her own criminality. Her crime, the most conspicuous and fatal crime of all, was permitting him to be the umpire in such a case. It was really the trial of Massachusetts. Every moment that she hesitated to set this man free, every moment that she now hesitates to atone for her crime, she is convicted. The Commissioner on her case is God; not Edward G. God, but simple God."

Who shall say that even in such audacity there is not righteousness? If the Recording Angel had to write it down, who does not believe that it also dropped a tear to blot it out? But pray tell me what would that pitying angel do with this utterance:

"It was while in the Lower House of Congress that Franklin Pierce took that stand on the slavery question from which he has never since swerved by a hair's breadth. He fully recognized, by his votes and his voice, the rights pledged to the South by the Constitution. This, at the period when he declared himself, was an easy thing to do. But when it became more difficult, when the first imperceptible murmur of agitation had grown almost to a convulsion, his course was still the same. Nor did he ever shun the obloquy that sometimes threatened to pursue the Northern man who dared to love that great and sacred reality—his whole united country—better than the mistiness of a philanthropic theory."

Before Heaven's Chancery I would rather be the hot-blooded Thoreau than the author of the "Life of Franklin Pierce". Well and truly did Thoreau say,

"What is wanted is not men of policy, but men of probity,—who recognize a higher law than the Constitution or the decision of the majority. The fate of the country does not de-

pend on what kind of paper you drop into the ballot box, but
on the kind of man you drop from your chamber into the
street every morning."

When voting is only a matter of counting noses, when it becomes a game in which Judas Iscariot is as "strong" as Jesus
Christ—as Carlyle declared—Thoreau disclaimed the ballot.
He repudiated his allegiance to the Commonwealth and refused to pay taxes that were used to uphold slavery. He was
put in jail. His friend, Mr. Emerson, learned of his arrest and
hastened to see him. He stood before the cell door and asked,
"Henry, why are you here?" and from the cell came the suggestive reply: "Why are you NOT here?"

Of this event in Thoreau's life John Burroughs says, "His
carrying his opposition to the State to the point of allowing
himself to be put in jail rather than pay a paltry tax, savors a
little bit of the grotesque and the melodramatic." It has been
already affirmed in your hearing that "the most subtle
critical essay" which aims to sum up a man gives only the
measure of its writer; he betrays his own limitations.

John Hampden refused to pay a "paltry tax" of twenty
shillings "Ship money." That is not "grotesque and melodramatic," but tragic and sublime because in the end a king's
head dropped from his shoulders "in the open street before
Whitehall."

Considering their respective worldly goods, John Hampden's twenty shillings sterling was the paltrier tax. But the
PRINCIPLE (which a President's "advertising agent" failed to
discern)! Tried by results that the world takes note of, one
resistance decapitated a man; in the ultimate, the other
enfranchised six million slaves, and in a manner neither
"grotesque nor melo-dramatic"—to any other than advertising agents! Some weak-backed friend, mayhap of the
advertising agent species, ever after paid Thoreau's taxes and
so his one night's imprisonment "savors a little bit of the
grotesque and melodramatic"—but what if the "salt" in the

man had lost its savor? All advertising agents whatsoever will do well to consider that!

Hampden's recalcitration ushered in a tragedy. Because of non-payment? Because the Hampdens and Pyms and Fairfaxes and Cromwells—not being of advertising agent limitations—said, "resistance to tyrants is obedience to God"—and the great heart of England throbbed its Amen!

Thoreau could live up to a conviction though to do it were a minority of one with the universe against it. Burroughs sees only a "paltry tax"—so different the measure of men. And yet, look at the contradictions of these same "critics," for this identical John Burroughs, in the same essay says of this very Thoreau, "His devotion to principle, to the ideal was absolute; it was like that of the Hindu to his idol. If it devoured him or crushed him—what business was that of his? There was no conceivable failure in adherence to principle." Yet such "devotion" can become "grotesque and melodramatic" on occasion! Such are the paper flowers of rhetoric.

On the 30th of October, 1859, Thoreau spoke in defense of John Brown, when to do that required a moral backbone whose every vertebra was as solid as the everlasting hills. It is an unequivocal endorsement of Brown in the face of the most overwhelming public opinion—a deprecatory murmur even among anti-slavery men. Emerson says, "Before the first friendly word had been spoken for Captain John Brown, after the arrest, Thoreau sent notices to most houses in Concord that he would speak in a public hall on the condition and character of John Brown, on Sunday evening, and invited all people to come. The Republican Committee, the Abolitionist Committee, sent him word that it was premature and unadvisable. He replied "I did not send to you for advice, but to announce that I am to speak."

Burroughs calls this event "the most significant act of his life. It clinches him: it makes the colors fast. We know he means what he says after that . . . It shows what thoughts he fed his soul on, what school he had schooled himself in, what his devotion meant." If virtue were only contagious and Thoreau's speech were read in our churches from time to time it might change the relative value of Jesus and Judas at the polls!

James Russell Lowell has written that Thoreau "looked with utter contempt on the august drama of destiny of which his country was the scene, and on which the curtain had already arisen"—an awful charge to make over a dead man's grave.

The name of HENRY D. THOREAU does not appear on the roster or on the muster-roll of any Massachusetts regiment because, while he lived, the war was only for the preservation of a Union that sanctioned Slavery, and occasion would make him a slave-hunter. Before the Emancipation Proclamation was written Thoreau was in his grave; Lowell's relatives went to death in that "august drama of destiny," but Lowell lives— in the capacity of a Massachusetts "mugwump." Such is the difference between carbonate of lime and cartilage in the man's backbone.

I have dwelt at this length on Thoreau as an abolitionist in order to show him unswervingly steadfast to principle, and to correct an unrighteous aspersion. I think the time well spent, although it makes my remaining moments too few for an adequate glance at Thoreau as a "loafer" a loafer; "by Divine right," an inspired loafer.

Novalis called Spinosa a "God-intoxicated man"; Thoreau was Nature-intoxicated. "If he waked up from a trance in a Concord swamp, he could tell by the plants what time of the year it was within two days." His knowledge of nature was microscopic; trees, plants, animals, birds, fishes, all told him their secrets, almost unasked,—and he lived chiefly amongst them. In an essay entitled "Life without Principle" he says: "To have done anything by which you earned money MERELY, is to have been idle or worse."

He was a good gardener, an excellent surveyor, unusually handy with tools; said he had "as many trades as fingers;" was also college bred, and yet with all this equipment he devoutly believed that the worst use you could put a man to was to—hang him? No; set him to "Making Money."

He proved that a man could earn enough in six weeks to support him a year—did so support himself, for he lived in his shanty at Walden Pond on some fifteen dollars a year. He says of that episode in his life, "I went to the woods because I wished to live deliberately, to front only the essential facts of life, and see if I could not learn what it had to teach, and not, when I came to die, discover that I had not lived. I did not wish to live what was not life, living is so dear, nor did I wish to practice resignation, unless it was quite necessary. I wanted to live deep and suck out all the marrow of life, to live so sturdily and Spartan-like as to put to rout all that was not life, to cut a broad swath and shave close, to drive life into a corner, and reduce it to its lowest terms, and if it proved to be mean, why then to get the whole and genuine meanness of it, and publish its meanness to the world: or if it were sublime, to know it by experience, and be able to give a true account in my next excursion."

"Able to give a true account of it in my Next excursion"— that journey made with closed eyes and folded hands!

All around him was a surging humanity, toiling, sweating, and groaning in travail, as if "resignation" to life were necessary; and yet he said, "I am convinced that to maintain oneself on this earth is not a hardship, but a pastime, if we will live simply and wisely; as the pursuits of simpler nations are still the sports of the more artificial."

"The essential facts of life"—the pearl of great price—were an ever-present and a solemn reality to Thoreau. The thought of them filled him with "a feeling of awfulness" just as it did John Woolman, and George Fox, and Mohammed, and him of Nazareth. I think it must have been some day when these essential facts had gotten obscured in the murky mist arising from the Slough of Despond that he wrote: "It is hard to be a good citizen of the world in any great sense; but if we do render no interest or increase to mankind out of that talent God gave us, we can at least preserve the principal unimpaired."

This is he of whom Lowell said, "Did his life seem a selfish one, he condemns doing good as one of the weakest of superstitions"—and he the while sweating in the arena, despairing of "interest or increase," and yet girding up his loins to "preserve the principal unimpaired."

Says Moncure D. Conway, "Emerson took me to see Thoreau, and I remember that he asked me what we were studying at Divinity College. I answered, 'The Scriptures.' 'Which?' he asked. I was puzzled until Emerson said, 'I fear you will find our Thoreau a sad Pagan.' " Thoreau recognized several Bibles in which men were gasping for God in atmospheres more or less respirable. He did not seek the solution of the great secret in printed Bibles. Men had sought it there for thousands of years: that they had found it there was a postulate contradicted by their conduct of life. He contrasts men and animals, and finds a large balance in favor of the brute. He says, "I must receive my life as passively as the willow leaf that flutters over the brook. I must not be for myself, but for God's work, and that is always good. I will wait the breezes patiently, and grow as they determine. My fate cannot but be grand so. We may live the life of a plant or an animal without living an animal life. The constant and universal content of the animal comes of resting quietly in God's palm."

The animal is wiser than man, he concludes; and at once a great suspicion dawns upon his mind: the animal lives nearer to Nature, lives more in accord with her, more in obedience to her, and it is through Nature—God's Bible—that the Creator reveals himself to the creature. A Revelation in Nature: all earnest souls seek that! That much-misunderstood Walt Whitman writes, "While I cannot understand it or argue it out, I fully believe in a clue and purpose in Nature, entire and several; and invisible spiritual results, just as real and definite as the visible, eventuate all concrete life and all materialism through time."

From that supreme moment onward, to this man Thoreau every created thing was a divine message from its Maker and his. Oh, if he could but catch the meaning of the message or of the messenger! Hence his mystical allegory: "I long ago lost a hound, a bay horse, and a turtle dove, and am still on their trail. Many of the travellers I have spoken to concerning them, describing their tracks and what calls they responded to. I have met one or two who had heard the hound, and the tramp of the horse, and even seen the dove disappear behind the cloud, and they seemed as anxious to recover them as if they had lost them themselves." Alas for us all! they had lost them, even as we have: for what is the hound but the divine scent that finds the trail: what the bay horse but sagacity and strength to carry us in pursuit; what the turtle-dove but innocence to secure us the Divine protection? And we have lost them all. Are we still on the trail? Thoreau kept there "till he disappeared behind the cloud."

The vision of "the constant and universal content of the animal" was Thoreau's apocalypse, and from that moment he put his ear to the great heart of Nature as lovingly as a child lays its head on its mother's breast. He wrote in his journal on the 31st of March, 1852 (just ten years before he was translated), "The song-sparrow and the transient fox-colored sparrow, have they brought me no message this year? Is not the coming of the fox-sparrow something more earnest and significant than I have dreamed of? Have I heard what this tiny messenger has to say while it flits from tree to tree? God did not make this world in jest, no, nor in indifference. These migratory swallows all bear messages that concern my life. I do not pluck the fruits in their season. I see that the sparrow cheeps and flits, and sings adequately to the great design of the universe, that man does not communicate with it, understand its language, because he is not at one with it." I suppose it was considering the respective messages they brought that led him to rank the D. D's below the Chick-a-de-dees—one preaches for a stipend, the other brings word from Heaven. The "practical man" can see nothing in this sentimental "twaddle about sparrows": the "practical man" is too often the Devil's "right bower" for that very reason. An old Book, somewhat obsolete now-a-days, but in precious esteem with aged people, says:

"Are not five sparrows sold for two farthings? and not one of them is forgotten of God."

I notice many sparrows in this little leafy town of ours; I find them about our streets in the dead of the harshest winter; I do not learn that any of them has ever made application to the overseer of the poor—they "rest quietly in God's palm." Is there no "message" in this?

I crave your patience for one more quotation which may, or may not, have meaning for you:

"The ultimate expression or fruit of any created thing is a fine effluence which only the most ingenuous worshiper perceives at a reverent distance from its surface even. The cause and effect are equally evanescent and intangible, and the former must be investigated with the same reverence with which the latter is perceived. Science is often like the grub which, though it may have nestled in the germ of a plant, has merely blighted or consumed it, never truly tasted it. The rude and ignorant finger is probing in the rind still, for in this case, the angles of incidence and exidence are equal, and the essence is as far on the other side of the surface or matter, as reverence detains the worshiper on this, and only reverence can find out this angle instinctively. Shall we presume to alter the angle at which God chooses to be worshipped?"

This "fine effluence" is that "invisible spiritual result" for which Thoreau hungered and thirsted and ceaselessly sought, though he had lost hound, horse and turtle-dove. Sir Galahad sought the Holy Grail: The Concord "loafer" had a higher quest.

If I have attained my highest expectation, this glimpse of Thoreau will leave you wholly unsatisfied. Can you be persuaded to turn from the contemplation of such sacerdotal scarecrows as "Robert Elsmere," and "John Ward" to read the writings of a rare man, a flesh-and-blood reality, whose whole life was a strenuous endeavor to apprehend—lay hold of—eternity? His books contain so much that will "find" you, as Coleridge says. Let me give you a thought of his that comes home most touchingly to those of us who are "ayont" the fifties. He says, "The youth gets together his materials to build a bridge to the moon, or, perchance, a palace or temple on the earth, and at length the middle-aged man concludes to build a wood-shed with them." (My white-haired friend, how is it?) And yet he finely reproaches us for being content with a "wood-shed." "If," he says, "you have built castles in the air, your work need not be lost: that is where they should be. Now put the foundations under them." Aye, the boulders of truths eternal.

Of any earnest man he declares, "In proportion as he simplifies his life, the laws of the universe will appear less complex, and solitude will not be solitude, nor poverty poverty, nor weakness weakness." Thus grandly doth he "justify the ways of God to man." He says with ever increasing emphasis, "If life is with us a soul-wearying struggle, the fault is in us: we are violating those laws of the universe which, unbroken, make heavenly harmony."

Emerson called this man "a sad pagan," and there is deep meaning in the word spoken in jest, for, with the Elizabethan writers, "sad" and "serious" were synonymes—and a serious "pagan" Thoreau most surely was. The only other "pagan," known to me, equally serious in the consideration of that mystery we call "Life," is Marcus Aurelius.

Looking beyond the stars on a cloudless night we can easily imagine them walking hand in hand in fields of amaranth and asphodel.

Thoreau: An Appreciation

Apparently speaking of the lecture "Thoreau: An Appreciation," Dr. Jones wrote Fred Hosmer on 11 February 1891 (letter 44 in Toward the Making of Thoreau's Modern Reputation):

Next Monday night I am to speak of Thoreau's ideal life that is possible for all men. Of course, I mean as far as I am capable of understanding it, for one must be as tall as Thoreau to see as far, and as great to see as deep. I am only doing my little best, and only my sincerity can palliate my audacity. It is to me even as a religious exercise, and I assure you I feel my unfitness. But Thoreau is not popular, and somebody has got to assert him and assert him until the many begin to look into him for themselves. Then such as I must keep silent.

Dr. Jones did not keep silent after he delivered this essay, but the essay is a good example of his attempt to make Thoreau known to a larger public. The poem near the end of this essay is Dr. Jones's own.

G OLDSMITH tells of a traveller who once upon a time, found himself in a Swiss village where goitre was universal; and with one accord the lump-decorated inhabitants began to ridicule the stranger who lacked the lump under his chin. In following the trend of his genius, Thoreau eschewed Church, State, and Society. None of these had been able to develop its particular "lump" in

20

him. He never went to church; never voted; never found the companion that was so companionable as solitude. Said his friend Emerson, "The man of genius may scorn worldly matters in his devotion to his thought, but the scorned world will have its revenge." It is having this with Thoreau. He has already suffered the extremes of criticism from the fling of the fictile Lowell to the flout of the flippant Lang; both of whom must undergo a series of ascending transmigrations before they can see above his knees. Indeed, the whole Lilliput of "polite literature" cannot contain him whom Church, State, and Society could not include.

It is the critic's "lump" that determines the criticism; it is the Church's "lump," the State's "lump," Society's "lump" that makes Church, State, and Society coincide with the criticism. To all these "such a man as it takes ages to make, and ages to understand" is simply incomprehensible. They measure him by their pattern instead of making his measure the standard. They condemn a specimen because it condemns a species. They combine to punish him for his singularity because in his sturdy non-conformity they read their rebuke. It is not so much what he says as what he does that offends. "If you could convince a man that *he* does wrong, do *right* and so he does!" His living example is the lash that chastises. Their aims are debased and their ideals cheapened by his achievements. It is far easier to contradict than refute him. Easiest of all to misconceive him. He has been considered as a botanist, a naturalist, and a Man of Letters. He is all of these; but they are only the fringe of his life. He has been called a pseudo-hermit; stamped as a loafer, and stigmatized as a "skulker." He was none of these except from a wrong point of view. It is the penalty of vulgarity to call him a "crank"; but Socrates and Jesus received the same tribute. It was reserved for a professor in the University of Michigan, in his capacity as a teacher, to refer to him as "a half fool," but it would appear that some professors outdo him by half.

Justice to his genius demands that he be judged from the standpoint of his own ideal, however much that may differ from our own; and the honest student of his life and work will spend his strength in earnest endeavor to comprehend an ideal which may be in its every feature the opposite of his own.

Thoreau did not consider himself either an accident or a superfluity in the universe. *Here*, therefore, he was an essential. There was a purpose in his being, and he deemed it the chief duty of his life to find out that purpose and adjust himself thereto. He did not believe in the "Self-Renunciation" that Goethe and Carlyle preached without practising; he did not think that the world was a hospital for sick souls which were to be cured by taking bitters. He saw in the universe only the Me and Not-Me, and he did not rate that which he felt lower than that which he saw. He is the Apostle of the Ego. He formulated no creed; but he lived one, singularly, seriously, unswervingly. His every step resounds with the force of a conviction. He has triangulated the great problem, and his conclusions are mathematical certainties. He shaped his course thereby, and not a wind of doctrine could change it; he planted himself on his convictions, and not the wreck of the universe could displace him. He had found an anchor for his soul, and he had found it early in his search; found it when he turned his face from the flesh-pots of Egypt; found it when he repelled the old tempter who said to him, as he says to each soul: "all these will I give thee *if*." And whilst he was making this search and achieving such a finding, he was thought to be "disappointing the natural expectations of his family and friends." So was Christian when he turned and fled from the City of Destruction.

To Thoreau the most important thing in the universe was his own life. That was supreme. This was to be lived to its uttermost; he must leave no capacity unemployed, no opportunity unimproved. He must obey his genius implicitly; he must follow it fearlessly; he must see that nothing dims its clear light. He is like Socrates in his devotion to his *daemon*. Hence the charge that he is an egotist. Ah, but every soul is as supreme to itself as his to him. Rate your own as high. His privilege is your privilege. Perhaps he recognized his duty, and teaches yours. "What shall it profit a man if he gain the whole world and lose his *own* soul?" Which is supreme? Is it a question?

He never chanted,

> "A charge to keep I have,
>   A God to glorify,
> A never-dying soul to save
>   And fit it for the sky."

He did not deal in Church coupons of any description; he was not curious about the "reserved seats" of eternity. He lived in the present. His philosophy forbade a retrospect; his faith needed no glimpse beyond. The present moment is all-sufficient. He says, "God himself culminates in the present moment, and will never be more divine in the lapse of all the ages." When he was nearing his end, the shadows darkening around him, a solicitous friend asked him about "the other world." With the splash of the Styx in his ears he said: "One world at a time!" I have seen a letter from that very friend describing this event. It was written twenty-eight years after the occasion, but the scene burnt itself into his memory. He writes, "It was to me that he uttered the memorable words, 'one world at a time'; too weak to but gasp them; his ever-watchful, faithful mother standing over him at the time, with fan and hartshorn phial in hand. The interview lasted no more than two or three minutes, but was made memorable by the few words he gave me." Even so!

He had an innate, inherited and intense love of Nature. It was more than a love; it was a passion. A passage in his journal makes me think that it was deepened by his disappointment in another love which is common to us all. Nature mollified "that aching in the breast, the noblest pain that man endures, which no ether can assuage." Moreover, the untainted air, the murmur of the streamlet, the fragrance of the fields, the freshness of forest breeze were necessary for his well-being; he could not be confined for a day or two without being conscious of a falling-off in his life. Like Antaeus, when he touched the earth he renewed his strength. Nature never failed him:

> "Whenever the way seemed long,
>   And his heart began to fail,
> She would sing a more wonderful song,
>   Or tell a more wonderful tale."

One blessed day he made a memorable discovery. You recollect what he wrote of it to the class secretary: "I have found out a way to live without what is commonly called employment, or industry attractive or otherwise. Indeed, my steadiest employment, if such it can be called, is to keep myself at the top of my condition, and ready for whatever may turn up in heaven or on earth." There is a great deal "between the lines" here. Not so much that he shall be "ready for anything that may turn up in heaven or on earth," though, as I understand it, that is the end of all so-called religion; but his desire to keep himself, body and soul, at the top of his condition. A physiological epicure; he the guest, life the feast. He must keep himself at the top of his condition to get from both of these their zest. Seven years before writing this letter he had made another discovery, namely, "A man is never inspired unless his body is also. It, too, spurns a tame and commonplace life. They are fatally mistaken who think while they strive with their minds that they may suffer their bodies to stagnate in luxury or sloth. The body is the first proselyte the soul makes. Our life is but the soul made known by its fruits, the body. The whole duty of man may be expressed in one line. Make to yourself a perfect body."

Seriously, strenuously, sedulously strove he for this. He was an utter stranger to stimulants, narcotics, and all defilements. He kept his body as one who knew it to be the temple of a God. This he did to make the uttermost of the life that had been lent him.

He was equally assiduous in regard to the keeping of his mind. He writes in his journal: "With a certain wariness, but not without a slight shudder at the danger often-times, I perceive how near I had come to admitting into my mind the details of some trivial affair, as a case at court, and I am astonished to observe how willing men are to lumber their minds with such rubbish, to permit idle rumors, tales, incidents, even of an insignificant kind, to intrude upon what should be the sacred ground of the thoughts. Shall the temple of our thoughts be a public arena where the most trivial affair of the market and the gossip of the tea-table is discussed, a dusty, noisy, trivial place? or shall it be a quarter of the heavens itself, consecrated to the service of the gods? I find it so difficult to dispose of the few facts which are to me significant, that I hesitate to burden my mind with the most insignificant, which only a divine mind can illustrate. Such is, for the most part, the news in newspapers and conversation. It is important to preserve the mind's chastity in this respect. Think of admitting the details of a single case at the criminal court into the mind to stalk profanely through its very *sanctum sanctorum* for an hour—aye, for many hours; to make a very bar-room of your mind's inmost apartment, as if for a moment the dust of the street had occupied you,—aye, the very street itself, with all its travel, had poured through your very mind of minds, your thought's shrine, with all its filth and bustle. Would it not be an intellectual suicide? By all manner of boards and traps threatening the extreme penalty of the divine law, excluding trespassers from these grounds, it behooves us to preserve the purity and sanctity of the mind. It is so hard to forget what it is worse than useless to remember. If I am to be a channel or thoroughfare, I prefer that it be of the mountain brooks, the Parnassian streams, and not of the city sewers. There is inspiration, the divine gossip which comes to the attentive mind from the Courts of Heaven, there is the profane and stale revelation of the bar-room and the police court. The same ear is fitted to receive both communications. Only the character of the individual determines to which source chiefly it shall be open, and to which closed. I believe that the mind can be profaned by the habit of attending to trivial things, so that all our thoughts shall be tinged with triviality. . . . I think we should treat our minds as innocent and ingenuous children whose guardians we are, be careful what objects and what subjects are thrust on their attention. I think even the facts of science may dust them by their dryness, unless they are in a sense affaced each morning, or rather rendered fertile by the dews of fresh and living truth. Every thought which passes through the mind helps to wear and tear it and to deepen the ruts, which, as in the streets of Pompeii, evince how much it has been used. How many things there are concerning which we might well deliberate whether we had better know them. Routine, conventionality, manners, etc.; how insensibly an undue attention to these dissipates and impoverishes the mind, robs it of its simplicity and strength, emasculates it." How he turns the subject over and over, follows its ramifications, enlarging, illustrating, emphasizing it, and in his eagerness tautologically repeating himself. It is not the smooth rhetoric of a complacent writer on ethics; it is not the studied pose of an artful actor; it is the burning conviction of a man who realizes that a complete scheme of Sanitary Science must include the dietetics of the Soul. A man whose ultimatum is: *A clean bill of health for body and soul.* With nothing short of this could he keep himself at the top of his condition; with nothing less than this could he realize the possibilities of life; the life that he so magnified, so exalted, so guarded as the gift of gifts.

But, he had found out "a way to live without what is commonly called employment." It is in this matter that he is so commonly and so largely misunderstood. Lowell calls him "indolent." To which Higginson replies, "You might as well speak of the indolence of a self-registering thermometer; it does not go about noisily, yet it never knows an idle moment." Stevenson says he "had as good as stolen his livelihood," and all because the man could get a year's subsistence by six weeks of labor. The Lowells, Stevensons, and their like live by the law of the ledger; their yard-stick is stained with the de-filements of the marketplace; their standard is that of the money-changers who were driven out of the Temple with stripes. Thoreau computed by an arithmetic they never learned. He determined the cost of a thing by an equation in which the value of x is absolute. He says, "The cost of a thing is the amount of what I will call life which is required to be exchanged for it." O Life, Life, that "unknown quantity" with the multitude, who toil and groan and fardels bear, when, as the gift of the Infinite, it was meant for a beatitude! What amount of it can he afford to exchange for the tinselled toys of Vanity Fair?

If a man is to keep himself at the top of his condition in order that he may make the most of his life, and if his genius, his daemon, the voice within, is to be his guide, how shall he obey it at all times, follow it in all places, if he be not free, his own master, the slave of neither time, place, nor circumstance? This was his problem, and this he went to Walden Pond to solve. He says, "I went to the woods because I wished to live deliberately, to front only the essential facts of life, and see if I could not learn what it had to teach, and not, when I came to die, discover that I had not lived. I did not wish to live what was not life, living is so dear; nor did I wish to practice resig-nation, unless it was quite necessary. I wanted to live deep and suck out all the marrow of life, to live so sturdily and Spartan-like as to put to rout all that was not life, to cut a broad swath and shave close, to drive life into a corner, and reduce it to its lowest terms, and, if it proved to be mean, why then to get the whole and genuine meanness of it, and publish it to the world; or if it were sublime, to know it by experience, and be able to give an account of it in my next excursion."

He first asked what are the absolute necessaries of life for man in this climate, and by actual experience he proved that they are simply Food, Shelter, Clothing, and Fuel. Such of these as he found *essential* for himself could be supplied by six weeks of labor in each year; that is, of every year of a man's life his body could claim six weeks, leaving more than seven times six for his soul. This is a division of labor of which Ministers to the Court of St. James and modern novelists do not dream; it is even stranger than the case of Dr. Jekyl and Mr. Hyde. Having thus simplified the problem of mere subsistance, and finding it so cheap, there stretches before him the broad highway to wealth; but just here he found "the parting of the ways" that so puzzles the Lowells and Stevensons and other worldly wise. He says, "When a man has obtained those things which are necessary to life, there is another alternative than to obtain the superfluities; and that is, to adventure on life now, his vacation from humbler toil having commenced." This is the alternative that the Lowells and Stevensons of this life never choose, and it is for his deliberate choice that they condemn him. It is also to be remembered that his choice accuses theirs and ours of ineptitude, is a living reproach to us, and that pride puts them and us and the multitude in antagonism to him. By actual count of hands he is a minority of one against the world: and the majority cannot be wrong. This is the logic which satisfies society. It were well if it also satisfied the soul—a function of logic that "society" is apt to overlook. Think of the audacity of this uncouth man to thus arraign Society; to set such an example, contravening the experience of the centuries; challenging civilization to give account for itself; denying its time-old conclusions; scorning its crowning results.

It was a question with Thoreau whether Civilization civilizes. Certain it is that Civilization affords some singular spectacles, and his not the only eye to see them. Looking from his study window one March day in 1833, Maurice de Guerin then wrote in his journal, "I see laborers digging in the garden. These poor people thus expend their whole life to gain wherewith to eat their bread from day to day—their dry and black bread. What a mystery is that of all these existences, so rude and lowly—and they are almost the whole of the human race. A day will come when all these drudges of society will show their blackened and callous hands, seamed with grasping the handles of their tools, and will say, 'Thou, Lord, who hast said, Blessed are the poor and lowly, behold us!'

'To you, good God, we make our last appeal.'

Who made these fellow creatures the "drudges of society"—God, or man? If six weeks of labor will provide sustenance for a year, what spell dooms these wretches to constant toil? If six weeks suffice to feed, shelter, clothe, and warm, who has stolen their other forty-six? If Man, woe to him in the day when at the bar of Heaven's Chancery those blackened and callous hands shall make their last appeal.

Thoreau does not ask these terrible questions directly; but an alert conscience can hear whispers in the pages of his "Walden" that are not to be silenced by flinging the book aside and calling the author all manner of names, a vain dreamer.

Thoreau's accepted alternative, "to adventure on life," is filled with unspeakable meaning. It is to grapple with the "mystery of all these existences" in order to find out whether the Creator has provided for the created; to learn if life is a mean misery, or a sublime sufficiency, declaring the plenitude, not the penury of God. It is to "justify the ways of God to man."

He says, "When we are weary with travel, we lay down our load, and rest by the wayside. So, when we are weary with the burden of life, why do we not lay down this load of falsehoods which we have volunteered to sustain, and be refreshed as never mortal was? Let the beautiful laws prevail. Let us not weary ourselves by resisting them." This is the core of his philosophy: that beautiful laws constitute the Divine Economy; that we resist them; that we make a grievous burden of a beneficent boon. He could find no other meaning for this Universe that did not contravene its Maker; he could see no other solution for the problem of the ages that did not impugn the Infinite; he could divine no other interpretation for the mystery of the blackened and callous hands that did not accuse the All-Just. This he believed. He put his life into his belief and his belief into his life.

He believed also that a man's soul was something better than a mere antiseptic to keep his body from stinking. Six weeks of a year would care for the body; forty-six were left for

the soul. He adjusted values accordingly. It was said to-night
that he saw in the universe only the Me and the Not-Me.
Himself, Nature and the Source of Nature. With the first two of
these he concerned himself. The last he worshipped not by
word but deed.

Thoreau lived far more with Nature than with man, and yet
was by no means a misanthrope as so many imagine. There
are to-day in Concord old men and middle-aged whose hearts
beat quicker at the mention of his name. They had learned the
depths of his tenderness, though he was so silent and un-
demonstrative that the superficial were deceived. His own
mother said there was one side of his nature that she might
never have known had it not been for his father's illness and
death. Then she found him the tenderest of nurses, and in her
bereavement an unfailing comfort. He has been thought rude
and selfish because he refused to share his walks indiscriminately; he said bluntly he had no walks to throw away on anybody. It is easy to misunderstand him in this. Not everyone is
qualified to commune with Nature in the same spirit. There
are degrees. Only the High Priest could enter the Holy of
Holies. In Thoreau was developed to its utmost that faculty
which, De Guerin says, "we all have, however veiled, vague,
and almost totally bereft of energy,—the faculty which
gathers the beauty of Nature, and hands it over to the soul,
which spiritualizes it, harmonizes it, combines it with ideal
beauty, and thus enlarges its sphere of love and adoration."
Not everyone could fitly approach the shrine with such a man.

I am glad to be able to illustrate what Nature was to
Thoreau by De Guerin's testimony. "When I go out to walk in a
pleasant mood and free from all care, I feel dawning in the
depth of my soul an unwonted, a singularly lively joy. The
farther I go into the country, it rises and diffuses itself, now
rapidly, now slowly, according to the incidents by the way and
the time it takes to reach the finest part of the walk. Once there
and established to my liking, and always in a way to receive
most vividly on all sides impressions from the surrounding

horizon, this growing feeling of indefinable delight attains its fulness, diffuses itself through my being, and fills it to over-flowing" (De Guerin's Journal).

Again: "As often as we allow ourselves to penetrate to Nature, our soul opens to the most touching impressions. There is something in Nature, whether she decks in smiles during the bright days, or becomes, as in autumn and winter, pale, gray, cold and tearful, which stirs not only the surface of the spirit, but even its most secret recesses, and awakens a thousand memories which have, apparently, no connection with the external aspects, but which, without doubt, sustain a relation to the soul of Nature by sympathies to us unknown. This marvellous power I have experienced to-day, stretched in a grove of beeches, and breathing the warm spring air."

Here is an April day from the pencil of De Guerin that might have been painted by Thoreau himself: "A beautiful day as one could wish. Some clouds, but only as many as are needed to give picturesqueness to the sky. They assume more and more their summer forms. Their scattered groups repose motionless under the sun, like flocks of sheep in the pastures during the heat of day. I have seen a swallow, and I have heard the bees humming over the flowers. Seating myself in the sun, in order that I may be saturated to the marrow with divine Spring, I have experienced some of the impressions of my childhood; for a moment I have regarded the sky with its clouds, the earth with its forests, its songs, its murmurings as I did then. This renewing of the first Aspect of things, of the expressions which our first thoughts put upon them is, to my thinking, one of the sweetest influences of childhood on the current of life."

Thoreau has said that he was not isolated when all alone in field or forest. De Guerin reveals the secret of this. "There is no isolation for the man who knows how to take his place in the universal harmony, and to open his soul to all the impressions of that harmony. Then one comes to have almost a physical consciousness that we live from God and in God."

It was one of Thoreau's friends that said,

"And when I am stretched beneath the pines,
Where the evening star so holy shines,
I laugh at the lore and the pride of man,
At the sophist schools and the learned clan;
For what are they all in their high conceit,
When man in the bush with God may meet?"   (Emerson)

Thoreau thought that he deteriorated in society, that he could recuperate only by a retreat to Nature. Mr. Lowell is of the opinion that "to a man of wholesome constitution the wilderness is well enough for a mood or vacation, but not for a habit of life." In the matter of "constitution" considered all round the author of the *Centaur* will compare favorably with the writer of *The Bigelow Papers*, and I beg leave to give De Guerin's estimate of the respective influences of society and solitude. "To leave solitude for the crowd; the green ways, and the solitary, for the obstructed streets with their clamors, where instead of a breeze circulates a current of warm, tainted human breath; to pass from quietism to turbulent life, and from the vague mysteries of Nature to the harsh reality of society, has ever been a terrible change for me, a return to evil and misfortune. As I go on my way, and advance in the discernment of the true and false in society, my inclination to live, —not as a savage nor a misanthrope, but as a solitary man on the confines of society, on the borders of the world,—is strengthened and extended. The birds flutter, pilfer, build their nests about our dwellings, they are like fellow-citizens of the farms and hamlets; but they fly in the sky, which is immense; the hand of God alone distributes and meassures out to them the day's food; they build their nests in the hearts of the thickets, or hang them on the tops of the trees. Thus I would wish to live, hovering about society, and having always behind me a field of liberty, vast as the heavens. If my faculties are not yet formed, if it is true that they have not attained their growth, they will develop only in the open air and under a somewhat wild exposure. My last sojourn in the country has confirmed my conviction on this point." It would appear that Lowell must scrape his shoes on a tapestry carpet to elicit his little spark. It is the touch of the turf that inspires genius.

Thoreau's "adventure on life" was, then, a life-long communion with Nature. It is safe to say that five-eighths of his life was spent in the open air. He was as apt to take a walk by night as by day being eager to see Nature in her every aspect. His descriptions of Nature charmed an Emerson as completely as they did the child. Said Emerson's son, in a recent lecture on Thoreau, "We children, when we heard his step at the door, would rush to him, and, clinging round his knees, would drag him to the fireplace, when he would sit down and tell us stories of what he had seen in the woods, and of the manner of living of the animals and birds." Not long since, George William Curtis, from pure love for this dead man's memory, found time to write me this sketch: "One of my most vivid recollections of my life in Concord is that of an evening upon the shallow river with Thoreau in his boat. We lighted a huge fire of fat pine in an iron crate beyond the bow of the boat and drifted slowly through an illuminated circle of the ever-changing aspect of the river bed. In that House Beautiful you can fancy what an interpreter he was."

Thoreau's harshest critic acknowledges that "he had watched Nature like a detective that is to go upon the stand." Day after day, for twenty-five years of his life he recorded in his journals his seeings, doings, and thinkings, and the same critic felt obliged to say, "as we read him, it seems as if all out-of-doors had kept a diary, and become its own Montaigne." These journals comprise some thirty volumes, and they are a transcendentalist's *Apologia pro Vita Sua.*

Thoreau says, "The true harvest of my daily life is somewhat as intangible and indescribable as the tints of morning and evening. . . . Perhaps the facts most astounding and most real are never communicated by man to man."

He has this entry in his journal, "The Secretary of the Association for the Advancement of Science requested me, as he probably has thousands of others, by a printed circular from Washington, the other day, to fill the blanks against certain questions, among which the most important one was what branch of science I was specially interested in, using the term science in the most comprehensive sense possible. Now, though I could state to a select few that department of human inquiry which engages me, and should rejoice at an opportunity so to do, I felt that it would be to make myself the laughing stock of the scientific community to describe to them that branch of science which especially interests me, inasmuch as they do not believe in a science which deals with the higher law. So I was obliged to speak to their condition and describe to them that poor part of me which alone they can understand. The fact is I am a mystic, a transcendentalist, and a natural philosopher to boot. Now I think of it, I should have told them at once that I was a transcendentalists; that would have been the shortest way of telling them that they would not understand my explanation. How absurd that though I probably stand as near to Nature as any of them, and am by constitution as good an observer as most, yet a true account of my relation to nature should excite their ridicule only. If it had been the secretary of an association of which Plato or Aristotle was the president, I should not have hesitated to describe my studies at once and particularly."

What is there here that eludes us? Is it only the "poor part" of him that we can understand? The preparation of a bibliography of Thoreau has led me to read all that I could lay hold of pertaining to him, and after all that I have read I still feel that an indefinable something has eluded the subtlest critical analysis. Perhaps it is a true conception of his "relation to nature." I do not know. To me the missing quality is simply and only an indefinable *something*.

I believe he went to Nature for answers to questions the solutions of which we seek far elsewhere. If once it dawns upon a man that our Bible is only one of many Bibles; that a special revelation of Himself to a favored people is the delirium of spiritual pride; that every yearning soul, in every time and every clime, has had access to the one only God, and these were his convictions, then shall he seek his revelation of God in Nature. Where else can he go?

He says, "We may live the life of a plant or an animal without living an animal life. This constant and universal content of the animal comes of resting quietly in God's palm." That is simply, the animal conforms to Nature's laws, lets "the beautiful laws prevail." These laws are as perfect and as beneficent for us as for the animal, and we can have "the constant and universal content of the animal" by a like obedience. What earthly use had such a man for the Westminster Catechism? The animal is guided by an instinct that is to it inviolate, and that implanted instinct is the Creator's provision for the creature. The same Wisdom has given to Man his good genius, the voice within, and if he will implicitly follow *that* it shall be well with him. To Thoreau this is the sum and substance of all Bibles whatsoever. He distinctly says, "If one listens to the faintest but constant suggestions of his genius, which are certainly true, he sees not to what extremes, or even insanity, it may lead him; and yet that way, as he grows more resolute and faithful, his road lies. . . . No man ever followed his genius until it misled him. Though the result were bodily weakness, yet perhaps no one can say that the consequences were to be regretted, for these were a life of conformity to higher principles."

He believed that his life was given to him to be lived to the utmost realization of its every possibility, and that fidelity to his genius alone could enable such a realization. I am not alone in thus interpreting his science of life. His most favored correspondent and oldest living student says, "He declined from the first to live for the common prizes of society, for wealth or even what is called a competence, for professional, social, political, or even literary success; and this not from a want of ambition or a purpose, but from an ambition far higher than the ordinary, which fully possessed him,—an ambition to obey his purest instincts, to follow implicitly the finest intimations of his genius, to secure thus the fullest and

freest life of which he was capable. . . . Perhaps the highest
lesson of all to be learnt from him is that the only way of salvation lies in the strictest fidelity to one's own genius"
(Blake).

He differs from all iconoclasts in the fact that "he desired no
servile imitation of his own methods." "I would not have anyone adopt my mode of living on any account; for, beside that
before he has fairly learned it I may have found out another
for myself, I desire that there may be as many different persons in the world as possible; but I would have each one be
very careful to find out and pursue his own way, and not his
father's or his mother's or his neighbor's instead."

Nor did he pose as a reformer though the very air he
breathed was rife with reforms. Brook Farm, Fruitlands, the
Phalansteries that sprung from the spawn of Fourierism did
not deflect him from his orbit. Alone he went to Walden to
learn for himself if life is mean or sublime. That is a problem
which every soul must solve for itself. It is between man and
God. He recognized no mediator that can come between man
and God. It is a relationship that knows no middle term. The
soul has no vicar. Of all whose example has in it any lesson for
Man, he is singularly *solitary*—the apostle of the Ego as we
have called him. He lifts us from the slough of self abasement
into the sunshine of self reliance.

"He condemns doing good as one of the weakest of superstitions," said Lowell with a sneer. That is, "doing good to
another," as the phrase goes. To consider this conceit a superstition is a depth of insight denied to not only Lowell. It was
such a "superstition" as Lowell shares that filled Tetzel's
money chest. "The perseverance of the saints" reaches no
farther than *to* and *for* the saint that perseveres. The kingdom
of Heaven is not won by proxy. Not all the saints can "do
good" to a single sinner; it is the soul's prerogative, a possibility to itself alone. He who so recognized the soul's su-
premacy could acknowledge no other reformer than itself;
could find no other field for one beyond itself.

He made all things subsidiary to the higher life, a means to
that end; and he never made immortality a conjecture. To him

that was no more to be questioned than that the setting sun implied the rising. In the divine order the one followed the other. He did not calculate probabilities. He never lived behind or beyond the present moment. He made that his sole concern. The Infinite Purpose would fulfill itself. His was the consummation of faith.

It proved a sustaining faith. When he was summoned in the very prime of manhood from a world that he found so full of beauty, and from pursuits in which he stood preeminent, Emerson said sadly, "It seems an injury that he should leave in the midst of his broken task, which none else can finish,—a kind of indignity to so noble a soul, that it should depart out of Nature before yet he has been really shown to his peers for what he is. But he, at least, is content." True; I cannot find that he ever uttered one repining word.

Up to almost the day of his death he was busy arranging his manuscripts, aided by his sister Sophia. Last summer I saw the manuscript of his essay on Walking, and it shows three differ[ent] handswriting: two of them his own and one his faithful sister's. When too feeble to use the pen he had resorted to the more convenient pencil, and where his strength had wholly failed there came passages written by Sophia from dictation. As I read it seemed as if I were looking over the dying man's shoulder.

Then the Concord Library faded from my sight, and I heard the part of his last letter as he spake the words that his sister wrote:

"I have not been engaged in any particular work on Botany, or the like, though, if I were to live, I should have much to report on Natural History generally.

You ask particularly after my health, I suppose that I have not many months to live; but, of course, I know nothing about it. I may add that I am enjoying existence as much as ever, and regret nothing.

Yours truly,
HENRY D. THOREAU,
by SOPHIA E. THOREAU."

It was, indeed, a fitting sunset:

> He kept the temple as divine
>   Wherein his soul abided;
> He heard the voice within the shrine
>   And followed as it guided;
> He found no bane of bitter strife,
>   But laws of Love's designing:
> He quaffed the brimming cup of Life,
>   And went forth unrepining.

His career remains a shining instance of a high endeavor to find out the meaning of Life. We know that we can make it mean enough; he has shown that it may be made grand enough.

He is not quoted as an authority in bank parlors; he is disdained in the world's market places; Society disowns him, and yet he has shown the way to that Promised Land wherein the wise may dwell.

Of the ten volumes of Thoreau's works but two were published by him. The papers that he arranged in his last illness were printed in the *Atlantic Monthly* immediately after his decease, and in the year following appeared his first posthumous volume, edited by his faithful sister with the assistance of Emerson and William Ellery Channing. Two other volumes appeared in 1864, one in 1865, and the last of Sophia Thoreau's editing in 1866. Dying herself in 1876, she bequeathed her brother's Journals and all his MSS. to his earliest disciple, the Rev. Harrison G. O. Blake, of Worcester, Mass. From the Journals Mr. Blake has since eidted and published three volumes, and now has a fourth in preparation. These books are called *Early Spring in Massachusetts, Summer,* and *Winter*, each *"From the Journal of Henry D. Thoreau."* The forthcoming volume will be entitled *Autumn*. In his editorship, Mr. Blake has followed a suggestion made by Thoreau himself, namely, "to make a Journal of the seasons." Mr. Blake has gone through the 30 manuscript volumes and made a selection from the entries on the same day of the month for the various years. Of course, the result of this labor of love is not such a diary of the seasons as Thoreau would have made, but it is a priceless contribution to American literature. In these books the sincere student can hear trumpet blasts that will nerve him for the highest endeavor; he will turn from their pages refreshed and renewed, and he will recur to them for counsel and inspiration so long as his aim is worthy and his life is true.

I am thankful for these books as they are, and I do not know how else Mr. Blake could have opened Thoreau's Journals to us; but yet they are unsatisfactory to one who desires to study Thoreau *thoroughly*, because they do not allow us to trace the steps of his development. The plan of these books necessitated the disruption of continuity; the current of Thoreau's thought is not followed from year to year. We can but hope that one as faithful as Mr. Blake may be found to take up the torch when he shall go to join his long-loved friend.

14th February, 1891.

Thoreau's Inheritance

This essay originally appeared in the Inlander *3 (1893): 199–204 and was reprinted in* Thoreau: A Glimpse, *pp. 28–35. (The text used here is from* Thoreau: A Glimpse.) *In this article, Dr. Jones attempts to do justice to Thoreau's parents, who, he believed, had been dealt with unfairly by Sanborn. Dr. Jones made frequent use of material supplied by Horace Hosmer, who had attended the school operated by the Thoreau brothers. The poem that concludes the article was composed by Dr. Jones. For additional material, see* Remembrances of Concord and the Thoreaus: The Letters of Horace Hosmer to Dr. S. A. Jones.

THOREAU'S shanty-life at Walden is the episode by which he is chiefly known and from which he is generally misunderstood. That really serious and far-reaching experiment in "plain living and high thinking" is considered a transcendental fête champetre or as one of the various freaks of the disciples of "The Newness." It was unfavorably judged by Lowell, whose criticism of Thoreau's life and aims has given the cue to that respectable majority who think by proxy when they think at all. In Lowell's opinion, Thoreau at Walden was masquerading as a "hermit" whose whole environment proclaimed him a pretence; and even the genial genius who presides "over the teacups" mentions him as "the Robinson Crusoe of Walden pond, who carried out a school-boy whim to its full proportions." The atmosphere in which alone a Lowell and a

Holmes could burst into blossom would only stifle a Thoreau, and men so different can never interpret, much less comprehend, each other.

Thoreau's adventure at Walden was a crucial experiment in the science and art of living; an earnest grappling with the mysteries that vex and perplex this earthly existence. He had concluded that "the mass of men lead lives of quiet desperation. What is called resignation is confirmed desperation," and in the very soul of him he believed that such lives impugn the wisdom, the justice, and the compassion of the Divine Arbiter. Moreover, he had found that a man who was willing to live sanely, "close to the bone, where life is sweetest," could earn by six weeks' labor sufficient to support him for the remainder of the year. The richest of the Concord farmers were not doing so well as that; they were "so occupied with the factitious cares and superfluously coarse labors of life that its finer fruits cannot be plucked by them." Yet these very fruits— an intercourse and intimacy with Nature, whose countless delights made life one ceaseless round of rapture—were his continual harvest, spring, summer, autumn and winter.

Thoreau was happily constituted; he was strong and alert; a tireless pedestrian, and endowed with such a refinement of the special senses as made him a marvel to his intimates. His sight was almost microscopical; his scent so acute that he detected a peculiar odor coming from such inhabited houses as he happened to pass at night, and he heard rapturous harmonies in the vibrations of a wind-shaken telegraph wire. He revelled in the luxury of these gifts and became the epicure of Nature. Now it was the austere flavor of a wild apple from his well-stored pockets or that of some simple bark which he stripped as he walked; then it was the perfume of the clethra or the fern as he strode through them on his daily ramble; again it was the song of the birds, which he was so skillful in translating into syllabic similitudes; and always there was the painted landscape of the varied year, the gilded sunsets and the calm night's silvered clouds. Did HE make all these for the deaf and the blind! Did HE tempt the children of men with these ineffable visions and then so order their lives that they should have "no time" to enjoy them! It is what the fool hath said in his heart: they are wide-spread as the earth, free as the air, and to drink in their delights is verily "to glorify God and enjoy Him forever." Thoreau recognized his inheritance and entered upon it with joy.

But his inheritance included also the endowment of heredity: a potent factor which has not yet had just and due consideration from any of his biographers.

A gentleman who attended the school kept by the Thoreau brothers once wrote to me: "Henry Thoreau was not a superior scion upon an inferior stock, neither was he begotten by a North-west wind, as many have supposed. There were good and sufficient reasons for the Thoreau childrens' love of, and marked taste for, Botany and Natural History. John Thoreau and his wife were to be seen, year after year, enjoying the pleasures of nature, in their various seasons, on the banks of the Assabet, at Fairhaven, Lee's Hill, Walden and elsewhere; and this too without neglecting the various duties of their humble sphere. Indeed, such was Mrs. Thoreau's passion for these rambles that one of her children narrowly escaped being born in a favorite haunt on Lee's Hill.

"The father was a very cautious and secretive man, a close observer, methodical and deliberate in action, and he produced excellent results. His marbled paper and his pencils were the best in the market, while his stove polish and his plumbago for electrotyping have never, to my knowledge, been excelled. He was a French gentleman rather than a 'Yankee,' and once having his confidence, you had a very shrewd and companionable friend to commune with. Then, when there were no unauthorized listeners about, the otherwise quiet man, who had such a faculty for 'minding his own business,' would sit with you by the stove in his little shop and chat most delightfully.

"When I recollect, too, what an exacting woman his excellent wife was, and that he fully met her inflexible demands, I can by no means regard him as the mediocre 'plodder' depicted by one of his famous son's biographers. No; the tree is known by its fruits, and John Thoreau begot brains of a high order, with sound, healthy bodies to go with them; and I feel certain that his highest earthly aspirations were realized in his children."

Nor was this sterling man yoked with an unworthy help-mate, despite the biographer who represents her as a gossip-monger prompt to "take her share in the village bickerings." This ascription, so sadly at variance with the sweet charity that spares the dead, was sharply contradicted by a lady friend of Mrs. Thoreau in the Boston "Daily Advertiser," but, alas! the ephemeral newspaper perishes with the day that brought it forth, while the printed book lives on and

"Like a tall bully, lifts its head and lies."

One biographer bears glowing testimony to the high moral altitude of the Thoreau children, but quite forgets to explain how they could possibly attain to such a lofty ethical grandeur in the atmosphere of a home that was moulded and managed by a gossip-loving mother. Such a discrepancy should not be left to disfigure and disgrace the American Men of Letters Series. Marcus Antonius was indeed the putative father of that Commodus whose ear was deaf to the stirring "Meditations" that were written for his guidance; but we feel assured that Faustina corrupted the stream of gentle blood which came untainted from the heart of Annius Verus, and her son sustained the calumnies that without him would have perished. There is no baleful cloud to cast this dark shadow on John Thoreau's village home, and in that favored environment—of which it is written, "Perpetuity, indeed, and hereditary transmission of everything that by nature and good sense can be inherited, are amongst the characteristics of Concord"— the Thoreau children throve and were a blessing to their home.

Such were the human sources of Thoreau's inheritance; enviable on both the spear side and the spindle; but most probably his ruling passion can be traced to one of them chiefly. A mother whom the woodland nymphs are surprised to see smitten with the throes of maternity while she is straying in their haunts, is likely by the rule of heredity to impress her deepest-rooted trait upon the son that most closely resembled her, and it is more than probable that Henry D. Thoreau's intense Nature-love caught its life-long fire from his mother's fervor; while the clear sanity of his genius is as distinctly attributable to the plain but solid virtues of his sire. The marriage of quiet John Thoreau and vivacious Cynthia Dunbar was a happy conjunction of diverse temperaments and opposite traits, of substantial virtues and of simple habits; and with bodies undefiled by luxury and minds unsophisticated by social dissimulation they made a home, and its lowly hearth became a shrine whose incense brought blessings to their offspring.

That impulse, the culminating momentum of which impelled Thoreau to seek the solitude of Walden, was a two-fold force: the mystery of Life pressing upon him for solution and the maternal love of Nature sending him to Nature with his burden. Of a certainty he was swayed more by instinct than reason; it was a sacred oestrus soliciting the marriage of Nature and Man's soul—better say the re-marriage, for in the golden age these two were one.

Thoreau says he does not know why he went to live in Walden woods and on looking back long after he had forsaken his shanty, he frankly acknowledges that he is equally at a loss to say why he left it. But whether in that sojourn he correctly settled the problem or not, he has left us in "Walden: or Life in the Woods," one of the most sanative books in all literature. This volume is equalled only by the example of his clean, pure life, which is like a winter morning, austere to the rebuking of all slothfulness; clear as the water of Life, serene as an Alpine summit and bracing as its atmosphere; and the lesson of his trustful death, which is like the setting of a summer sun ere yet the harvest time has fully come: there is still need for the ripening rays to longer linger, but still the ineffable glory of the fading effulgence has in it the Eternal's promise of another day.

Emerson once playfully called him "a sad pagan," and many, not Emersons, to this day deem him irreligious, and from the manner in which he flouted their false gods, even sacrilegious. As Schiller says, "Against stupidity the gods themselves contend in vain." Take a retrospect of his life—the only "religion" that will "smell sweet and blossom in the dust"—and what are its gleaming mountain-tops? A sacred care for his body to keep it undefiled, and a sleepless vigilance to preserve unsullied the purity of his mind; an obedience to the Voice within fully as pious as the devotion of Socrates to his daemon; a justification of the ways of God to man that makes a "back number" of all catechisms; a resignation to death that needed not the agony of Gethsemane.

Who can read unmoved that last letter of his, written at dictation and signed by proxy:

"I have not been engaged in any particular work on Botany" [Oh, the perfume of the young buds in the wind!] "though if I were to live, I should have much to report on Natural History generally.

"You ask particularly after my health. I suppose I have not many months to live; but, of course, I know nothing about it. I may add that I am enjoying existence as much as ever, and regret nothing."

In the matter of "religion" it would appear that his began where so many are apt to fall away—at the yawning brink of a grave.

He kept the temple as divine
  Wherein his soul abided;
He heard the Voice within the shrine
  And followed as it guided;
He found no bane of bitter strife,
  But laws of His designing;
He quaffed the brimming cup of Life
  And went forth unrepining.

Prefatory Note to

Some Unpublished Letters of

Henry D. and Sophia E. Thoreau

Dr. Jones located Thoreau's Michigan correspondent Calvin H. Greene in 1897 and obtained from him six letters that he had received from Thoreau, three letters from Sophia Thoreau, and one each from F. B. Sanborn and Ellery Channing. Greene also gave Dr. Jones the Maxham daguerreotype of Thoreau.

Dr. Jones first made public announcement of this literary find in "Some Unpublished Letters of Henry D. and Sophia E. Thoreau," a lecture for the benefit of the ladies' gymnasium at the University of Michigan in January of 1898. He then returned to the preparation of a publish- *able manuscript. Greene, however, objected to certain language in the manuscript: he particularly disliked Dr. Jones's characterization of him as "lowly born and lowly bred"; Greene understood that the phrase was used to contrast him with Froude and knew that the contrast was meant to be complimentary. Still, Greene believed that he was being damned with faint praise. The conflict over language accounts for one peculiarity in* Some Unpublished Letters: *Greene is not mentioned by name, rather he is Thoreau's "Western correspondent."* See Toward the Making of Thoreau's

Modern Reputation *(Urbana: University of Illinois Press, 1979) for a full account of the Greene-Jones relationship and for the history of the Froude letter.*

Some Unpublished Letters of Henry D. and Sophia E. Thoreau: A Chapter in the History of a Still-Born Book *was published by the Marion Press of Jamaica, N.Y., in 1899. The Prefatory Note is reprinted here. Many of the letters in the text were reedited by Walter Harding and Carl Bode and appear in* The Correspondence of Henry David Thoreau; *their readings are more accurate than Dr. Jones's transcriptions.*

The discovery and publication of the Thoreau materials in the possession of Calvin Greene were among Dr. Jones's most notable literary achievements. (All bracketed and parenthetical remarks in the text are Dr. Jones's unless otherwise noted.)

L EARNING that Thoreau had once a Western correspondent, and knowing that these of his letters had not been published, it occurred to the slightly irascible and somewhat eccentric ex-professor that it were worth while to make search therefore: possibly that correspondence might be recovered. Thoreau's correspondent was found without difficulty,—an aged and venerable man,—and to the great surprise of the ex-professor the holographs were transferred to his keeping, and are used by the present editor in preparing the text of this book.

Thoreau's letters are in themselves but a trifle, yet they give characteristic glimpses of him; those of his sister reveal a phase of his character that is not so widely known as it deserves, and in justice to a dead man should be.

The story of these simple letters is briefly as follows: George Ripley's review of *Walden; or, Life in the Woods*, led a distant reader to write to Ticknor and Company for a copy, the chief incitement being the liberal citations from the book itself. Upon receiving the volume it was almost literally devoured; a somewhat peculiar spiritual experience had prepared the way for it with that remote reader; he then found it sweet in the mouth, and after forty years it has not proven bitter in the belly. Of course the book had "found" its reader, as Coleridge would say of such a divine conjunction, and like the famishing charity boy, that particular reader wanted "some more." That earnest man, reading *Walden*, and one of the few of that day able to read it "between the lines,"—reading and pondering under the burr-oaks in the silence of the forest solitude,—

> "—felt like some watcher of the skies
> When a new planet swims into his ken."

From the title-page of *Walden* he learned that Thoreau was also the author of another book, *A Week on the Concord and Merrimack Rivers*. Failing to obtain a copy of this from the publishers of *Walden* or any other source then known to him, the seeker managed to get Thoreau's address and made application directly to him; and there the correspondence begins.

Thoreau and his Western correspondent never met, though at one point of the hopeless journey to Minnesota in search of health one hour's ride would have brought them together; but the doomed pilgrim knew that he must speedily return to put his house in order, for he was not deceived in regard to his bodily condition. "I think," he wrote to Mr. Ricketson, "that, on the whole, my health is better than when you were here; but my faith in the doctors has not increased."

The correspondence with Sophia E. Thoreau arose from a letter of condolence, on the death of her brother, written more than a month after that event. A subsequent visit to Concord brought the distant friend and the Thoreau survivors face to face: it was the *res angustoe domi* alone that had prevented such a meeting with Thoreau himself. The visitor from afar was tenderly received by both the mourning mother and sister and Thoreau's friends Alcott and Channing. Before returning, the pilgrim was requested by both Mrs. Thoreau and Sophia to select from the library of his departed friend some books for keepsakes. Thus it came that both the ex-professor and the present editor saw and touched the very copy of Lemprière's *Classical Dictionary* that had been Thoreau's when he was an undergraduate in Harvard College,—the first flyleaf bearing the autograph: "D. H. Thoreau." This is written in ink, while on the succeeding leaf is the pencilled inscription, "Mr. . . . from S. E. Thoreau." The book selected as a memento for the visitor's wife is an American edition of *The Spectator*, two volumes in one, Philadelphia, 1832. On the title-page is an autograph, in a fine clerkly hand: "J. Thoreau." It is the signature of Thoreau's father, a man, according to one biographer, "who led a plodding unambitious and respectable life in Concord village." It is not mentioned whether he "kept a gig"; but commend us always to the "plodder" who, from his scanty means, provides his family book-shelf with a substantially bound and well printed copy of the *Spectator*. One can readily believe that such a man was respected, gigless though he be; but few would have the hardihood to declare that a father who furnishes the *Spectator* for his children's reading is "unambitious." Perhaps the highest ambition lies in a wise forecast that is not for one's self;

"But Brutus says he was (un) ambitious;
And Brutus is an *honorable* man."

The sterling native worth of Thoreau's Western correspondent was quickly discerned by not only Thoreau's mother and sister: Thoreau's friends recognized and honored it. The transparent-souled Alcott was moved to the highest issues of friendship, as sundry inscribed presentation copies of the writings of that belated Platonist amply testify; and William Ellery Channing, the "man of genius, and of the moods that sometimes make genius an unhappy boon," was thawed into human warmth, as specially inscribed copies of his books— perhaps the most elusive "first (and only that) editions" that ever mocked the book-hunter's desire—amply show, on those precious shelves, where the ex-professor and the present editor saw them for the first and only time. One who has been allowed access to those richly laden shelves may be allowed, without violating the sanctity of hospitality, to bear witness to the simplicity, sincerity, and serenity investing the eventide of a true life with that ineffable splendor which has in it the soul's strongest assurance of a dayspring beyond the mists of Life's mirage.

The Froude letter and that which authenticates it are not considered irrelevant. The English historian's letter to the Concord "loafer" is introduced to show that although his first book was "despised and rejected" of men, Thoreau had the assurances that are always vouchsafed to the solitary thinker, and these from sources so diverse as Oxford University, justly proud of the achievements of its scholars, and the primeval oak forest of a remote young State,—a raw settlement, as it had been called only fifty years before. [*At this point Dr. Jones has an asterisk directing the reader to this quotation from Harriet Martineau's* Society in America: *"At Ypsilanti I picked up an Ann Arbor newspaper. It was badly printed, but its contents were good; and it could happen nowhere out of America that so raw a settlement as that at Ann Arbor, where there is difficulty in procuring decent accommodations, should have a newspaper."—G. H.*] It is not whence the apprehension, the agreement, the assent; it is who agrees, assents, and by the cordial handgrasp conveys to the solitary scholar, whose meditations have disturbed Mammon's market-place, the calm, unfaltering courage that is ever a marvel to the multitude, which quietly "bears the fardels" of unthinking servitude.

The difference between the fibre of a Froude and a Thoreau will be quickly distinguished by those who have read the exculpatory preface especially written for the second edition of Froude's *Nemesis of Faith*. Froude faced the angry storm of incensed detraction with the courage of a well-equipped scholar and the dignity of a true gentleman; nevertheless he had made an "explanation": not the whole world could have moved Thoreau's lips to anything other than a smile of infinite commiseration; he would not have foregone a single furlong of his accustomed "walk"; he might indeed have whispered to his own heart,

> "Time cannot bend the line which
>   Truth hath writ."

The present editor has assured himself that Froude's presentation copy of his self-sacrificing *Nemesis of Faith* is to this day in Emerson's library at the old home, but he has not been able to learn that Froude also sent a copy to Thoreau; so it is a safe inference that Thoreau read Emerson's. A phrase in Froude's letter to Thoreau shows conclusively that Thoreau had learned of Froude from Emerson and that Thoreau had read Froude's ill-starred *Nemesis*—the "wild protest against all authority, Divine and human," as that gentlest of Quakeresses, Caroline Fox, terms it. Froude writes this phrase within inverted commas: "not on account of his [Emerson's] word, but because I myself have read and know you." This can refer only to a complimentary copy of *A Week on the Concord and Merrimack Rivers* that had been previously sent to Froude either by Thoreau or their mutual friend Emerson. Thoreau himself has recorded that of his still-born book some "seventy-five copies were given away."

Froude's *Nemesis of Faith* could transmit no seismic tremors to the man who would have nothing between him and Heaven—not even a rafter. The blue dome with its inscrutable mystery: nothing must obstruct the soul's view of that! The chapter in Thoreau's *Week* entitled "Sunday" could readily carry to Froude the assurance that possibly he, too, had

> "Builded better than he knew,"

that very possibly the angry Anglican hierarchy had merely mistaken a Church colic for a universal cataclysm.

These two recalcitrants never touched hands, albeit the "steam bridges" were both commodious and convenient. Their perigeum occurred during Froude's much later visit to Emerson, and it was in Sleepy Hollow burying-ground; but that perihelion was sadly incomplete: six feet of graveyard mould and death, the mystery of mysteries, intervened. For both of them *now*, no more of that mystery. Oh, the boon of "crossing the bar"!

A word in regard to the unusual manner in which the Letters are presented to the reader. One with whom, of all men living, the present editor is best acquainted (an effete ex-professor, gouty, grouty, and gray-headed) made these Letters the subject of a lecture delivered in aid of a Women's Gymnasium ("More power to their elbows!" said the ex-professor) located—it is not necessary to specify where. The text as written for that occasion has been followed: a convenience which all editors will fully appreciate. At the risk of marring the symmetry of the printed page the labor-saving editor will take the liberty of superimposing such patches of his own plain homespun upon the ex-professor's tapestry as occasion seems to demand (though he may be tempted of the devil to take undue advantage of so rare an opportunity). Being himself "as mild a mannered man as ever cut a throat," he owes it to himself to gently but plainly deprecate the ex-professor's lapses into the sarcastic. Both the editor and Herr Teufels-dröhk believe that sarcasm is the Devil's patois. As that is perilous stuff, he'll have none of it; the ex-professor must stand for his own petard: a proposition which he will be the last man to reject.

The typewritten text of the ex-professor's lecture is disfigured with pen-and-ink interlineations, and this is something so unusual that one who knows him so well as doth the editor could not resist the very natural curiosity which led to the asking for an explanation. This, as it fell from the ex-professor's lips, is too characteristic of him to be withheld; so it shall be shared with the reader—though this complaisance involves the editor in not a little personal peril.

Be it known then, first of all, that the ex-professor himself takes Thoreau very seriously; does not by any possible interpretation consider *him* a "glittering generality," but rather a "blazing ubiquity" wherever and whenever the blunt, plain truth is needful—which time and place he also believes is always and everywhere. Perhaps an excerpt from the ex-professor's lecture on "Thoreau" will best serve to show his attitude. (This lecture, it may be as well to add, was written for and delivered in a nameless territory where "success" is a matter of the bank-book rather than of that old-fashioned Hebrew Book.)

"I am chiefly desirous of enforcing one consideration regarding this man Thoreau, namely: that the brief episode in his life by which he is commonly known—the shanty life at Walden Pond—was not the vagary of an enthusiast. Reared in a family to every member of which 'life was something more than a parade of pretensions, a conflict of ambition or an incessant scramble for the common objects of desire,' Thoreau never lost sight of the high ideal which inspired that humble household.

"While yet an undergraduate he believed that the mere beauty of this world transcended far all the convenience to which luxury would debase it. He then thought 'the order of things should be somewhat reversed; the seventh should be man's day of toil, wherein to earn his living by the sweat of his brow, and the other six his Sabbath of the affections and the soul,—in which to range this widespread garden, and drink in the soft influences and sublime revelations of Nature.'

"With darkened eyes Milton dreamed of Paradise Lost; with an unfaltering trust in the beneficence of God Thoreau went forth in the broad daylight to find it. Who shall say of him that he failed of his quest; who shall declare to the struggling millions of Earth's toilers that Paradise is, indeed, irretrievably lost!

"Once before there came to the race a man wearing a garment of camel's hair, eating locusts and wild honey, and bearing a Message: perhaps this, too, is the veiled purpose of him who abode in that much-derided shanty at Walden Pond.

"Do we not hear the sounds as of satanic revelry coming from high places in the land; is not every breeze burdened with the muttered curses of ill-requited labor toiling for the taskmasters until the sweat of the brow is that of a Gethsemane which is only the Devil's?

"The message-bringer to the nineteenth century said: *Simplify your lives!* It is indeed a simple message, but it is fraught with terrible meaning for us all. If the foundations of this republic are to remain unshaken in the stress of the struggle that is even now looming darkly before us, it is the application, by *all*, of Thoreau's teachings that will avert or mitigate the disaster; if the end is to be only ravined ruin, then will his memory live in Literature as our everlasting reproach."

Verily our ex-professor doth take Thoreau seriously; but there are other matters that he takes as seriously, namely, the *mis*conceptions of Thoreau by all and sundry inepitudes; and on such occasions the ex-professor certainly forgets the amenities—but righteous wrath hath also its own peculiar *Amen!* Having said this much, it is due the reader that he should be allowed to get a glimpse of the ex-professor in a "spate." Here is an instance from the same lecture:

"Now let us return to the shanty at Walden Pond wherein Thoreau dwelt alone for some two and a half years, supporting himself solely by his own labor and living so 'close to the bone.' Lowell has written that Thoreau went there in the self-assertive mood of a hermit whose seclusion is a declaration of his non-dependence upon civilization. 'His shanty life was a mere impossibility, so far as his own conception of it goes, as an entire independency of mankind. The tub of Diogenes has a sounder bottom. Thoreau's experiment actually presupposed all that complicated civilization which it theoretically abjured. He squatted upon another man's land; he borrows an axe; his boards, his nails, his bricks, his mortar, his books, his lamp, his fish-hooks, his plough, his hoe, all turn state's evidence against him as an accomplice in the sin of that artificial civilization which rendered it possible that such a person as Henry D. Thoreau should exist at all.' I question whether in all the history of criticism a blinder misconception can be found."

[Just here the ex-professor was evidently heated. He took the customary sip of water with which the professional lecturer prepares his learned larynx for its next innings. Having returned the handkerchief to the left hand coat-tail pocket, the ex-professor resumed.]

"In the two royal-octavo volumes edited by Professor Norton, *Letters of James Russell Lowell*, there is a photogravure showing the poet sitting on the ground, by the bole of an ancient elm. His hat is off, his hair is parted in the middle (and this was fifty years ago!), his head is thrown forward so as to put his face in the most favorable position for pictorial effect; his whole attitude is of studied ease, and the hand nearest the spectator is—kid-gloved! Oh, the significance of that picture! Posing under an elm in whose branches the robins had built their nests long before the Norsemen's prow had grated upon the sands of the New England coast; the small birds singing around the petted poet, the fragrance of summer filling the air, the scented breeze toying with his curled locks, and he carrying into *that* sanctuary—the kid glove of 'Society'! Is this the man to comprehend the aim and purpose of Thoreau,—this leather and prunella combination of 'civilization' and 'culture'!

"Yes; I am aware that I am speaking of a dead man, of a man whose pig weighed more than he thought it would, if one may judge from the tone of his own early letters; of one whose living tongue tasted the seducing sweetness of earthly fame; but there is another dead man, one who was called away 'in the midst of his broken task, which none else can finish,' and him the kid-gloved favorite of fame and fashion has flouted. There is a time for all things; a time for the sweet charity of silence, a time also for asserting the grandeur of simple and sincere manhood: brown-handed manhood that never saluted Nature with a kid glove. *De mortuis nil nisi bonum?* Yes; I'll stand by that sentiment; but it can also be read, *De mortuis nil nisi verum*: it is well also to stand by that!

"It was Thoreau's purpose at Walden Pond to find out just how much of Lowell's confessedly 'complicated civilization' was absolutely necessary in order that Man's sojourn in Nature might be as sane and serene as became an immortal soul. Did he not plainly write, 'I went to the woods because I wished to live deliberately, to front only the essential facts of life [kid gloves not being found in that inventory], and see if I could not learn what it had to teach, and not, when I came to die, discover that I had not lived. I did not wish to live what was not life, living is so dear; nor did I wish to practice resignation, unless it was quite necessary. I wanted to live deep and suck all the marrow out of life, to live so sturdily and Spartan-like as to put to rout all that was not life, to cut a broad swath and shave close, to drive life into a corner, and reduce it to its lowest terms, and, if it proved to be mean, why then to get the whole and genuine meanness of it, and publish its meanness to the world; or if it were sublime, to know it by experience, and be able to give a true account of it in my next excursion.'

"*In my next excursion*—that journey made with closed eyes and folded hands; hands not kid-gloved; bare hands to lay hold on the realities beyond this Vanity Fair that we in our ignorance call 'Life.'

"Of a truth, Lowell, a clergyman's son, could not read the simple chart by which the son of the Concord pencil-maker shaped his course amidst the sunken rocks of Conventionality."

But the ex-professor's foibles are making us forget the pen-and-ink interlineations that are yet awaiting their explanations.

"I did not imagine," said the ex-professor on the morning after his lecture on the Letters, "that any but sensible people would sit an hour to hear an old fellow talk about Thoreau; but, sir, on going to the appointed place, I found myself, and most unexpectedly, facing a parlour full of frills and fine linen. An exceedingly well-dressed young man sat down at the piano, and he was immediately joined by another even more extraordinarily arrayed. One played and the other warbled something in a tongue unknown to the builders of Babel, I'll warrant. I have never in all my life felt so much out of place since the only woman to whom I ever proposed laughed outright in my face. But there was no escape; I was fairly in for it, and I did some curious thinking whilst that nice young man was warbling. The music ceased, and there was a small storm of kid-gloved hand-clapping. That disconcerted me still more; for there was my audience applauding some artistic noise which I felt in my very bones they did not understand. I had to to make peace with myself before I could begin with my exposition of the Thoreau letters; so I just told them right out what I had been thinking of whilst they were listening to that incomprehensible singing. I told them I had been thinking of the rude homeliness of that shanty at Walden Pond, and that my peculiar environment just then nearly paralyzed me, and only that I had the courage of my convictions, I could not read the Thoreau letters then and there. Just then a distinguished-looking gentleman, with the greatest expanse of shirt-front I had ever seen during all my earthly career, adjusted an English monocle to his right eye and politely stared at me. Worse than all, it had not entered my mind that I should have bought a pair of kid gloves for the occasion.

"It is astonishing how much 'punishment' well-bred people will take fully as smilingly as do all the 'fancy'; but I held them down, sir, for a full hour of torment; and certainly some things got into the talk that were not in the text. The next day a friend, whose wife was present, told me that when she was putting on her cloak, behind a screen in the robing room, she heard one ultra-fashionable lady say to another of the same species: "Well, I never was *bored* so in all my life!" Then I knew that I had scored a success.—Suppose I had talked down to the level of her comprehension!"

The ex-professor thereupon filled his pipe; the present editor found himself filled with reflections of which there is no need to make farther mention.

Thoreau's Incarceration

(As Told by his Jailer)

"Thoreau's Incarceration" appeared in the Inlander 9 *(December 1898): 96–103 and has been reprinted as* Thoreau Society Booklet, No. 4 (1946). *As Walter Harding has noted in* A Thoreau Handbook, *Dr. Jones wrote the most complete account of Thoreau's night in jail. Curiously enough, Dr. Jones did not reprint Fred Hosmer's letter of 22 May 1894 (letter 180 in* Toward the Making of Thoreau's Modern Reputation) *to Jones. Hosmer wrote that Staples was an easy-going jailer and that "Emerson could easily have seen Thoreau—as the jail was easy of access, and he might have talked with him from the outside of the wall." The omission of quotations from this letter is particularly difficult to understand since Dr. Jones believed (though he had no direct proof) that Emerson did visit Thoreau in jail.*

Mr. S. is Sam Staples; Miss H. is Miss Eliza Hosmer, and Mr. X is A. W. (Fred) Hosmer.

"THERE'S the man that locked up Thoreau; I'll introduce him to you." The speaker was a Concord lady who was kindly acting as a guide to a stranger and pilgrim in that renowned village. We were returning from a visit to an ancient woman who had known the Thoreau family intimately, when my friend espied a man sitting on the porch of a fine looking dwelling upon the main street. I followed her through the gate, and as she approached the veranda a cheery voice said, "Good afternoon, Miss H." "Good afternoon, Mr. S.; are you enjoying this fine day?"

I was thereupon presented to a substantial, bluff-looking specimen of mankind who, though past sixty years of age, was exceedingly well preserved; which fact one was speedily led to ascribe to the good humor that fairly bubbled from every pore of him. He was evidently "at ease in Zion," and apparently he thought everyone else should be. It was not that boisterous humor which to a stranger would appear "put on," but a spontaneous outflow of spirits as unaffected as the ripple of a brook or the song of a bird.

Mr. S. was above the medium stature, straight as a pine tree, browned by outdoor life, well-fleshed enough to pass for a "solid" citizen, and time had dealt so kindly by him that he still had his own dark hair and lustrous brown eyes that fairly seemed to sparkle. Everything about him was in good keeping except the large diamond that flashed from a rather dirty shirt front and was silently reproached by the condition of the linen. In striking contrast to this misplaced luxury was his clothing, which was of good material, quiet in color and wholly free from that suspicion of foppery suggested by the glittering gem. His language fully explained the incongruous situation of the diamond, for that stone denotes the social extremes represented by culture and by vulgarity; and unfortunately the present wearer was in the vortex of the latter category. He impressed you as being a man who had learned his manners in the market-place rather than the drawing room and who, in the storm and stress of life, had kept his eye well to the windward, thereby escaping shipwreck. He had evidently prospered, whatever may have become of his companions in the struggle of life. Indeed, something about him said plainly enough, "I have no fault to find with fate; I can afford to gratify my desires; and, begging your pardon, I ask no odds of anybody." More than this, he made you feel that he regarded life as a huge joke; that he was wholly devoid of any conception of the tragic; that, in fact, he would have considered his own funeral as a part of the great and ever present joke. Yet with all, there was nothing disagreeably offensive about him; you could regard even the diamond discrepancy as only a pardonable vagary,—in him.

When he learned that I was "one of them Thoreau fellows that comes 'round here every summer" it seemed as if his every recollection of his famous townsman suddenly swarmed into his memory and was at my service. His flood of reminiscences constantly associated Emerson with Thoreau; but of all these I recall but one, and perhaps that is remembered because it presents Thoreau in an unsuspected character; that of a joker.

It seems that a question had arisen regarding the boundary line between land owned by Emerson and Mr. S. himself, which the latter told me had recently become his through a "dicker" with someone whose name I did not catch. Thoreau was employed to make the necessary survey ("and he did it right slick, I tell you"); and having finished his work, he had appointed a meeting at Emerson's house to make his report. I can never forget how Mr. S. in his statement of that meeting made me feel the bland mildness of Emerson's nature. "He was a man, sir, that wouldn't hurt a fly," said Mr. S. most emphatically. Then he went on to explain that there had been no "quarrel" between Emerson and himself; they only "just wanted to know, you know, which was which."

Thoreau was already at Emerson's house when Mr. S. arrived, and they plunged into business without delay. Much to Emerson's surprise, Thoreau said and proved by a map of the survey that his, Mr. Emerson's, partition fence intruded several feet upon the adjoining property; and without waiting for a word from the utterly unconscious intruder, he went on to declare that the appropriation of the land was intentional, only Mr. S. had proven too sharp to be imposed upon; and all these years you've been holding up your nose as an upright citizen and an example to everybody, yet every time you reset your fence you knowingly shoved it in a little farther and a little farther, until you've stolen land enough to almost feed a yearling heifer; but Mr. S. has been too smart for any of you sly fellows, and I'm glad to have a hand in exposing you; though "it's an awful disappointment to me.

"Why," said Mr. S., "if Emerson hed been ketched pickin' pockets at town meetin' he could n't a looked more streaked. Thoreau was talkin' in downright earnest, and you could have heard him way out on the Lexin'ton road. I felt so all-fired mean, I could n't do nothin' but look at the floor; but whilst Thoreau was a rakin' of him and had just said somthin' darned haa'sh, I just had to look at him, and when I saw his eye I laughed 'til you could a heard it up to the top of the Hill buryin' ground. You see, he was just guyin' Mr. Emerson, and when he see it, he did n't take it amiss at all. He was the nicest man that ever lived."

Surely, this surprising spirit at the expense of the "sage of Concord" will make a companion piece for that famous extemporized dance in Mr. Ricketson's parlor—and yet this was the Thoreau of whom Lowell said, "he had no humor!"

Just how the matter of Thoreau's imprisonment entered into our talk I do not remember, for the jailer's reminiscences followed each other as indiscriminately as the autumn leaves that fell at our feet that day. In the flood tide of his recollections he said: "Henry knew that I had a warrant for him, but I did n't go to hunt for him, 'cause I knew I could git him when I wanted to."

Thoreau was arrested early in the evening, while on his way to get a shoe that was being repaired preparatory to his piloting a huckleberry party on the morrow. The serving of a warrant had no novelty in it for the reminiscential jailer, so he mentioned no details of the arrest, but simply stated that he locked up Thoreau "and the rest of the boys" for the night. A little later he himself went up town on some business. During his brief absence someone rapped at the door of the jailer's private apartments. His daughter opened it, when a veiled young woman said: "Here is the money to pay Mr. Thoreau's tax," and immediately departed. The demand of the law being satisfied, Thoreau was no longer a culprit, and should have been instantly set free on the jailer's return; but when telling me of it, that worthy, in the coolest manner imaginable, said, "I had got my boots off and was sittin' by the fire when my daughter told me, and I was n't goin' to take the trouble to unlock after I'd got the boys all fixed for the night, so I kep' him in 'till after breakfast next mornin' and then I let him go."

It was indeed a surprise to learn how nearly the recalcitrant reformer had escaped his one night in prison, only for the free-and-easy jailer's love of his ease we had lost the raciest experience that Thoreau has recorded. I said nothing at the time, though inwardly I questioned the jailer's statement; but on subsequently reading Thoreau's account of the event, I found that it tallied in the fact that he was discharged after having breakfasted in the Concord jail.

I asked Mr. S. if he knew who it was that paid Thoreau's taxes. He replied that he did not know, but believed it was Judge Hoar—"the girl that brought the money had somethin' wrapped 'round her head so't you could n't see her face"; but he guessed it was Elizabeth Hoar. He said Thoreau was "as mad as the devil when I turned him loose."

I had long been interested in the fate of Thoreau's roommate on that uneventful night, and I enquired what became of him. "He was a first-rate fellow," replied Mr. S. and he went on to say that at the following session of the court he had been set free. He had been arrested for arson, but was really innocent, as Thoreau had shrewdly surmised would be found to be the case.

When I left Concord in 1890 the question, Who paid Thoreau's tax? was unsettled, although I had made diligent research in all directions. Four years later I saw a newspaper article by Mr. Irving Allen in which it was definitely stated that the veiled lady was Thoreau's Aunt Maria. I at once wrote to Mr. Allen to learn the source of his information, and received this reply:

NORWICH, CONN., May 7, 1894.

My Dear Sir:—In reply to yours of the 5th inst., received this morning I am compelled to confess that I can furnish no evidence of the exact truth of my statement regarding the payment of Thoreau's tax. The old ladies Jane and Maria Thoreau were intimate and valued friends of mine in my youth and I have no doubt that the statement was made—to me or in my hearing by one of them.

When I wrote the article of which you speak, it did not occur to me to question the source of my conviction in this matter; it seems to me that I have known for years that it was good old Aunt Jane who came to the relief of her eccentric nephew; yet I cannot prove that I was right. I suggest that you write to Professor E. J. Loomis, Washington, D.C.; he was a very intimate friend of the Thoreaus, and is quite likely to have evidence on the question at issue.

Professor Loomis wrote:

WASHINGTON, May 12, 1894.

Dear Sir:—In regard to the question who paid Henry Thoreau's tax, I have always understood that it was paid by his aunt, Miss Maria Thoreau, not Jane, who was very deaf, and all matters concerning either of them were attended to by Maria.

I have tried to recall to my mind whether Maria Thoreau ever told me that she paid the tax, but although I fully believe she did, I cannot say positively that she told me so. But in order to have something definite and authentic to tell you I have written to a friend in Concord to find the fact and let me know. As soon as I hear from him I will write you again. The question of the payment of the tax rests between two persons, Miss Maria and R. W. Emerson.

Mr. Emerson visited Thoreau at the jail, and the meeting between the two philosophers must have been interesting and somewhat dramatic. The account of the meeting was told me by Miss Maria Thoreau—"Henry, why are you here?" "Waldo, why are you *not* here?"

I received yesterday a photograph of Henry which is quite different from Rowse's crayon likeness.

I was at Mr. Thoreau's house spending the summer at the time Rowse was making the portrait, and Henry and I walked, boated and talked over the whole of old Concord. Those were ambrosial days to be always remembered by me.

Excuse this rather gossippy letter; I hope to have something definite to write you soon.

The Concord friend to whom Professor Loomis proposed to write proved to be a correspondent of mine, and from him came this communication:

CONCORD, May 17, 1894.

My Dear Doctor:—I had a letter from Professor Loomis after sending him one of the photos of Thoreau, in which he asked in regard to the payment of Thoreau's tax, "for a gentleman from Ann Arbor."

I called on Mr. S., the jailer, last evening, and he told me that he committed Thoreau about sundown; that about nine or half past, while he was away from the house, a lady called at his front door, and on his daughter answering the bell, this lady handed her an envelope with the remark, "that is to pay for Henry Thoreau's tax." His daughter did not recognize the lady, as it was dark and she had a veil on. He said he always thought it was Elizabeth Hoar. I wrote to Judge Hoar in regard to it and his answer is that he was out of town at the time, but he always understood that it was Aunt Maria who paid it. He does not believe his sister did. There is one sure thing about it; Emerson did *not*.

S. thinks that Emerson could not have seen Thoreau in

jail, as he was committed at sundown, or thereabout, and the jail was soon locked up. The tax being paid that evening, Thoreau was turned out immediately after breakfast— as S. expressed it, "as mad as the devil." He says he always liked Henry Thoreau; that he was thrown in with him a great deal in running the lines of different farms, etc.

When I told him for whom I wanted the information, he burst out laughing, "Oh, yes, that little fellow with the G. A. R. suit on." Then he gave me a resume of his talk with you, saying, "Tell him he must not place too much dependence on what I say, for when I get to talkin' I am apt to say more than I mean."

If Professor Loomis says Aunt Maria told him Emerson visited Thoreau in jail, I should call it so, as the story is too good to lose and also shows the difference between the men. "Henry, I am sorry to find you here." "Mr. Emerson, why are you *not* here?" I repeated this to S., with the remark that Thoreau was ready to back up his principles, while Emerson was not. "Yes, X. . . *that is so*," was his reply."

It is seen that Judge Hoar (Senator Hoar) corroborates Professor Loomis in regard to the paying of Thoreau's tax. The fact was not mentioned during Thoreau's life, as he would have bitterly resented it; so that matter may be considered settled.

As to the Emerson-Thoreau interview in Concord jail, Professor Loomis writes:

WASHINGTON, May 21, 1894.

Dear Sir:—I have just heard from Mr. X., of Concord, Mass., to whom I wrote for information regarding the payment of Thoreau's tax, and his information, which I understand he has already forwarded to you, agrees with my own recollection of the story as told me.

In regard to the meeting of Mr. Emerson and Henry Thoreau in Concord jail, that story was told me by Henry's

Aunt Maria; "Henry, why are you here?" "Waldo, why are
you *not* here?"

I have heard her tell the story several times, and always
the same, never varying a word.

There is no reasonable doubt of its truth. It was first told in
print in 1862, by George William Curtis, in an obituary notice
of Thoreau—*Harper's Monthly*, vol. xxv, p. 279. It has never
been contradicted, and it is characteristic of the men. Emerson was the man of thought, Thoreau of action. It was
Thoreau, not Emerson, that first raised his voice in defence of
Captain John Brown.

Henry D. Thoreau:

Emerson's Obituary

Dr. Jones wrote the Note for this reprinting of Emerson's obituary of Thoreau which appeared in the Boston Daily Advertiser *on 8 May 1862. Edwin B. Hill printed the pamphlet* Collectanea Henry D. Thoreau, *No. 1, in 1904. Mr. Hill was quite slow with his printing and the copy was prepared by Dr. Jones long before publication. Thoreau's Michigan correspondent mentioned in the Note was Calvin Greene. (The Thoreau letter, Dr. Jones says in a footnote, is from* Some Unpublished Letters.)

D<small>IED</small> at Concord, on Tuesday, 6 May, Henry D. Thoreau, aged 44 years.

The premature death of Mr. Thoreau is a bitter disappointment to many friends who had set no limit to their confidence in his power and future performance. He is known to the public as the author of two remarkable books, "A Week on the Concord and Merrimack Rivers," published in 1849, and "Walden, or Life in the Woods," published in 1854. These books have never had a wide circulation, but are well known to the best readers, and have exerted a powerful influence on an important class of earnest and contemplative persons.

Mr. Thoreau was born in Concord, in 1817; was graduated at

Harvard University, in 1837. Resisting the example of his companions, and the advice of friends, he declined entering either of the learned professions, and for a long time pursued his studies as his genius led him, without apparent method. But being a good mathematician and with an early and controlling love of nature, he afterwards came by imperceptible steps into active employment as a land-surveyor,—whose art he had first learned in the satisfaction of his private questions,—a profession which gave him lucrative work, and not too much of it, and in the running of town lines and the boundaries to farms and woodlands, carried him precisely where he wished to go,—to the homes of new plants, and of swamp and forest birds, as well as of wild landscape, and Indian relics. A man of simple tastes, hardy habits, and of preternatural powers of observation, he became a patient and successful student of nature in every aspect, and obtained an acquaintance with the history of the river on whose banks he lived, and with the habits of plants and animals, which made him known and valued by naturalists. He gathered a private museum of natural curiosities, and has left a large collection of manuscript records of his varied experiments and observations, which are of much more than scientific value. His latest studies were in forest trees, the succession of forest growths, and the annual increment of wood. He knew the literature of natural history, from Aristotle and Pliny, down to the English writers on his favorite departments.

But his study as a naturalist, which went on increasing, and had no vacations, was less remarkable than the power of his mind and the strength of his character. He was a man of stoic temperament, highly intellectual, of a perfect probity, full of practical skill, an expert woodsman and boatman, acquainted with the use of tools, a good planter and cultivator, when he saw fit to plant, but without any taste for luxury, without the least ambition to be rich, or to be popular, and almost without sympathy in any of the common motives of men around him. He led the life of a philosopher, subordinating all other pursuits and so-called duties to his pursuit of knowledge and to his own estimate of duty. He was a man of firm mind and direct dealing, never disconcerted, and not to be bent by any inducement from his own course. He had a penetrating insight into men with whom he conversed, and was not to be deceived or used by any party, and did not conceal his disgust at any duplicity. As he was incapable of any the least dishonesty or untruth, he had nothing to hide, and kept his haughty independence to the end. And when we now look back at the solitude of this erect and spotless person, we lament that he did not live long enough for all men to know him.

E.

NOTE

It is believed that a peculiar interest attaches to this reprint of Emerson's obituary on the death of Thoreau. Perhaps the history of the "copy" from which it is now reprinted will make this plain.

It is known to but a few that Thoreau had a correspondent in Michigan and as early as 1856. The reading of "Walden" had filled the earnest Michigan man with a fierce hunger for Thoreau's first book, "A Week on the Concord and Merrimack Rivers," and failing to find a bookseller who could supply a copy, he had written directly to Thoreau, whose reply we are permitted to publish through the courtesy of the present owner of the holograph:

CONCORD, Jan'y 18th, 1856.

Dear Sir:

I am glad to hear that my "Walden" has interested you—that perchance it holds some truth still as far off as Michigan. I thank you for your note.

The "Week" had so poor a publisher that it is quite uncertain whether you will find it in any shop. I am not sure but authors must turn booksellers themselves. The price is

$1.25. If you care enough for it to send me that sum by mail (stamps will do for change), I will forward you a copy by the same conveyance.

As for the "more" that is to come, I cannot speak definitely at present, but I trust that the mine—be it silver or lead—is not yet exhausted. At any rate, I shall be encouraged by the fact that you are interested in its yield.

Yours respectfully,
HENRY D. THOREAU

The correspondence thus begun ended in November, 1859, at which time Thoreau was devoting himself to defending the despised Captain John Brown and fervently advocating his cause.

It was not until the month following Thoreau's death that his Michigan admirer learned of it, and he at once wrote a letter of condolence to the surviving mother and sister. Then, beside letters from Sophia Thoreau, the following came to him, in reply to a direct enquiry which had been directed to one of Thoreau's Concord intimates:

CONCORD, June 11th, 1862

My Dear Sir:

Your letter of the 8th instant inquiring concerning the death of Henry Thoreau is just received, and I hasten to answer it.

A slight notice of the funeral was printed in the Boston "Transcript" of May 10th (I think), and the "Advertiser" of the 9th had a notice of himself by Mr. Emerson.

A more extended notice, consisting of the Eulogy spoken at the funeral, with additions, will appear in the "Atlantic Monthly" for August—and will be the answer to many of your enquiries.

His illness was a lingering one—a year and a half, at least, the last six months of which he was able to go out doors but little. He endured it with great patience and sweetness, preserving his gayety and wit to the last. I was often with him, having known him well for the last seven years.

You have indeed missed much in not having met him, for he well supported the impression left by his writings.

His mother and sister, who survive him, Mrs. Cynthia and Miss Sophia Thoreau, desire me to say that they remember your friendly letters to Mr. Thoreau, and have desired to send some token of their remembrance. They therefore enclose these verses of Ellery Channing's and Mr. Emerson's "Advertiser" sketch.

At the funeral, which was in the church, Mr. Emerson spoke after the clergyman—Mr. Channing's hymn was sung, and Mr. Alcott read some passages from the writings of Mr. Thoreau.

I hope you may carry out your purpose of visiting Concord, and shall be glad to talk with you then on a subject so dear to us both.

Yours truly,
F. B. SANBORN

After being carefully kept for thirty-five years the original recipient of these posthumous tributes transferred them to the present editor, and thus it is that they are no longer entrusted to the precarious keeping of a scrap-book.

Doubtless many who read Emerson's obituary notice in the "Advertiser" some forty years ago (when Thoreau's fame was but "a cloud out of the sea, as large as a man's hand") thought the eulogium only the fond exaggeration of a fervent friendship, but to-day Time, the incorruptible Arbiter, has confirmed the judgment pronounced while yet the mother's tears were warm upon the face of her dead son. Not only confirmed, but enlarged the judgment; for Emerson himself had not fully known the extent of Thoreau's acquirements and capacity. It will be a matter of astonishment and of surprise to many other than the few now living in "old Concord" who had known Thoreau in the flesh, to learn on the best of authority that as a classical scholar he was far superior to Emerson and fully the equal of the over self-conscious Lowell; and as an original Thinker, it is safe to declare that Thoreau will be read when Lowell is forgotten and Emerson remembered chiefly as the leading exponent of "the Transcendental movement" in the United States. The charm of personality perishes with the memory of those who felt its spell; the inspiration of the Thinker is the deathless inheritance of the race: and this pronouncement confidently abides the incorruptible arbitration of the coming centuries.

It is noteworthy that Emerson's obituary notice, written as it was while yet Thoreau's clay was uncoffined, contains all of real worth and importance that was included in the more carefully prepared eulogy which was spoken in the very church wherein Thoreau had made his impassioned "Plea for Captain John Brown" and which subsequently appeared in the "Atlantic Monthly," but without the "additions" predicted by the Concord correspondent: at least any additions that are now detectable, for Emerson's spoken words were not "reported."

As the "Atlantic" paper forms the biographical introduction to Thoreau's first posthumous book, the student of literature can pass an interesting hour by comparing the germ from the Boston "Advertiser" with the later and carefully finished product of the scholar's study; the former reveals Emerson as a friend, the latter shows his consummate art as a writer.

SECTION TWO

Dr. Jones on Thoreau's

Biographers, Editors, and Critics

Thoreau and His Biographers

"Thoreau and His Biographers," which appeared in Lippincott's Monthly Magazine *48 (August 1891): 224–228, is the only one of Dr. Jones's Thoreau articles to be published in a major journal. Dr. Jones's praise of Salt and his questioning of Channing, Page, and Sanborn have stood the test of time. (In the original, an asterisk after the title directs the reader to the following biographies:*

Thoreau, the Poet Naturalist, *by Wm. Ellery Channing, Boston, 1873*; Thoreau: His Life and Aims, *by H. A. Page, Boston, 1877;* Henry D. Thoreau, *by F. B. Sanborn, Boston, 1883;* The Life of Henry David Thoreau, *by H. S. Salt, London, 1890. The information from two other asterisked notes has been placed in brackets and inserted into the text of the essay.)*

WHAT more delightful anticipation is there than when we cut the leaves of a new Life of an author whom we have long loved? And if the reading prove only a "bootless bene," how absurdly inefficacious do we find dear Mary Lamb's "shoeless pea"! Beyond question there is a special limbo for the inept biographer.

It is Thoreau's good fortune to have biographers who improve upon each other. The initiatory endeavor, by Channing, though published eleven years after Thoreau's death, was still too near that event to allow his chosen companion to write anything other than a rhapsody. For a more satisfactory glimpse of Thoreau the student was obliged to have recourse to Emerson's calmer obituary sketch. From it and the subsequent volume of "Letters," edited by Emerson, has been derived that conception of Thoreau which is at once the most general and the most unjust. It was Emerson's desire to display Thoreau as "a most perfect piece of stoicism." He elided from the letters the evidences of Thoreau's human tenderness so unsparingly that Sophia Thoreau remonstrated: "it did not seem quite honest to Henry." Mr. James T. Fields seconded her protest, and a few passages which evinced "some tokens of natural affection" were retained. Emerson, we are told, "fancied" that this pious interference of a bereaved sister "had marred his classic statue."

Channing's book is valuable as containing much of Thoreau's "Journal" that has not been published elsewhere; and many of his selections are of singular beauty. For instance, Thoreau is at Clematis Brook watching the dispersion of milkweed seeds as the summer breeze catches their silken wings, and he derives this corollary from so commonplace an incident: "Who could believe in the prophecies of a Daniel or of Miller, that the world would end this summer, while one milkweed with faith matured its seed?"

The succeeding Life by H. A. Page, now known as Dr. A. H. Japp, was written at too great a distance from its subject and too near Thoreau's books to be of any other use than to whet the reader's curiosity and make him eager for a more extended knowledge of its hero. Dr. Japp is the introducer and chief disseminator of the figment that the shanty at Walden was a station of the underground railroad. He infers this from a cursory statement of Channing's: "Not one slave alone was expedited to Canada by Thoreau's personal assistance." R. L. Stevenson accepts this myth as the *raison d'être* for Thoreau's abode in Walden woods, and even Mr. Salt repeats the story in his excellent Life. The writer has made this a matter of special investigation, and the truth is that there were specially-prepared houses in "Old Concord" which afforded infinitely more secure resting- and hiding-places for the fugitive slave.

Moreover, the survivors who managed Concord "station" declare that Thoreau's hut was not used for such a purpose.

With Mr. Sanborn's Life began the era of personal misrepresentation; and soon after its publication a highly-incensed lady called its unfortunate author to account in the Boston *Daily Advertiser*. We have not been able to learn the whereabouts of Mr. Sanborn's reply. Living in Concord, and having known Thoreau personally, Mr. Sanborn had at hand the materials for an interesting book; but it appears that he felt called upon to write at once Thoreau's biography, and a history of Concord, and at the same time to make "honorable mention" of all its worthies, living or dead, past, present, and to come. It is, however, an entertaining volume if you possess the patience to unravel it and the skill to follow an often-hidden trail. Lacking these qualities yourself, the book is still deserving of the encomium that Dr. John Brown says a Scotch shepherd awarded to a boiled sheep's-head: "There's a deal o' confused eatin' aboot it." But this Life has left a smart in the hearts of those who knew and loved the Thoreaus that needs only to be known to nullify the false witness.

Mr. Salt's Life is purely a labor of love. To him Thoreau's "gospel of simplicity" is both chart and compass: he is not so much an "admirer" as an earnest follower of the sincere man whose life he both writes and lives. When precept and practice go hand in hand and love walks with them, the printed page becomes refulgent. Mr. Salt has done more than any other writer, living or dead, to correct the errors that are current concerning Thoreau and to enable a just conception of his character to be made. Preceding this Life is an essay on Thoreau, *Temple Bar*, No. 78, p. 369, so felicitous that all students of Thoreau should read it; and since the appearance of the more formal Life Mr. Salt has published an "Introductory Note" [Anti-Slavery and Reform Papers, *Swan, Sonnenschein & Co, London, 1890*] and a paper on "Thoreau's Gospel of Simplicity" [The Paternoster Review, *March, 1891.*] which form an all-sufficient reply to certain objections by Professor Nichol and James Russell Lowell. Writing in a foreign country, with only a scholar's access to his materials, and, of all who had known Thoreau personally, having met only Mr. Sanborn, Mr. Salt's Life is singularly correct. A few trivial mis-statements are found: its one great blemish is owing solely to his having accepted Mr. Sanborn's estimate of Thoreau's parents and their relatives as trustworthy. It is to be feared that Mr. Sanborn has judged Thoreau's father from the exterior alone,—a shallow judgment! John Thoreau had in his veins the blood of Huguenot, Covenanter, and Quaker,—an ancestral blending to be coveted; Mr. Sanborn could discern only a "little," "deaf," "plainly-clad," "unobtrusive," "unambitious," "plodding" man whose shrug and snuff-box were the only reminiscences of his French extraction. They who knew him believe that John Thoreau is to Mr. Sanborn like the cathedral window described by Hawthorne: "Standing without, you see no glory, nor can possibly imagine any; standing within, every ray of light reveals a harmony of unspeakable splendors." But it isn't the window's fault!

That Mrs. Thoreau, her sister, and her sisters-in-law were vilified, after every one of the name Thoreau was dead, the best blood in and of Concord will this day testify. *De mortuis nil nisi bonum* should also be read *nil nisi verum*. Alas that the printed page should still be able to reiterate the lie that has been branded in the market-place!

There is another feature of Mr. Sanborn's Life that perplexes the thoughtful reader,—namely, the exalted character which he ascribes to the Thoreau children. Not that their moral status is to be questioned: the puzzle is to explain the phenomenon. The fountain, according to Mr. Sanborn, rises *so* much higher than its source. A "plodding, unambitious" father, but children living up to the highest ideals. A mother given to "flashes of gossip and malice," yet growing up around her hearth-stone sons and daughters whom such an atmosphere would have stifled! The problem darkens when Mr. Sanborn says, "Perpetuity, indeed, and hereditary transmission of everything that by nature and good sense can be inherited, are among the characteristics of Concord." (Life, p. 38.)

The whole household—father, mother, Helen, John, Henry, Sophia: the last of their name in America—are gathered together on that little hill-top in Sleepy Hollow which the morning sun is the first to visit and the last to leave; and if the reader shall ever stand a pious pilgrim there in the solemn silence of a summer's night, shadows below and starlight above, he will be devoutly thankful that nothing of earth can break their peace.

No man's life can be fully written by a contemporary. *Pace Tua*, James Boswell. If thine angry shade shall threaten vengeance, then shalt thou be referred to Dr. Birkbeck Hill, whose editorship has made old Ursus Major better known to us than ever he was to those who supped with him at the Mitre or helped him to beguile the nights he so dreaded. Death and time break the seals of reticences that are sacred to coevals, and posterity is permitted to make the most searching post-mortem examinations. Meanwhile, the falsities that for a time batten on a dead man's memory one by one drop into oblivion, shrivelled by the light of Truth. Time is doing its kindliest offices for Thoreau. One after the other misrepresentations are being brought to judgment, and there is "reversal with costs." Lowell, the chief offender, is already condemned by all but the vulgar. Thoreau is no longer considered a "misanthrope," nor is he deemed a "hermit" who masqueraded at Walden Pond. The seriousness of his life is being recognized, his earnestness is seldom questioned, and the wisdom of his philosophy is more than suspected. Before the end of Plato's year he may find disciples in very deed.

That he was sincerity incarnate is the first necessary lesson to be learned concerning him. That he studied the problem of life as profoundly and as continually as did Marcus Aurelius, and that he lived it as regally, will soon be seen. Then it will be time to consider what was to him the outcome of his philosophy. It will be found that his religion grew out of his philosophy; not the philosophy from the religion. This reversal of the sacerdotal order produced precious fruit. He learned that life is not from the Divine *design* a soul-wearying struggle, but, truly lived, a pastime worthy of the soul. His spiritual ear discovered the source of the discords that mar the harmony of the psalm of life: "When we are weary with travel, we lay down our load and rest by the wayside. So, when we are weary with the burden of life, why do we not lay down this load of false-hoods which we have volunteered to sustain, and be refreshed as never mortal was? Let the beautiful laws prevail. Let us not weary ourselves by resisting them."

Volunteered to sustain. There is the hammer-stroke that buries the nail. The Eternal Unspeakable One is *not* the bungler: it is *we* who will not "let the beautiful laws prevail." Thus devoutly doth he justify the ways of God to man.

He inculcated the supremest care of the body: "A man is never inspired unless his body is also." He insisted that man should accept his "genius"—the voice within—as the unerring guide: not Socrates was more obedient to his daemon. He declares "that if one advances confidently in the direction of his dreams, and endeavors to live the life which he has imagined, he will meet with a success unexpected in common hours." Ay, more, "in proportion as he simplifies his life, the laws of the universe will appear less complex, and solitude will not be solitude, nor poverty poverty, nor weak-ness weakness. If you have built castles in the air, your work need not be lost; that is where they should be. Now put the foundations under them."

When our latter-day mad race for wealth, only wealth, shall have brought to us the inevitable result and a chastened people shall seek "the better way," it will be the "hermit" of Walden, not the Sage of Concord, that will lead them.

Though called away when his capabilities were at their highest and his cherished work undone, it is difficult to think of Thoreau's life as incomplete; still harder to believe with his distinguished friend that it was only "pounding beans." His end was presaged by that sublime outburst of supreme man-hood, his defence of Captain John Brown "sick and in prison."

When all other lips were sealed, Thoreau's flamed with living fire, for even God had touched them.

After that came the slow decay, and the sleep for one whom the grandest occasion in his life had found sufficient. But every vouchsafed moment was piously husbanded: manuscripts were arranged and essays revised before the hand had forever lost its cunning. One of these may be seen in Concord Library, and three handwritings are found in it,—his own with pen and ink, and, when he wearied, with the more convenient pencil, and, when too weak for even that, his sister Sophia wrote at his dictation.

He went forth at his prime, having "much to report on natural history," but obliged to take it all into the inexorable grave. Yet no repining; instead, the declaration from lips that were never sullied by a lie, "I am enjoying existence as much as ever, and regret nothing."

"A man's religion is the chief fact with regard to him." What was Thoreau's? He "rested quietly in God's palm." He was so filled with confidence in the Unspeakable One that he asked no curious questions; and, in our ignorance, perhaps that is the wisest attitude for any soul. Better than all, the moral grandeur of his exit shows that he had not only the courage but also the comfort of his convictions.

Thoreau and His Works

"Thoreau and His Works," a review of the ten-volume Riverside edition of the works of Thoreau, appeared in the Inlander *4 (February 1894): 234–240. The review helps explain why Thoreau, in spite of much wrong-headed criticism, was beginning to be recognized as a greater writer than Emerson. (Full publishing information about the reviewed edition is placed in brackets and inserted into the text of the second paragraph.)*

O<small>N</small> the last morning of his life, with his mother and his sister by his bedside, Thoreau suddenly said, "Lift me up!" They did so; his breathing grew fainter and fainter, and he speedily departed.

His last words were prophetic; for, thirty-two years after his death, they find a fitting fulfillment in the issuing of the *Riverside edition* of his works [The Complete Writings of Henry David Thoreau, *10 vols., Boston: Houghton, Mifflin & Co., 1894*]. The ten volumes thereof present the reader with the imperishable record of his life-work. There we find his earliest contribution to the Dial—rejected by Margaret Fuller, against the judgment of Emerson—and his last fervid testimony to the high and heroic qualities of Captain John Brown. There also, exhumed from the rare pages of the long-defunct Dial, are his translation of the Prometheus Unbound of Aeschylus, and his rendering of fragments from Pindar. Each of these ten volumes contains an index, and a voluminous general index completes the series. Six of the volumes have each a prefixed introductory note, containing such information that will be new to the large majority of readers. We find only one trivial error therein, namely, it is stated that the paper on "The Last Days of John Brown was read by the author at North Elba." It was presented and read at that meeting by the secretary, to whom Thoreau had given it when the former was passing through Concord on his way thither.

The first volume of the *Riverside edition* contains two typographical errors, and we note them with surprise, as evidencing that this work was not set up from the text of the original edition. As Sir Boyle Roche would say, there are two first editions of Thoreau's "Week." That of James Munroe and Company, 1849, and the one bearing the imprint of Ticknor & Fields, 1862, are really the same. The unbound sheets of the still-born book that Munroe had returned to Thoreau in 1853, were lying piled up in his mother's garret when their author died. They were bought by James T. Fields for his firm, and were issued with a new title-page. When these copies—some seven hundred and odd—were sold, a new edition was published by Ticknor & Fields in 1867, and then crept in the errors that have since been reproduced in every subsequent edition, English and American. On page 339 of the *Riverside edition* "souls" is printed instead of "stools," and on page 517, "interrupt" instead of "interpret."

In the second volume of the *Riverside edition,* Walden is printed without the time-honored picture of the shanty at Walden Pond, and Thoreau's topographical and hydrographical survey of the Pond itself—a fine specimen of Thoreau's skill as a surveyor—is omitted. These missing features will enhance the value of the original edition.

A very gratifying addition pleasantly surprises the reader of the *Riverside edition* in the three portraits of Thoreau: The early crayon by Rowse, the later daguerreotype, taken for Mr. H. G. O. Blake, and the ambrotype thoughtfully secured by Mr. Daniel Ricketson the year before Thoreau's death. The second of these is said to best represent the "hypaethral" Thoreau of the Concord fields.

There are forty long years between the ejection of Thoreau's still-born book from Munroe's cellar, and his apotheosis in the *Riverside Press* gallery of the gods, and "the art preservative" insures the fulfillment of that last request: "Lift me up!"

When Thoreau died his fame was to be discerned as a cloud no larger than a man's hand, but now, says an English critic, "it is an axiom of latter-day culture that you must know something about Thoreau." And the larger that something, the better, for "Thoreau's name has of late years become more and more prominent, until now the reputation of Emerson's "moral man" almost predominates over that of Emerson himself.

Undoubtedly Thoreau's first recognition came from Emerson, but that did not much avail when George William Curtis wrote of him in *The Homes of American Authors,* nor when Duyckinck found him "occasionally rash and conceited" in the pages of his "Week," and declared that he "sometimes stumbles into the abysmal depths of the bathetic" in his "Walden." A later critic pronounces this very volume to be "the only book yet written in America, to my thinking, that bears an annual perusal." Whilst the critics were reconciling their discrepancies, the readers had found use for some twenty-five editions of "Walden."

Thoreau found a toilsome road from the *Dial* to the publishing of his "Week." The "Walk to Wachusett" was written for money, though, at the time, Thoreau was not aware of Horace Greeley's opinion: "In my poor judgment, if anything is calculated to make a scoundrel of an honest man, writing to sell is that very particular thing." For this his first endeavor to open the oyster for himself there was no pay forthcoming, although so keen a collector for a friend as Emerson bearded the bankrupted publisher in Thoreau's behalf. With two contributions to the *Democratic Review,* for which Hawthorne had opened the way, Thoreau was more fortunate, but still the "shower of shillings" was by no means copious. "Literature comes to a poor market here, and even the little that I write is more than will sell." Then Horace Greeley came to the fore with his knowledge of the literary market and the avenues thereto, and found place for Thoreau's pen in the columns of *Graham's* and the *Union Magazine*. In the year following, after many futile endeavors to find a publisher, James Munroe & Company printed the firstling, "A Week on the Concord and Merrimack Rivers," at Thoreau's risk. On the 28th of October, 1833 [1853], the 706 unsold copies were expressed to him, and his debt made a heavier load for him than even they did when he carried them up to his garret. Meanwhile the fruits of his shanty life had been garnered and winnowed, and he bravely published "Walden" in 1854. In the year following four chapters of "Cape Cod" were published in *Putnam's Magazine,* and in 1858, the paper entitled "Chesuncook" in the *Atlantic Monthly*. His sinews were strengthening for the supreme effort of his life, and John Brown, wounded and in prison, found in him the only fearless friend in all America— startled, shocked and stupefied America! He defied the threatening avalanche of public opinion, the blind fury of party passion, and spake as one commissioned by the Lord God Omnipotent. It was the crowning consummation of his life; the divine moment in which he was found fully qualified. Then the baleful war cloud overshadowed the land, and whilst a sinning nation was being baptized in blood, the Messenger came and Thoreau arose and followed him.

When the turf had knit over his grave, a loving sister and some old-time friends began to gather up his papers, and the first five posthumous volumes were their harvest. "A Yankee in Canada"—the last of their gleaning—was published in 1866, and the seven volumes were left to testify of him.

In 1863-4 William Ellery Channing published his "Reminiscences of Henry D. Thoreau" in the *Boston Commonwealth,* and at the instigation of Mr. F. B. Sanborn he enlarged these, and "Thoreau: the Poet-Naturalist" appeared in 1873. This volume is largely made up of citations from Thoreau's journal—it contains much that has not been published elsewhere—and one would think that it must emphasize a hint that had already been given by Alcott: "A delightful volume might be compiled from Thoreau's Journals by selecting what he wrote at a certain date annually, thus giving us a calendar of his thoughts on that day from year to year."

That Journal was the quarry from whence Thoreau got his boulders, and the supply was by no means exhausted by the existent posthumous publications. In 1881 Mr. H. G. O. Blake, Thoreau's literary executor, began to work this mine after the plan suggested by Alcott, and within eleven years has given us "Early Spring in Massachusetts," "Summer," "Winter," and "Autumn." The Journal is not wholly depleted and Thoreau's faithful friend may be spared to give us the completion of his long labor of love.

The career that we have outlined may be said to have begun in the youthful journal that Thoreau commenced to keep in 1834 and continued for nearly thirty years. To its pages he resorted for the materials of his lectures, essays and much of his books, and from it we can get the measure of the man, the mode of his thought and the manner of his living. This is the only tribunal before which he should be tried, for therein he testifies in his own behalf, and with the unhesitating frankness and blunt sincerity of one who has nothing to conceal. But even in this court he can be understood by only those who are as earnest and as truthful as himself, and who, like him, have but single end and aim, namely, the simplification of the mystery of our earthly existence.

It is the manner with some critics to consider Thoreau as a naturalist; but this he was not, in their sense. He feasted upon the beauty of nature, but he was not an observer who could botanize upon his mother's grave. John Burroughs urges against him as a naturalist that he made no discoveries, whilst Thoreau himself frankly avows that the "fine effluence" which is alike in flower, and bird, and sunset, and the many-changing robe of the seasons—and which alone he sought—forever eluded him. That is a "discovery" which does not concern the fancy field ramblers upon whom Thoreau would not waste a walk, and for all of whom he certainly would not lose one.

Others have considered Thoreau as an author, and dwelt

upon his "style" and sundry other rhetorical trimmings pertaining to the conventional conception of that thing of the schools. He himself cared little for the varnish of scholarship and, to use his own words about John Brown, "He would have left a Greek accent sloping the wrong way, and righted up a fallen man." But he was skillful in the use of the writer's file. Passages from his journal reappear in his essays with its marks upon them, and always for their betterment. Under the date July 7, 1851, he wrote:

"With a certan wariness, but not without a slight shudder at the danger oftentimes, I perceive how near I had come to admitting into my mind the details of some trivial affair, as a case at court, and I am astonished to observe how willing men are to lumber their minds with such rubbish, to permit idle rumors, tales, incidents, even of an insignificant kind, to intrude upon what should be the sacred ground of their thoughts. Shall the temple of our thoughts be a public arena where the most trivial affair of the market, and the gossip of the tea-table, is discussed, a dusty, noisy, trivial place? or shall it be a quarter of the heavens itself, consecrated to the service of the gods, a hypaethral temple? I find it so difficult to dispose of the few facts which to me are significant, that I hesitate to burden my mind with the most insignificant, which only a divine mind can illustrate. Such is, for the most part, the news in newspapers and conversation. It is important to preserve the mind's chastity in this respect. Think of admitting the details of a single case of the criminal court into the mind to stalk profanely through its very sanctum sanctorum for an hour,—aye, for many hours; to make a very bar-room of your mind's inmost apartment, as if for a moment the dust of the street had occupied you,—aye, the very street itself, with all its travel, had poured through your very mind of minds, your thought's shrine, with all its filth and bustle."

Prepared as an essay for the *Atlantic Monthly*—"Life without Principle"—in 1861, this passage presents the following changes:

> *Not without a slight shudder at the danger, I often per-ceive how near I have come to admitting into my mind the details of some trivial affair,—the news of the street; and I am astonished to observe how willing men are to lumber their minds with such rubbish,—to permit idle rumors and incidents of the most insignificant kind to intrude on ground which should be sacred to thought. Shall the mind be a public arena, where the affairs of the street and the gossip of the tea-table chiefly are discussed? Or shall it be a quarter of heaven itself,—an hypaethral temple, conse-crated to the service of the gods? I find it so difficult to dis-pose of the few facts which are to me significant, that I hesitate to burden my attention with those which are in-significant, which only a divine mind could illustrate. . . .*
>
> *Think of admitting the details of a single case of the criminal court into our thoughts, to stalk profanely through their very sanctum sanctorum for an hour, aye, for many hours, to make a very bar-room of the mind's inmost apart-ment, as if for so long the dust of the street had occupied us,—the very street itself, with all its travel, its bustle, and filth, had passed through our thought's shrine.*

But he did not live for authorship, and his "writings" are the accidents of his life. It is curious how differently the fellow-craft interpret him. Robert Louis Stevenson writes: "He was not one of those authors who have learned, in his own words, 'to leave out their dulness.' He inflicts his full quantity upon the reader in such books as 'Cape Cod,' or (surely, he means and) 'The Yankee in Canada.' " On the contrary, we are as-sured by Horace E. Scudder, "Cape Cod" and "Walden" are likely to remain as the most finished and agreeable books by the writer.

There are other judgments upon record of the fashion of those made by a naturalist-*savant*, who takes a pickled fish from a glass jar and solemnly declares it to be without either life or motion. "He was devoid of compassion, devoid of sympathy, devoid of generosity, devoid of patriotism, as these words are generally understood," says one in a snore of comatose "criticism." From the same family came that other pronouncement: "Thoreau had no humor." It is a critic with the influenza affirming that the rose has no perfume. It is not mustard, but a fragment of ambergris that is put into the Sultan's coffee, and if the ambrosial beverage is given in charity to the beggar at the palace gate, how shall he who has but fed upon the husks that the swine did eat recognize the rare aroma?

Thoreau must be regarded neither as a naturalist, nor as an author, but simply as one who "did not wish to live what was not life." He followed the voice within, as did the wisest of Greece, though it declared for the cup of hemlock rather than the Prytanaeum. To the transcendental Puritan that monitor was supreme, and he followed it so unswervingly that there was never one moment of his existence in which he could not read his title clear to all that life had in it for him. To "enjoy existence" was his aim; to "regret nothing," his religion. A serene sanity attended him and his life is a perpetual challenge to ours. Judged by his daily walk for the brief forty-four years of his life, and by the calm dignity of his exit from this mad Vanity Fair, the burden of proof is upon us to show that his philosophy is wrong. By actual count of noses in the market place, he is in the minority; but heaven's chancery will award "reversal, with costs."

"Vox Clamantis in Deserto"

*"Vox Clamantis in Deserto"
appeared in the* Inlander
*8 (March 1898): 222–230. It
is one of Dr. Jones's most
forceful statements about
Thoreau and* Walden. *His
defense of Thoreau from the
misinterpretations of Lowell
and Bradford Torrey is
particularly well argued.
(The material within the
brackets in this essay comes
from Dr. Jones's original
footnotes.)*

T$_o$
one who has seen an *editio princeps* of "Walden" ["*Walden, or
Life in the Woods." By Henry D. Thoreau. With an Introduction by Bradford Torrey. Illustrated with Photogravures. In
two volumes. Boston and New York: Houghton, Mifflin &
Company.* 1897] these superb volumes will bear emphatic testimony to the enterprise of the publishers, and the exquisite
skill of "The Riverside Press." Involuntarily the question
leaps from the lips—"What would Thoreau say if he could see
this edition?" To be sure, "Walden" was not so *dear* to him as
the almost still-born "Week"; he did not groan for some years
under his debt to its publishers. He could write to a correspondent in 1856: "The *'Week'* had so poor a publisher that it is
quite uncertain whether you will find it in any shop. I am not
sure but authors must turn publishers themselves." And a
month later, replying to a friendly enquiry about his books:
"You ask how the former ["Walden"] has been received. It has
found an audience of excellent character, and quite numerous,
some 2,000 copies having been dispersed. I should consider it a
greater success to interest one wise and earnest soul, than a
million unwise and frivolous." [Autograph letters, unpub-

lished. *Penes nos.*] This was within two years after its publication, and it testifies to not only the popularity of Thoreau's second book: perhaps the declaration about his estimation of the "success" of a book affords the reply to Col. Higginson's enquiry,—"It will always be an interesting question, how far Thoreau's peculiar genius might have been modified or enriched by society or travel." After Thoreau had finished "cancelling," it is quite probable that the "modification" would prove to be microscopical. Or do "society or travel" turn up wise and earnest souls as the cornfields did arrowheads when Thoreau trod them?

The publishers are fortunate in their photogravures, but the readers of Thoreau who cannot expect to visit Concord are far more so. "Fred" Hosmer's camera has done faithful work; doing it as for very love of Thoreau's memory. If there is a haunt of his that "Fred" has not found, then there is just that pleasure yet in store for him: and having had the felicity of being piloted by "Fred," the writer might very easily say much more, though in common gratitude he could not less.

Especially to be commended is Miss Wheeler's sketch, vol. 1, p. 20. Thoreau's grand-mother's house (in which he was born) has been removed from its original location, but Miss Wheeler's pencil depicts it as it once stood, and with all the old-time appendages. This, too, from the descriptions of ancient people who remember it, and who are fast passing away. A second boon for the latter-day purchaser of "Walden" is the reproduction of Thoreau's map of Walden Pond—the original of which a friend of Emerson's enjoyed hugely, thinking it a burlesque of sundry government surveys. "Against stupidity the gods themselves contend in vain," as Thoreau's friend, William Ellery Channing, has written.

The vignette on the title page is, perhaps, all that we can expect today, but it is the "shanty" glorified and seen in a

"Light that never was on sea or land."

Every picture of Thoreau that has become historical has been reproduced; the early crayon by Rowse, the faithful and rustic-like Blake daguerreotype, and the pathetic, death-sealed Ricketson ambrotype. Even Mr. Walter Ricketson's almost-speaking profile medallion is pictured. Between them all the reader can clothe his conception of Thoreau in the habit in which his familiars beheld him. Opposite p. 498, vol. ii, is a photogravure of the house from which he started on his last "excursion," and in the gable on the left hand of the picture can be seen the window of that garret to which, "up two flights of stairs," Thoreau carried the seven hundred and six copies of the "Week" which Munroe cast out of his cellar to make room for better literature—from the ledger side of the computation.

The portrait of Emerson, opposite p. 80, vol. i, is a singular felicity. There he stands in the attitude that the old-time lecture-goers will remember; so self-poised, so serene, so utterly unaffected—and now there is only the mound in Sleepy-Hollow: O Time!

If any real Thoreauite can withstand the picture of the site of the "shanty," p. 436, vol. 1., it were difficult to comprehend how he is made: most of us, certainly, are not "built that way."

Striking and significant is the difference in tone and color between Lowell's review of Thoreau's "Week" in the *Massachusetts Quarterly* in 1849 and his final pronouncement upon the collected writings of the dead author in 1865.

The *raison d'être* for this critical change of base is not to the credit of the younger and far more "popular" writer. In his "Sketches from Concord and Appledore," Mr. Stearns, once a schoolboy in Concord, writes: "James Russell Lowell (as he himself tells us) was sent to Concord to rusticate while he was at college, and conceived at that time an aversion for Thoreau which never left him. In his celebrated "Fable for Critics" he satirized him as an imitator of Emerson, and so plainly that there was no mistaking the portrait." And Emerson said in his familiar talks with Mr. Woodbury: "James Russell Lowell is a man of wit; a genial man, of good inspirations, who can write poems of wit and something better. It does one good to read him. He has a good deal of self-consciousness, and he never forgave Margaret Fuller and Thoreau for wounding it."

But the day had been when Thoreau was to Lowell what Fuseli said Blake was to his fellow artists: "d— good to steal from." In the "Week," which Lowell had reviewed so patronizingly but on the whole admiringly, Thoreau had written:

"As we thus dipped our way along between fresh masses of foilage overrun with the grape and smaller flowering vines, the surface was so calm, and both air and water so transparent, that the flight of a kingfisher or robin over the river was as distinctly seen reflected in the water below as in the air above."

This was to be read in the "Week" in 1849, remember, and in the winter of 1855, when lecturing before the Lowell Institute on "English Poets," Lowell said:

"Who can doubt the innate charm of rhyme whose eye has ever been delighted by the visible consonance of a tree growing at once toward an upward and a downward heaven, on the edge of the unrippled river; or as the kingfisher flits from shore to shore, his silent echo flies under him and completes the vanishing couplet in the visionary world below." [Lectures on English Poets, p. 10. Rowfant Club. Cleveland: 1897.]

It is very plain "whose eye" had, indeed, "been delighted" by Thoreau's sylvan picture. Wordsworth borrowed Landor's "Shell" and Lowell "conveyed" Thoreau's landscape as only a poet could—but the pity of it, Iago, the pity of it.

Some inimical influence darkened Lowell's critical insight when he endeavored to interpret the purpose of Thoreau's shanty-life at Walden Pond. The elegant scholar could see in that episode of a serious life only an awkward attempt to masquerade as a "hermit"; and the parlor wit makes merry over the suggestion that Alcott's axe, and the boards, nails, bricks, mortar, books, lamp, fish-hooks, plough, hoe, "all turn state's evidence against him as an accomplice in the sin of that artificial civilization which rendered it possible that such a person as Henry D. Thoreau should exist at all." Lowell is not content to speak for himself: "Thoreau's experiment actually *presupposed* all that complicated civilization which it theoretically abjured." "His shanty-life was a mere impossibility, *so far as his own conception of it goes*, as an entire independency of mankind." Was ever merry critic so sadly caught *in flagrante delictu?*

The *Holy Grail* sought by the rustic *Sir Launfal* of the hermitage in Walden Woods was the *Simplification of Life;* his high quest, "to drive life into a corner, and reduce it to its lowest terms, and, if it proved to be mean, why then to get the whole and genuine meanness of it, and publish its meanness to the world; or if it were sublime, to know it by experience, and be able to give a true account of it in my next excursion." Doubtless, Thoreau had far less need for the blandishments of an "artificial civilization" than entered into the *summum bonum* of Lowell's drawing-room ideal. Thoreau's only inquiry was: How far *must* a man defile himself with the fleshpots of Egypt? Strange that such a "pagan" as Thoreau should set an example to the pampered son of a clergyman in denials of the fleshly appetite; but the fact remains.

Holmes, another Mr. Worldly-Wiseman, stumbled upon a truth unwittingly when he made mention of Thoreau as "the Robinson Crusoe of Walden Pond, who carried out a schoolboy whim to its full proportions." It was not a "whim," but a scholar's *settled purpose* carried out to such fair proportions as Holmes had not the "angle of aperture" to perceive. At the graduation of his Class Thoreau was appointed to participate in a "Conference" upon *The Commercial Spirit of Modern Times, considered in its Influence on the Political, Moral and Literary Character of a Nation.*" Thoreau said: "Let men, true to their natures, cultivate the moral affections, lead manly and independent lives; let them make riches the means and not the end of existence, and we shall hear no more of the commercial spirit. The sea will not stagnate, the earth will be as green as ever, and the air as pure. This curious world which we inhabit is more wonderful than it is convenient; more beautiful than it is useful; more to be admired than enjoyed. The order of things should be somewhat reversed; the seventh should be a man's day of toil, wherein to earn his living by the sweat of his brow; and the other six his Sabbath of the affections and the soul—in which to range this widespread garden and drink in the soft influence and sublime revelations of Nature." This conclusion in regard to the philosophy of life was an under-graduate's day-dream in 1837; it was *realized* at Walden within eight years. Reducing life to its lowest terms, *Food, Clothing, Fire, and Shelter*, Thoreau found that *he* could range this beautiful garden of God's for six days out of the seven and yet earn an honest living by the sweat of his brow: a demonstration in the face of which no one can sacrifice an ideal and be guiltless of a base deed.

Besides writing the volume that was to embalm his dead brother's memory, it was Thoreau's purpose at Walden to find out just how much of Lowell's confessedly "complicated civilization" was absolutely necessary in order that man's sojourn in Nature might be as sane and serene as became an immortal soul; a problem having unknown quantities the determination of which denotes the difference between existence and subsistence: a distinction that is only

"caviare to the multitude."

The only discordance in this illustrated edition of "Walden" is found, unhappily, in Mr. Bradford Torrey's "Introduction." It certainly savors of the superfluous to "introduce" a book which has seen some thirty editions within the forty-four years that it has been a significant integer in the world's literature. One would as soon expect an "introduction" to Shakespeare—unless, indeed, Bacon were in the company. But such an introduction as Mr. Torrey's must give a startling pause to those who have learned to believe Thoreau nothing if not sincere. "It is to be remembered always," writes Mr. Torrey, "that 'Walden' is a young man's book. A philosopher of thirty may be pardoned for holding the truth somewhat stiffly; finding the ideal truer than the actual, and his own faith a surer guide than other people's experience. At that age the earnest soul still believes it possible to live according to one's inner light. With added years, *of course*, there come added wisdom and a tempering of desire. We no longer expect the moon for a plaything. The thought of personal perfection mostly ceases to haunt us. Our mood has grown humbler, and we wear an easier yoke. We have learned to take things as they are, to feel less confidence in our own intuitions and more respect for traditional and collective opinion. . . . We no longer cultivate poverty as a garden herb; on the whole, as we now think, a good house and money in the bank are more desirable." All of which are very "proper" sentiments; but they are Mr. Torrey's, not Thoreau's.

"Walden" certainly is "a young man's book," if the gods are kind, but not in the sense of Mr. Torrey's misconception. Thoreau was never a "young man" of the complexion imagined by Mr. Torrey. He was nearly forty-five years of age when he died, and "Walden" was finished some eight years before his death. Eight from forty-five does not leave "a philosopher of thirty." Why does Mr. Torrey cheapen, or lessen, his "philosopher's" years? Does the early death of Novalis make his philosophy immature? Do Kit Marlowe's twenty-four years rebuke old Goethe for admiring how "greatly his Dr. Faustus is Planned"? Was it indeed a spring chicken that hatched "Walden" in the woodshed of the shanty while Thoreau was hoeing his beans? Oh, no; it is only Mr. Bradford Torrey "reconciling" Thoreau's "sentiments" to the charitable consideration of the "modern reader."

But how about that prudent aftermath of later life regarding the "good house and money in the bank" being "more desirable"—for Thoreau? Will Mr. Bradford Torrey have the hardihood to assert that!

The clear light of eternity shining into his eyes; too feeble to

write but dictating to his sister a letter responding to a
friendly enquiry about his health, the philosopher of forty-five
years declares: "I *suppose* that I have not many months to
live; but, of course, I know nothing about it. I may add that I
am enjoying existence as much as ever, and regret nothing."
Can we imagine Thoreau facing death with a lie on his lips;
and were it not a lie if so sincere a soul felt that he had held a
spurious philosophy, yet left it to debauch the young minds
that are drawn to him so trustingly, and this without the
shadow of a "regret"?

When the critics, of every degree, have done their worst with
Thoreau, they have still to find in him one fibre of the propa-
gandist. If Emerson is the Melancthon of Transcendentalism,
Thoreau is its Luther, fervid in the intensity of his convictions, but refusing alike the surplice and the creed. He is
wholly, but only, the apostle of the Ego:

> "The life that I aspire to live,
>   No man proposeth me;
> No trade upon the street
>   Wears its emblazonry."

He had learned that the Soul is solitary, and to him its
privacy was sacred. He doubted the philanthropy of the
parish and he despised its philosophy:

> "To all true wants Time's ear is deaf,
>   Penurious States lend no relief
>   Out of their pelf:
> But a free soul—thank God—
>   Can help itself.

> "Be sure your fate
> Doth keep apart its state,—
> Not linked with any band,
> Even the noblest in the land."

His whole sojourn here was one strenous endeavor to find out the *meaning of life*; he wished to be able to give a true account of it in his "next excursion." He made his triangulations, and he had both the courage and the comfort of deductions therefrom that no cataclysm could disturb:

> "I will not doubt for evermore,
>   Nor falter from a steadfast faith,
> For though the system be turned o'er,
>   God takes not back the word which once He saith."

To read Thoreau for his style rather than the spirit that inspires him is to admire a flower for its color rather than its perfume; but all creatures having sufficient length of ear turn from the rose to crop the thistle. It cannot be helped, "it is their nature to."

Introductory Note to

Pertaining to Thoreau

Pertaining to Thoreau *contained the following selections: George Ripley's review of the* Week *from the* New York Tribune, *13 June 1849 (Horace Greeley undoubtedly wrote this unsigned review, not Ripley, as Jones believed); Lowell's review of the* Week *in the* Massachusetts Quarterly Review, *December 1849;* C. F. Brigg's "A Yankee Diogenes" *from* Putnam's Monthly, *October 1854; Edwin Morton's "Thoreau and his Books" from* Harvard Magazine, *January 1855;* "Town and Rural Humbugs" *from* Knickerbocker Magazine, *March 1855; "An American Diogenes" in* Chambers's Journal, *21 November 1857; Bronson Alcott's "The Forester" from the* Atlantic, *April 1862; Storrow (not "Storms") Higginson's "Henry D. Thoreau" in* Harvard Magazine, *May 1862; John Weiss's article in* Christian Examiner, *July 1865; and Henry Williams's sketch in* Memorials of the Class of 1837 of Harvard University. *The collection was printed in Detroit by Edwin B. Hill in 1901. Only Dr. Jones's Introductory Note is reprinted here.*

I_T

It is the purpose of this collection of papers *Pertaining to Thoreau* to preserve and make easy of access the earliest mentionings of him for such students of his writings as may be interested to know what was his reception at the hands of his contemporaries. To trace the growing river of his fame to the rivulets in which it had its beginning has been a pleasure to the compiler and he believes that these gatherings from out-of-the-way sources will be welcomed by the readers of Thoreau.

Thoreau's first book fell still-born from the press and Ripley's review, with its gentle remonstrance may point out the fault that caused its rejection by the audience which Emerson thought would welcome the young iconoclast.

Lowell's paper, though flippant and patronizing contrasts strangely with his later review, which alone finds a place in Lowell's collected writings. The altered tone of the critic is explained by Emerson in a remark dropped by him in one of his talks with Mr. Charles J. Woodbury:

"James Russell Lowell is a man of wit; a genial man of good inspirations, who can write poems of wit and something better. He has a good deal of self-consciousness, and never forgave Margaret Fuller and Thoreau for wounding it."

As editor of *The Atlantic Monthly*, Lowell had elided a passage from one of Thoreau's manuscripts, whereupon Thoreau refused to continue his contributions to the magazine.

Lowell had read the *Week on the Concord and Merrimack Rivers* to good purpose, for he appropriated a beautiful nature-picture from its pages when he delivered his *Lectures on English Poets* some few years later. In the first of these brilliant lectures he says:

"Who can doubt the innate charm of rhyme whose eye has ever been delighted by the visible consonance of a tree growing at once toward an upward and a downward heaven, on the edge of an unrippled river; or as the king-fisher flies from shore to shore, his silent echo flies under him and completes the vanishing couplet in the visionary world below."

But in his account of that now-famous river journey, Thoreau had written:

"As we dipped our way along between fresh masses of foliage overrun with the grape and smaller flowering vines, the surface was so calm, and both air and water so transparent, that the flight of a kingfisher or robin over the river was as distinctly seen in the water below as in the air above."

Thoreau found the nugget that Lowell so deftly coined: Thoreau had the seeing eye; Lowell the cunning hand.

The paper by Mr. Briggs is chiefly noteworthy for being the first published misconception of Thoreau as akin to Diogenes. Briggs was Lowell's *alter ego* and too much like him to comprehend Thoreau.

Mr. Morton's paper has an added interest from the fact that we know it was read by Thoreau himself. It is the enthusiastic greeting of an ingenuous undergraduate, not yet sophisticated enough to damn with faint praise; and it remains the first warm greeting that Thoreau had received. He presented the writer with a copy of the book.

The article from the old *Knickerbocker Magazine*, "Town and Rural Humbugs," is so plainly a needy scribe's "pot boiler" that it is reproduced only as showing to what sore straits your mere critic is sometimes reduced. To classify Thoreau with Barnum and to declare that "both were humbugs" is such an "excess of stupidity" as had hitherto been found only in Thomas Sheridan by Dr. Samuel Johnson.

"An American Diogenes" is clearly an echo from the preceding papers in *Putnam's Monthly* and the *Knickerbocker Magazine*. It is the first mention of Thoreau on the other side of the Atlantic; and while far from able to comprehend Thoreau, its writer was sufficiently favored of the gods to be able to declare: "If Barnum's autobiography be a bane, Thoreau's woodland experiences may be received as its antidote."

There is a pathetic interest attaching to the next two papers. Mr. Alcott's "Forester" was published the month before Thoreau died, and may have been read to him; so he had a foretaste of what the future would say of him and his life.

Mr. Alcott had every opportunity to know him of whom he wrote and his contribution must ever remain one of the most trustworthy sources to which the future biographers of Thoreau will have recourse in forming their conception of the "Poet-Naturalist."

Mr. Storms Higginson's contribution to the *Harvard Magazine* was published in the very month that Thoreau died, but after that event. It afforded a sad pleasure to the bereaved mother and sister, and is tenderly mentioned by Sophia in letters written at the time. For biographical purposes, Mr. Higginson's paper is the most valuable in this collection. It corrects the erroneous conception of Thoreau as being unsocial, cold and repellant. It refutes the false estimate of the Rev. W. R. Alger. A frank and earnest school-boy meets Thoreau in his woodland rambles and finds him anything but the stony "stoic" that a friend's mistaken fancy has depicted.

The Rev. John Weiss was one of Thoreau's classmates, and his paper embodies his matured recollections, twenty-eight years after graduation. There is in it an absence of the superlative that gives one confidence in the judgment pronounced: and amongst the recollections of Thoreau this paper must be allowed the highest rank.

The reprint from the *Memorials of the Class of 1837* is valuable as giving a portrait of Thoreau by his own hand. His brief and naïve retrospect of his school and college days and the schedule of his multifarious employments are a sufficient reply to those who say Thoreau had no humor, and his affirmation of the soundness of his philosophy, as regards the life he chose to lead, has the clear note of the best pages of *Walden*.

At Thoreau's funeral Emerson said: "The scale on which his studies proceeded was so large as to require longevity and we were the less prepared for his sudden dissappearance. . . . It seems an injury that he should leave in the midst of his broken task, which none else can finish,—a kind of indignity to so noble a soul, that it should depart out of Nature before he has really been shown to his peers for what he is." When this was spoken two books and a few magazine articles were all that the world knew of Thoreau; but within four years after his demise the tender solicitude of friends had prepared for the press five posthumous volumes. Then the "broken task" seemed not so grievous a disappointment and the "kind of indignity" proved to be a veiled benignity.

In these seven volumes "he has been really shown to his peers for what he is," but it still remained for his friend and literary executor, Mr. H. G. O. Blake, to show him to us in his daily walk and to reveal the "task" to which he devoted his days. In the broad light that is now thrown upon the Concord "loafer," the early misconceptions are fading away, the lesson of his life is being rightly read and the arbitrament of Time has in it the assurance of his immortality, for "there is no fame more permanent than that which begins its real growth after the death of an author; and such is the fame of Thoreau."

> He kept the temple as divine
>   Wherein his soul abided;
> He heard the Voice within the shrine
>   And followed as it guided;
> He found no bane of bitter strife,
>   But laws of His designing;
> He quaffed the brimming cup of Life
>   And went forth unrepining.

Thoreau as a Skulker

"Thoreau as a Skulker" was unpublished until 1976, when it appeared in the spring issue of the Thoreau Society Bulletin. *The manuscript is in the Albert E. Lownes Thoreau Collection, Brown University Library, and is produced here with permission. Dr. Jones wrote Edwin B. Hill on 22 November 1901 that in "Thoreau as a Skulker" he was "defending Thoreau's memory from the misapprehension of* ROBERT LOUIS STEVENSON *and* UN-ANSWERABLY *answering him, too. This will surely attract the attention of Thoreau lovers." Dr. Jones wanted the essay to appear as number 1 in the* Collectanea Henry D. Thoreau *leaflets. Instead, "Emerson's Obituary" appeared as number 1 and Mr. Hill did not print "Thoreau as a Skulker." (In this section, taken from the original typescript, I have corrected a few obvious typographical errors.)*

"In one word, Thoreau was a skulker. He did not wish virtue to go out of him among his fellow-men, but slunk into a corner to hoard it for himself."

R. L. Stevenson. *Familiar Studies, etc.*

"SKULK. To withdraw into a corner or into a close or obscure place for concealment; lie close or hidden from shame, fear of injury or detection, or desire to injure another; shrink or sneak away from danger or *work*."

Century Dictionary

ISN'T

it Mathew Arnold who intimates that one supreme test of any writer is that he can endure the "return upon himself?" He means more than I have time to state definitely, just now; so, please, read his lecture upon *Emerson*, and he himself will make his meaning far clearer than I can. Having gotten this, you will, I hope, be able to see that Robert Louis Stevenson suffers from the "return upon himself," in the matter of the judgement he pronounced upon him that was Henry D. Thoreau.

Yet Stevenson tried so hard to deal justly with the memory of Thoreau, and this, too, without the stimulus of Dr. Japp's vindicatory ire. Stevenson had made the fatal mistake of *reading* Thoreau before he attempted to "criticise" him,— thereby, as the wit said, "getting a prejudice in the author's favor." Nathless, we have only to read Stevenson's exculpatory *Preface, by way of Criticism*, to learn how very true it is that

> The best laid schemes o' mice an' men,
> Gang aft a-gley.

And this is by no means the worst of it, for it remains sadly true that the false judgement, the erring judgement, the *mis*-judgement, remains to do its damning work, when he who in good faith pronounced it is in the *lumen siccum* of Eternity —that "dry light" in which there is never a mirage!

Perhaps there is no audacity like that of the critic who presumes to utter his pitiful pronouncement upon, not a man's "life," but his "character and opinions." God help us all in so perilous an attempt! What is the best critical estimate of any man's "character" but a fellow-man's feeble endeavor to do that which the All-Seeing alone can do: read aright that inscrutable mystery a man's soul! (Of course, it is assumed that the reader has not *evolutionized* so successfully that the "theory" of a Soul is simply a very dusty "back number.") And

105

as for expressing another man's "opinion"—what temerity is that! Is it not *I* who am only telling what are *his* opinions without adding: *as I understand them*? Thus it is that Criticism is largely the unlicensed and unrebuked creation of *Frankensteins* without number. Perhaps it is from the benignant recognition of this truth that Burns was touched with sympathy and made to yearn for even "auld Nickie-ben"; perhaps, too, Judas Iscariot—yea, even he—seen through the benign refraction of an angel's tears, may be found far other than the unannealed wretch, at the mention of whose name so many of us shudder and thank God (if, indeed, we ever thank Him) that we are not such as he!

A friend of the writer has put this criticism of Thoreau in so cogent a manner that one can but, in simple justice, cite his very words: "If there ever was a man of genius who was fore-ordained by the peculiarity of his doctrines and the eccentricity of his actions to be misjudged by critics, it was Thoreau. It is not in the least surprising that his true character should to this day remain unknown to the majority of readers, while his place is usurped by a mysterious personage of whose origin I will presently speak"* (If the students of American Literature who are privileged to attend Professor Demmon's *Seminarium* will read Mr. Salt's Introduction, *in toto*, they will have no difficulty in apprehending the *man* Thoreau rather than the critic's *simulacrum*.)

In that self-sufficient riant manner, which is to him as his own skin, Stevenson wrote of Thoreau: "What we want to see is one who can breast into the world, do a man's work, and still preserve his first and pure enjoyment of existence." It is beyond question that a volume could not better prove Stevenson's utter inadequacy to comprehend Thoreau than does this most remarkable "want." But we, too, are in *want*, and our need is the evidence that our merry Scotch critic could recognise just such a piece of God's handiwork as Stevenson's

Selections from Thoreau, P. vi. London: Macmillan & Co. 1895.

ideal man. That evidence is certainly lacking in this instance; "but yet the pity of it, Iago!"

Another of Stevenson's grandoise ineptitudes is this dictum: "For six weeks of occupation, a little cooking and a little gentle hygienic gardening, the man, Thoreau you may say, had as good as *stolen his livelihood*." Some years ago a writer in THE INLANDER made this declaration: "Thoreau's shanty life at Walden is the episode by which he is chiefly known and from which he is generally misunderstood." Read it slowly, giving each word its due weight of meaning. Now tell us what "episode" means. Thoreau dwelt in the Walden shanty for a little more than two years; he lived amongst men for forty-two; but a Lowell could fasten upon a brief *episode* in a man's life and pretend to find in *it* that man's whole "life, character and opinions"—yet, "Brutus is an honorable man!"

For many years past two friends have been engaged in the pious work of defending Thoreau's memory as best they might with such limited abilities as are theirs. Being well acquainted with both of them, I am allowed to publish and for the first time, certain *data* bearing upon the charge that Thoreau *shirked work* and as good as stole his living. I shall give these *data* in the words of my friend's letter.

Concord, Mass., March 16, 1898.
"My dear X. Y. Z.:

I have just been reading carefully the records of the Concord Lyceum, and I send you the following in relation to Thoreau:—

He was secretary and one of the curators for
    the season of   1838-1839.
Ditto,   1839-1840.
He was secretary (John Thoreau, Jr. Curator) 1840-1841.
Jan'y 27th., 1841. Debate: "Is it ever proper to
    offer forcible resistance?" John Thoreau,
    Jr., and D. H. Thoreau, Affirmative; A. B.
    Alcott, Negative. (What one would not give

for a phonographic cylinder that could repeat that 'debate'? All the "pot-boilers" that
ever a hungry critic penned!)

Director (meaning one of them) for the season of		1842.
Lectured, no subject given, Feb'y 8th.,		1843.
" Topic: "Ancient Poets." Nov., 29th.,		"
" " "Concord River." March 25th.,		1845.
" " "Writings and Style of Thomas Carlyle." Mar., 25,		1846.
" "History of Himself." Feb'y 10th.,		1847.
" " " " 17th.		"
" "White Beans and Walden Pond." Jan'y 3rd.,		1849.
" "Cape Cod." " 23rd.,		1850.
" " " " 30th.,		"
" "The Wild." April, 23rd.,		1851.
" "Excursion to Canada." Jan'y 7th.,		1852.
" "Canada." " 30th.,		"
One of the curators again in		1853.
Lectured. "Journey to Moosehead Lake." Dec'r 14th.,		"
" "What shall it profit a man if he gain the whole world and lose his own soul?" Feb'y 14th.,		1855.
" Told the story of his excursion to Maine last Summer. Feb'y 25th.,		1858.
" "Autumn Tints." March 2nd.,		1859.
" "Wild Apples." Feb'y 8th.,		1860.
(Taken ill with pulmonary consumption.		1861.
Died. May 6th.,		1862."

Such is the incomplete record of a "skulker," and it must be remembered that this list of his activities pertains to only such lectures as were delivered before the Concord Lyceum, where such services, from Emerson, Alcott, and Henry D. Thoreau (who "had as good as stolen his living") were gratuitous.

I feel that I am safe in asserting that an examination of Thoreau's journals would enable one to increase this list of his lectures, at least, three fold. [From] 1838 [to] 1860: twenty-one years of "active service," during a lifetime of only FORTY-TWO years! Such is the "Skulker's" record; and alas, his critic has left a record also! "O Iago, the pity of it, Iago!"

A Notable New Book

This review of Thoreau's The Service *appeared in the* Detroit Journal *on 22 May 1902. Dr. Jones wrote Fred Hosmer on 10 March 1902 (letter 420 in* Toward the Making of Thoreau's Modern Reputation), *"I hope Sanborn can be flattered into publishing all Thoreau's under-graduate writings—which are very valuable for the proper appreciation of him." The review was, then, part of Jones's efforts to flatter Sanborn, but Dr. Jones could not resist noting that Sanborn was "selling" Thoreau, and all Thoreauvians know the ultimate destination of those engaged in commerce. In this review, Margaret Fuller joined Dr. Jones's list of deluded critics who failed to understand Thoreau.*

THE SERVICE, by Henry David Thoreau. Edited by F. B. Sanborn. Boston: Charles E. Goodspeed, 1902.

I_T is little more than half a century since Horace Greeley voluntarily essayed to exploit the then unknown Henry D. Thoreau: "Selling your (Thoreau's) articles and getting paid for them— the latter by far the more difficult portion of the business." Today, Mr. Sanborn is rendering a similar service to the genius of the "poet-naturalist"; selling Thoreau's articles and, let us hope, the publisher is getting that pay for them which "the nullifier of civilization" failed to get.

Every serious reader of Thoreau (and the number of these is

increasing at a rate that is a happy augury for the saving
"remnant" of which Matthew Arnold has spoken) can but be
grateful to Mr. Sanborn for preserving and publishing the
contribution to "The Dial," which the decidedly imperious
and somewhat imperial Margaret Fuller rejected, notwithstanding the gentle remonstrance of Emerson.

"Miranda," as Lowell delighted to call the critic who so
clearly discerned the tinsel on his toys and who cast for him a
horoscope which the next century will substantiate, and who
also had the hardihood to intimate that Longfellow's poetry
was largely *eau sucre*, "for family use," must have had
contributions "to burn" when she tardily returned "The
Service" to Thoreau, with the words: "The essay is rich in
thoughts, and I should be pained not to meet it again. But
then, the thoughts seem to be so out of their natural order that
I cannot read it through without pain." Alas, the sensitive
Margaret was born too soon, for there was no Lydia
Pinkham's remedy at that early day, so she had to endure her
pains. Poor-hyper-sensitive Miranda!

Sixty years later, when Margaret has "suffered a sea
change," and Thoreau has risen to his place amongst the fixed
stars in the firmament of literature, Mr. Sanborn's "service"
enables one to bring the critic before a tribunal where she is
not the judge, but where Thoreau is permitted to testify in his
own behalf.

One latter day reader of "The Service" must avow that he
has "read it through without pain," that he has found the
"essay so rich in thoughts" as to completely deafen him to
"the grating of tools on the mosaic." To be confidentially
frank, his opinion is that the Minerva of "The Dial" thought
Thoreau altogether too "cocky" in his utterances: that a
callow Harvard graduate spake too much as "one having
authority," that the entered apprentice had too confidently
made his pronouncement "in verbis magistri." Nevertheless,
after all the "service" that Thoreau was permitted to render
whilst in the flesh we feel that "He builded better than (s)he
knew."

Much more of true critical insight is found in Mr. Sanborn's appreciation: "One feels in this whole essay the spirit of youth—its confidence in itself, its haughty scorn for the conventional and customary—a singular blending of the aristocratic and the democratic in its tone towards other men— who are at once the dust of the earth and the superiors of the stars. Youth never forsook Thoreau; and though he moderated the peculiarities of this essay, he never quite abandoned them in his later writing." This is a singularly felicitous judgment, and its beauty is enhanced by its truth. One can but hope that Mr. Sanborn may be induced to edit every scrap of Thoreau's writing that now has no other shrine than his precious portfolio.

With all its somewhat sophomorical self-assertion and proneness to the paradoxical, "The Service" has in it the evidence that Thoreau's convictions were settled at a very early hour in his life, and were held without the shadow of turning until the last moment of his earthly sojourn. His whole life was one unswerving consistency, the fixedness of a settled purpose. Like the Sphynx in the desert, the varying winds of doctrine may bury him in the shifting sands, but there he remaineth, "a possession forever." Si sic omnes!

It is a matter for gratulation to every earnest reader of Thoreau that in Mr. Charles E. Goodspeed, Boston, Mass., "the hermit of Walden" is finding as appreciative a publisher, as sympathetic an editor; and it were ungracious to overlook the charming typographical dress in which The Merrymount Press is clothing some of the most sanative thought that has come to us from the New England "Transcendentalists."

It may be as well to add that the untraced quotation which has occasioned note 7 may be found in Sir Thomas Browne's Christian Morals, Part 1: "Sit not down in the popular forms and common level of virtues. Offer not only peace offerings but holocausts unto God: where all is due make no reserve and cut not a cummin seed with the Almighty. To serve Him singly to serve ourselves were too partial a piece of piety, not like to place us in the illustrious mansions of glory."

SECTION THREE

Dr. Jones's Last Thoreau Work

THOREAU AMONGST FRIENDS AND PHILISTINES

Dr. Jones wrote Fred Hosmer on 7 September 1901:
I have prepared the "copy" for a book to be called " Thoreau amongst Friends and Philistines." [Dr. Jones, in letters referring to this volume, placed a comma after "Friends." I have omitted the comma.] It is "Inscribed (without express permission) to that respectable majority which thinks by proxy— when it thinks at all." It is as plucky and as "sassy" as any friend of Thoreau could desire, and it will make more noise than the small boy's firecracker on the "glorious Fourth."

It consists of ten reviews of Salt's various Thoreau publications from English papers, and six [Dr. Jones revised this to five] American estimations of Thoreau. Interspersed throughout the text are comments of my own. . . .

A limited edition of it will surely prepare the way for a second and cheaper one.

Dr. Jones wrote Fred Hosmer two weeks later that the depression caused by the death of his favorite son kept him from getting on with his "sassy" book. In fact, he had one more section to finish: "I have found a criticism of Thoreau by Julian Hawthorne that makes me 'mad all over.' I have not yet been able to learn where it first appeared; but when I get the facts of it, my, but I'll try and answer him as he deserves. I have done his sister to the queen's taste, especially if she likes 'hot stuff,' and I want to tickle Julian in even better style." He asked Hosmer to inquire in Boston if Goodspeed would be interested in seeing the manuscript. "Once in print," he went on, "I am not at all afraid that the

115

book will not be heard from in many quarters, for it handles some folks without gloves and in a manner that will gratify those who love Thoreau."

Fred Hosmer called on Goodspeed, who did want to see the manuscript. Dr. Jones, on 29 September 1901, wrote that the manuscript was not ready because he had not found the Julian Hawthorne publication, only an abstract from it. Dr. Jones called the young Hawthorne's statements "the most shameful thing about Thoreau I ever read." Dr. Jones went on: "The book is sure to please Thoreau's admirers, and it is sure to make a noise, for I am going to handle the Hawthorne family—the father, 'rose' and Julian— without gloves. The book also adds something to our knowledge of Thoreau; corrects some prevalent errors concerning him, and it shows up the critics in fine style."

Perhaps Dr. Jones never found the essay that appeared in Julian Hawthorne and Leonard Lemmon's

American Literature *(Julian Hawthorne was undoubtedly the author of the essay). Dr. Jones does not seem to have written his reply to Julian Hawthorne, nor did he submit "Thoreau amongst Friends and Philistines" for publication. Henry Salt wrote for the return of the press clippings Dr. Jones had borrowed from him, but they remained in Dr. Jones's study; the manuscript was apparently put aside because of Dr. Jones's failing health. Some time after Dr. Jones's death, the manuscript and the clippings were moved to Urbana, Illinois, and I found them in June of 1974.*

I have added Julian Hawthorne's essay to the manuscript, for it was clearly Dr. Jones's intention to do so. Because Dr. Jones did not make final editorial changes on his typewritten transcripts of the Thoreau articles, I have presented the texts as I found them. The published texts have been altered in only one respect: all the footnotes have been italicized, placed in brackets, and inserted into the text at the points at which their corresponding asterisks occurred. This has been done whether the footnotes were the printer's or Dr. Jones's. "The editor" throughout is, of course, Dr. Jones.

Contents

Introductory Note.

Introductory Note

ON FRIDAY, the ninth of May, 1862, friendly hands laid all that was mortal of Henry D. Thoreau beside his earlier-departed brother John. Leaning over the face of his silent friend, Emerson said: "Wherever there is knowledge, wherever there is virtue, wherever there is beauty, he will find a home." This he spake to those who had known Henry Thoreau in the flesh; and they gave their mute assent.

The same eulogist, on the same occasion, had made another declaration: "The country knows not yet, or in least part, how great a son it has lost." And many of those who heard him thought it the fine exaggeration of a fervent friendship. Then the grave was filled and the mourners departed and the world went on its wonted way.

The widow Thoreau well knew that she had lost a dear son; but had not Emerson said a "great"? His very words were still echoing clearly in her ears and she murmured musingly, "Great?" She knew that at that moment there were lying in her garret over seven hundred copies of her dead son's still-born book: yet Emerson had distinctly said—"How great a son it has lost." It was not you have lost, but "the country." O mourning mother and sorrowing sister will "the country" ever learn in any part its loss?

The following pages form a part of Time's reply and that not only for Thoreau's country. Of the judgements and misjudgements gathered herein eleven are from the pens of friends, and of Philistines, each of whom are aliens; four only of these fifteen pronouncements speak for "the country" which the graveside prediction meant. And these scrap-book savings— some, of the precious material which loving appreciation provides; others, the sorriest stuff that ever boiled the pot for a needy scribe—these gatherings, which from the editor's store could have been almost indefinitely augmented, are yet only a tithe towards showing in what part the English-speaking world at length has learned to know how great a son it lost when Thoreau went forth to take his place in the galaxy of its Great Ones.

In the first five years after Thoreau's death, through the faithful service of his sister Sophia, Emerson, and Ellery Channing, five volumes were added to the couple that he had published; and twenty-seven years later Thoreau was canonized and enshrined in a Collected Edition, which so long as Literature is a delight shall show how great a son he is.

Surely the well-filled scrap-book is significant of much: acute appreciation, and stupid misconception; profound insight, and stark blindness; sweet sympathy, and sour sarcasm; the attraction of affinity, and the repulsion of diversity; praise, and condemnation,—all these, yet the subject one and the same; the judges many and the judgements so diverse! Perhaps the greater wonder is that Thoreau has been discerned at all: "Nobody, or hardly anybody, having in himself an earnest sense for the truth, how can anybody recognise an inarticulate Veracity, or Nature-fact of any kind; a Human Doer especially, who is the most complex, profound, and inarticulate of all Nature's Facts?"

In presenting the literary waifs that comprise this volume the editor, in five instances, has departed from the chronological order of their publication. The contribution from Great Thoughts is given first because it is considered as being the best adapted for introducing Thoreau to all and sundry who may not now know of him. Its writer displays an insight as unerring as it is rare: "Thoreau's devotion to nature was something as inevitable as it was unreserved. . . . It was his great and uncompromising sincerity, his strenuous devotion to truth and purity of life, that shaped his irrevocable career. . . . He was less a naturalist of the seen than of the unseen." These are rare notes in the interpretation of Thoreau: better still, they are true. They contrast strangely with that jeering voice which pronounced Thoreau "the nullifier of civilization, who insisted on nibbling his asparagus at the wrong end," and with that other ineptitude which considered the austere life at Walden Pond as being a "masquerade," or at best a "transcendental" pic-nic. Lowell misjudged Thoreau from a short episode in his life; a sincere critic surveying the whole life does not hesitate to declare it "a great illustration of the reward which comes to the man who is faithful to his ideal." In first coming to the study of Thoreau it is better to trust the hand of a friend than the boot of the Philistine.

The other lapses from chronological continuity are made in order that the English testimonials might be presented on the one hand and the American on the other. Even here a departure has been made and in the instance of the finely-discriminative review of the first collected edition of Thoreau's Works which appeared in the Boston Herald for December 18, 1893. The present editor felt that here and there a reader might have need for a corrective of some of the inanities (insanities?) which some of the pages of this book will have inflicted; and such a reader will take heart when he finds a critic declaring, "You feel in reading Thoreau that you are in a world of fact and observation which is beyond the ordinary range of thought and experience. There is a sense of the wholeness of life, apart from its traditions, which you find in no other writer."

Verily, here is one of the species critic who is by no manner of means a mere wood and leather device—may his tribe increase!

"It is as if a new world had been entered for a young person to take up the writings of Thoreau for study, but it is a world which every one ought to enter, and in which a truer side of life is approached and studied by one who had made himself master of his thought before he gave it expression." Many and heinous are the sins of the latter-day newspaper, but when one of them presents such a statement the sins of a century are shriven in an hour. Such a critic shall never write himself, as did Sam Johnson on occasion, Impransus, for of a truth he hath learned where to find the Bread of Life.

The editor must humbly apologise for the bracketted ad-
denda. Under some of the most grievous provocation—and
really smarting thereunder, as if it were a personal indignity
—he can still urge that he remembered the Irish laborer whose
sleep was being sorely disturbed by his wife's toothache:
"Biddy, darlin', be aisy; an' if you can't be aisy, be as aisy ae ye
can."

A few corrections of errors pertaining to facts have been
made in the interest of Thoreau's coming biographer; an assured advent because so delusive are the eyes of both friend
and of foe that no man's life can be rightly written by a contemporary.

Meanwhile, this little book has in it a lesson of patient for-
bearance. Here are various men, critics by profession, looking
at the same object but from widely different stand-points:

HAMLET: Do you see yonder cloud that's almost in shape of
a camel?

POLON: By the mass, it is like a camel, indeed.

HAMLET: Methinks it is like a weasel.

POLON: It is backed like a weasel.

HAMLET: Or like a whale?

POLON: Very like a whale.

The death of Ophelia and of Laertes did not leave old
Polonius without offspring, whatever history may declare to
the contrary. Not only the camel the weasel and the whale remain to vex all those who cannot see the man behind the
cloud.

HENRY DAVID THOREAU

The morning wind for ever blows,
The poem of creation is uninterrupted,
But few are the ears that hear it.

AMONG those who have joined in that modern pilgrimage which has been called a "Return to Nature," the Poet-Naturalist is one of the most significant and interesting. There have been poets of Nature, of whom Wordsworth is still the acknowledged master, and naturalists, among whom, I suppose, Charles Darwin stands supreme; but there are others who, though not great as these are great, either as poets or as naturalists, are yet great as these are not in the possession of a unique and impassioned feeling for Nature, which has in it something of both their qualities, and which, in a measure, transcends both. The temper of science *and* of poetry is theirs, and the blending of these gives to their vision of Nature a depth and richness we can hardly prize too well. They know her in ways which perhaps to the poet, as such, and to the specialised naturalist, are alike strange. They hear and see, not so imaginatively as the one, not so minutely or with such precision of detail as the other, yet with a clearness and directness of insight such as gives to their message a peculiar interest and charm. Take, in illustration, this brief passage from Thoreau's "Natural History of Massachusetts": "The universe is not rough-hewn, but perfect in its details. Nature will bear the closest inspection. She invites us to lay our eye level with the smallest leaf, and take an insect view of its plain. She has no interstices. Every part is full of life. I explore with pleasure the sources of the myriad sounds which crowd the summer noon, and which seem the very grain and stuff of which eternity is made."

The title "poet-naturalist" was employed first, I believe, by Ellery Channing. He used it as the best description of his friend Thoreau in a volume published in 1873. And Thoreau was, perhaps, the first to whom it could be fittingly applied. He originates a new order of Nature-students. Our own Gilbert White, of Selborne, and the great bird-naturalist Audubon might seem to have a prior claim. But in both these the scientific temper is too obviously in the ascendant, the poet too much in the background. They are strong and beautiful naturalists. They loved and observed Nature with a great enthusiasm, but they did not idealise her. They did not haunt through the imagination her hidden mysteries of life and thought. But Thoreau—let him be his own witness again, and note how the close observer and the spiritual seer are mingled in the rapt vision of beauty which his words enshrine. He has risen before the dawn on a summer morning that he may watch the opening of the water lilies in the first sun's rays. "Carefully looking both up and down the river I could perceive that the lilies began to open about fifteen minutes after the sun, from over the opposite bank, fell on them, perhaps three-quarters of an hour after sunrise, and one was fully expanded about twenty minutes later. . . . Found two lilies open in the very shallow inlet by the meadow. Exquisitely beautiful and unlike anything we have is the first white water lily just expanded in some shallow lagoon, perfectly fresh and pure, before the insects have discovered it. How admirable its purity! How innocently sweet its fragrance! How significant that the rich black mud of our dead stream produces the water lily! Out of that fertile slime springs this spotless purity." [*At this point, Jupp has an asterisk directing the reader to the citation at the bottom of the page: " 'Summer,' pp. 195 and 324."*]

PARENTAGE AND BIRTH

Henry Thoreau was born in the year 1817, in the village of Concord, in the State of Massachusetts, about twenty miles from Boston. It was here that the New England farmers withstood the English troops in 1775, and "fired the shot heard round the world." It has been called the "birth-place of American liberty." Thoreau's life was spent for the most part in and around his native village. His father, John Thoreau, was a pencil-maker, a silent, homely kind of man, poor for the most part, and of strict integrity, "wholly unpretending," as his son says of him, "and one who always studied merely how to make a *good* article, and was never satisfied with what he produced. Nor was he ever in the least disposed to put off a *poor* one for pecuniary gain, as if he laboured for a higher end." He was of French extraction, as the name imports, an emigrant from Jersey in 1773. Thoreau's mother was a clever and sprightly woman, "tall, handsome, quick-witted," says his biographer, "fond of dress, and fond of gossip . . . . and often monopolised the conversation by her unfailing flow of talk."

Henry was the third child of these, and the one to whom it was given to make their name famous wherever the literature of Nature and of the ideal was destined to be known. For a few years, from 1818 to 1823, they lived in Boston, but then returned to Concord, not to leave it again until the last survivor of the household had passed into the unseen. Around this village lay the farms and broad meadows and woodlands, where once the Indian had camped, and through it flowed the sluggish Indian stream Musketaquid, now called the Concord, and near it the swift flowing Assabet. Here the boy first met with Nature and put himself to school with her. He went to other schools, and at the age of sixteen entered Harvard University, graduating there four years later, but refusing his degree because it would cost him five dollars—more than he could afford, or more than he thought it worth. Then, for a few years, he maintained himself by teaching. Very soon, however, he discovered that this was not the work to which he was called, while it denied him the freedom essential to his true life. By labour out of doors, surveying, tilling of the soil, and occasional pencil making, he found it possible to earn all that was necessary without serious expenditure of time which he wanted for other and, to him, higher things. He lived a life of utmost simplicity. His aim was to be satisfied with fewest things, to be dependent in the least degree on external goods; and this in no ascetic temper, but in order to be free, to possess himself of the fullest possibilities of his own life and the higher activities of the spirit. "A man is rich," he said, "in proportion to the number of things he can do without." Socrates, Epicurus, Seneca, and Carlyle had said much the same before him. But he carried it home and pressed it to its extreme as these had not. He could boast that in six weeks, by the labour of his own hands, he had often earned sufficient to satisfy his material necessities for a whole year. He thus secured to himself the main part of his time for study, and for roaming the woods and fields, observing, absorbing, meditating there, living the noblest life he believed in, and gathering material for the books which remain to us as the product of his genius and industry. For two years, from 1845 to 1847, he dwelt alone in the woods in a small hut, built by his own hands, on the shore of Walden Water, about one mile from the nearest house in his native village. He lived thus, he will tell you, not as a monk or a hermit might, not from fear or dislike of his fellow men, not to live indolently, or shirk any legitimate social claim; but rather to put himself finally to school, to finish his education or to carry it forward into higher regions of spiritual activity. "I went to the woods because I wished to live deliberately, to front only the essential facts of life, and see if I could not learn what it had to teach, and not, when I came to die, discover that I had not lived."

DEVOTION TO NATURE

This man is set on getting his own original and direct vision of things, to know what for him those "sealed orders" of Providence may be—to break the seal and read his destiny, or, at least, his duty there. Each serious and awakened mind must have its own way of facing the realities. Thoreau's way was to get close to Nature, and since he could not get close enough while living among the habitations of men, he betook himself for a while to a home in the woods, to be calm, deliberate, thoughtful there. He does not want to be hurried away by the stream of custom and conventionality. He would find his own feet. "Let us spend one day as deliberately as Nature, and not be thrown off the track by every nutshell and mosquito's wing that falls on the rails. Let us rise early and fast, or break fast, gently and without perturbation; let company come and let company go, let the bells ring and the children cry, determined to make a day of it. Why should we knock under and go with the stream?" This may read unsocial and a little hard, as of a man indifferent to the great human world and its affairs. It is, and you must beware how you imitate it or catch its spirit. It may not avail for you. For some, misanthropy and narrowness of soul would lie that way. But this man, bent as he is on education and self-discipline, finds that with Nature he can train best and learn his deeper lessons. "Every morning was a cheerful invitation to make my life of equal simplicity, and I may say of innocence, with Nature herself. I got up early and bathed in the pond; that was a religious exercise, and one of the best things I did. . . . Morning brings back the heroic ages. . . . To him whose elastic and vigorous thought keeps pace with the sun, the day is a perpetual morning. Morning is when I am awake and there is a dawn *in me*. Moral reform is the effort to throw off sleep. To be awake is to be alive."

So the great days came to him clearly, and he took their grand lessons to heart. When the purpose of his self-chosen solitude was fulfilled he returned to his home, under his father's roof, where he spent the remainder of his years, though ranging still each day, and often at night, the lonely places he had found so fair.

Thoreau's devotion to Nature then was something inevitable as it was unreserved. He belonged to her as a pine tree or a wood nymph belongs to her. He was familiar with her from boyhood, and in manhood, the more wild and unfrequented her scenes, the more perfectly was he at home. In college days, though he loved books, and was no mean classic scholar, his heart longed for the woods, and the free life there which he knew so well. "Though bodily I have been a member of Harvard University, heart and soul I have been far away among the scenes of my boyhood. Immured within the classic walls of a Stoughton or a Hollis, my spirit yearned for the sympathy of my old and almost forgotten friend, Nature." To most who knew him, and to most, probably, who read his books, this devotion to Nature was too absolute and exclusive, leaving no room for human interests and affection. But to those who knew him closely, and to those who read him with clear eyes, this is the superficial view. It was his great and uncompromising sincerity, his strenuous devotion to truth and purity of life, that shaped for him his irrevocable career. A great loss and a great sorrow in the days of his early manhood thrust him perhaps more entirely into the arms of Nature than might otherwise have happened. Thoreau had one brother, older than himself by a few years, whom he loved with a great affection. With him he had lived in closest intimacy from boyhood. It was with him that the famous voyage was made in the boat they had built with their own hands, and of which we have such glorious record in his first published volume, "A Week on the Concord and Merrimac rivers." It is said that he once made the painful discovery that this brother and himself were in love with the same maiden, and learning this he resolved to restrain and conquer his own feelings, lest any rival claim of his should thwart his brother's joy. A few years later, abruptly, from the result of some slight accident, this brother was taken from him. He died of lock-jaw from a wound in the hand. It was the supreme personal grief of Thoreau's life. The only event that moved him more deeply than this was the execution of John Brown, of Harper's Ferry, the heroic anti-slavery martyr. "After the sad and unfortunate death of his brother, whom he tenderly loved," writes Joseph Hosmer, "he seemed to have no earthly companion." Telling of it to a friend twelve years after, "he turned pale and faint." He had great and honoured friends, such as Emerson, Bronson Alcott, and Ellery Channing, but no vital companion of his soul after this irreparable loss.

> Eternity may not the chance repeat;
> But I must tread my single way alone,
> In sad remembrance that we once did meet,
> And know that bliss irrevocably gone.
>
> The spheres henceforth my elegy shall sing,
> For elegy has other subject none;
> Each strain of music in my ears shall ring
> Knell of departure from that other one.

I think his devotion to Nature became more absolute and unreserved in consequence of this loss. With her he knew his brother had become entirely one, and to her he turned with lonely and surrendered heart. He found solace and recovery thus. "What right have I to grieve who have not ceased to wonder. We feel at first as if some opportunities of kindness and of sympathy were lost, but learn afterwards that any pure grief is ample recompense for all. That is, if we are faithful; for a great grief is but sympathy with the soul that disposes events, and is as natural as the resin on Arabian trees. Only Nature has a right to grieve perpetually, for she alone is innocent. Soon the ice will melt, and the blackbirds sing along the river which he frequented, as pleasantly as ever. The same everlasting serenity will appear in the face of God, and we will not be sorrowful if He is not."

THE FIRST OF HIS ORDER

And so, turning each day to where for him was wisdom and great peace, Henry Thoreau became the first and perhaps the greatest of that new order of enthusiasts, the Poet-Naturalists. A very intense and eager, though withal most serene and stainless life he lived there in the great open air, at all seasons and all hours; not an indolent easy-going life, as we might think, but ever in pursuit of a high and pure ideal. Very calm and innocent was his movement across this world's wide stage, but it was calm as Nature herself is calm, as the clear midnight heavens are calm, whose stars burn with intense and quenchless fires, and move for ever onward in their viewless, but surely destined way. His life was a long and strenuous pursuing. An ideal never attained, yet, in the seeking made truly his own each hour, kept him ever alert. In his college days, one of his class-mates says of him, "his eyes were sometimes searching as if he had dropped or expected to find something." And in the opening pages of "Walden," which is one of the rare and sincere autobiographies of our age, to be read with the "Confessions" of Augustine or Rousseau, and the "Prelude" of Wordsworth, he tells us, in his own quaint fashion, of this life-long search: "I long ago lost a hound, a bay horse, and a turtle-dove, and am still on their trail. Many are the travellers I have spoken concerning them, describing their tracks, and what calls they answered to. I have met one or two who had heard the hound, and the tramp of the horse, and even seen the dove disappear behind a cloud; and they seemed as anxious to recover them as if they had lost them themselves." The calm strenuousness of his life-long spiritual endeavor wrought itself into the features of his strongly marked countenance. It was weather-worn from without but etherealised from within. One who saw him for the first time in his mature years, was heard to say, "how deep and clear is the mark which thought sets upon a man's face."

When he came in from his long hours in the woods, or by the Concord stream, his face browned by the sun and wind, persons meeting him have seen his countenance, as it were, filled and interpreted with a great soul-light; not "sicklied o'er with the *pale cast*," but kindled and illumined o'er with the *radiant glow*, "of thought." Life, to him, was no child's play, but an eager, though joyous and exultant, contest. Nature's voices called him to the glad, victorious fray. "Then the sound of distant thunder," he writes in his journal, "though no cloud is obvious. Thunder and lightning are remarkable accompaniments to our life, as if to remind us that there is always a battle raging. They are signal guns to us." Yet see with what calm and deep receptiveness of mind he could take his rest in favoured hours. "There were times when I could not afford to sacrifice the bloom of the present moment to any work, whether of head or hands. I love a broad margin to my life. Sometimes, in a summer morning, having taken my accustomed bath, I sat in my sunny doorway from sunrise to noon, rapt in a reverie, amidst the pines and hickories and sumachs, in undisturbed solitude and stillness, while the birds sang around or flitted noiselessly through the house, until by the sun falling in at my west window, or the noise of some traveller's waggon on the distant highway, I was reminded of the lapse of time.

"I grow in these seasons like corn in the night, and they were far better than any work of the hands would have been. . . . The day advanced as if to light some work of mine; it was morning, and lo! now it is evening, and nothing memorable is accomplished.

"This was sheer idleness to my fellow-townsmen, no doubt." ["Walden," p. 121.]

HIS LIMITATIONS

Thoreau's limitations were many, as indeed most men's are. There is something touching at times, almost to pathos, in his solitude—the cold, inaccessible heights where his spirit so often roamed. One thinks of the many human affairs that had no interest for him. Perhaps, at heart, he was not an unsocial man. Yet he wrote once, in his diary, "If I am too cold for human friendship, I trust I shall not be too cold for natural happiness. It appears to be a law that you cannot have a deep sympathy with both man and Nature. Those qualities which bring you to the one estrange you from the other." Yet was he not indifferent to the real humanities of life. It was the insincerities, the trivial pursuits and ambitions of men, that he learned to hate. For the oppressed slave, and for the persecuted champion of the oppressed slave, he was full of profoundest sympathy. He sheltered the fugitive negro in his hut. And when Brown, of Harper's Ferry, was imprisoned and condemned to death for defending the slave, it was the Hermit of Walden's voice that was first raised in public protest and appeal against the national crime.

To many, I suppose, the egotism of Thoreau will often be offensive and repellent. It will be difficult for his greatest lovers always to defend this. Yet one remembers that, for the most part, it is the egotism of cheerfulness and gratitude, never of complaining or of self-pity. "Instead of singing like the birds, I silently smiled at my incessant good fortune." Sometimes, in reading him, I am reminded of Coleridge's saying of some of Milton's self-unfoldings: "Such egotism is a revelation of spirit."

Thoreau's life is a great illustration of the reward which comes to the man who is faithful to his ideal. Nature, to whom he devoted himself, seemed to have kept few secrets from him. Her creatures loved and trusted him, and he knew them, their form and habits and tempers of mind, as only the lover knows. He conquered them without gun or trap or collecting bottle. He made them his friends by watchfulness and sympathy and gentle wisdom. Trees and shrubs and obscure flowers of the swamp, as well as birds and squirrels and burrowing animals, were his boon companions. The mice crept to his hand to share his dinner; the partridge hatched her brood beneath or near his hut; a sparrow once, "as he hoed in his garden, alighted on his shoulder," a squirrel, "which he had taken home for a few days to observe its habits, *refused to be set at liberty*, returning again and again to its new friend, climbing up his knee, sitting on his hand, and at last gaining the day by hiding its head in the folds of his waistcoat—an appeal which Thoreau was unable to withstand." [*H. S. Salt: Life, p. 134.*] Much more, the visible forms and movements were the inner revelations of Nature; her ways were "ways of the spirit" to him. He was less a naturalist of the seen than of the unseen. He found his way to the inner heart of things and stood worshipping, reverent, yet exultant, almost proud in presence of a life more sacred and divine than his own finest thought or man's most perfect achievement. Writing on a winter's day of the stillness and solitude of wild scenes in his walk, he says—"It is as if I always met in those places some grand, severe, immortal, infinitely encouraging, though invisible companion, and walked with him." Again, in "Walden," he says, "Nearest to all things is the power which fashions their being. *Next* to us the grandest laws are continually being executed. *Next* to us is not the workman we have hired, with whom we love to talk, but the workman whose work we are."

Thoreau died on a morning in spring, 1862, in his fifty-fifth year. A painful illness, which kept him within doors for many months, had been endured with the fortitude of a serene and uncomplaining content. He worked at his papers to the last, and his superb courage and unfaltering trust sustained him through all suffering and the weary days and nights of a lingering disease. "I am enjoying existence as much as ever and regret nothing," were the closing words of a letter written but a few weeks before the end. Let us take farewell of him in words written in the days of his strength. "My greatest skill has been to want but little. For joy I could embrace the earth. I shall delight to be buried in it. And then I think of those amongst men who will know that I love them, though I tell them not."

Great Thoughts, January 19, 1895 [By W. J. Jupp.]

THE LIFE OF THOREAU

W HAT little there is to say concerning the life and opinions of Thoreau, the New England naturalist, has been
told so often that one might well imagine that this biography
would turn out to be one of the superfluities of literature.
Thirty years have not yet elapsed since Thoreau was laid in
Sleepy Hollow Cemetery. Yet, in that interval, at least three
separate volumes have been published regarding him, while
the mere list of magazine articles devoted to his ways and his
opinions fill four octavo pages of the latest addition to them.
And yet this bibliography, large as it is, cannot be considered
complete. The man in himself was wonderfully interesting—
a man whom it was impossible not to like, and even to love.
But he did little for that world which he forsook. [*Dr. Jones's
copy of this article has this sentence marked with an exclama-
tion point in the margin.*] He hid in the Massachusetts woods,
and yet natural history is not indebted to him for anything
like the data garnered by Gilbert White, the parish priest, or
Audubon, the forest painter, or John Burroughs, the farmer
poet of his own State, or by Richard Jefferies, who found the
world and its responsibilities quite compatible with the study
of bird and beast and flower. "Men of science," indeed, do not
recognise Thoreau as one of them. They are afraid to quote an
observer who eschewed the learned Societies, and tinctured
everything with the light of Transcendentalism. And to do
Thoreau justice, he never pretended to be either zoologist or
botanist, and though as a boy he collected for Agassiz, he
cared not a straw for any man's opinions. All he wanted was
to live as he liked, and think as pleased him best, without the
cut and dried conventions of mankind interfering with him.
Even his contributions to literature, though generally
pleasant, and often charming, are, with the exception of

"Walden," the "Excursions," and "Letters," no great bids for immortality. His poems lack music, while his "Cape Cod," "A Yankee in Canada," and "The Maine Woods"—all three published after his death—could have been written by a much feebler philosopher. The first is certainly a delightful book, but he generalises confidently from imperfect premises. He is always striving after paradox and antithesis, and, having seen little of mankind beyond the New Englanders within a few miles of his home, was apt to imagine that his experience was that of the big world which he despised. On the other hand, Thoreau, in close touch with Nature, and quaint in his description of his converse with her, will always remain an attractive character. In Europe he could not have failed to draw disciples to him. But not a little of our interest in the man and his writings lies in the fact that he presented so marked a contrast to the rest of his countrymen. Many of them are clever, and most of them are original, and in no other land have there been so many social experiments. But for a Harvard graduate to take to day labour by choice, and then only for long enough to earn the few dollars necessary to sustain him, was a paradox to those whose notions of the New Englander were based upon a study of Mr. Barnum's "Autobiography." "Walden" may, indeed, be described as the antidote to that volume. The gospel of the one is a glorification of money-making. The drift of the other is to cultivate literature on the Massachusetts representative of "a little oatmeal," and to prove how very low living is quite compatible with very high and pure thinking.

Thoreau's biography is really embodied in his books. The man who has read these will find even Mr. Salt's comprehensive "Life" at secondhand unnecessary. But, as only a thorough-paced Thoreauist will care to work through the entire series, the present volume will save him that agreeable toil. Mr. Salt's three hundred pages will unquestionably not be the last words upon "the American Rousseau," but they are so exhaustive, and so conscientious, that it is hard to see what is left for another Boswell to glean. After the ordinary life of a

country boy, and a career at school and college in no way remarkable, Thoreau tried schoolmastering, and then land surveying. But by-and-by, coming to the conclusion that the less
a man does over and above what the necessity of existence
demands, the better servant he is to his species, the land
surveyor threw down his chain, and, meeting Emerson, took
to Transcendentalism as a business, and to literature as an
amusement. Concord, his native village, was, indeed, in those
days (as it is still) a queer jumble of New England thrift and
Hegelian metaphysics. A "School of Philosophy" has of late
years given it a place in the lettered world. But even in 1844,
as the home of Emerson, Hawthorne, Margaret Fuller, Ellery
Channing, Bronson Alcott, and a number of other dreamers
after an ideal community, which by-and-by found expression
in Brook Farm, it was an extraordinary place. Thoreau built
himself a hut in the back woods, to live there a simpler life
than could be attained on three meals a day and regular office
hours. Mr. Salt insists that his intentions have been misinterpreted by all of his previous biographers, among others by Mr.
Stevenson, who falls in with his humour, and Mr. Lowell,
whose good sense rather rebels against the step. The recluse
wished, not to be quit of mankind, only to "adopt a more independent way of living than that which custom enjoins." In
any case, he could not get rid of his species, even if he had
tried. He got his cabin up, and it is curious to remember that
he borrowed an axe from Alcott, who is still alive, and was
helped in cutting the logs by George Curtis, a young enthusiast fresh from Harvard and Brook Farm, and then seeking the
better life as an agricultural labourer, though since these days
he has twice had the refusal of the post of Envoy to the Court
of St. James's, and is now a purifying influence in American
politics. Thoreau lived an extremely rough existence, but he
was not alone. Friends visited him pretty frequently, and he
found too often on returning from his rambles that curious
folks had been making up a party to see how a bachelor
philososopher managed to live without furniture, and
"women-folk to cook his victuals."

Yet the record of his life at Walden Pond is, in its way, a model of natural history observation, of quaint remarks, and of dry humour. But it lacks the human interest of Izaak Walton, of White's "Selborne," or of Jefferies's earlier and better books. He reduced economy to a fine art. He surveyed a little, tilled a patch of potatoes, did an odd job at gardening, fence-building, or whitewashing. In the book which is his masterpiece we have a minute account of his expenditure and income, told with a good deal of earnestness. He communed with bird and beast until they would answer his call, and forget that man was their hereditary enemy. Every flower he knew, and could, in the two years he spent in the woods, tell when and where to expect each one of them above the soil. Towards animals he was a humanitarian. He would neither shoot nor trap them for specimens. But, though a violent Abolitionist, and an admirer of the hero of Harper's Ferry so uncompromising that he loved all the race of Browns for the sake of Captain John, except for children and old folk he appears to have had little more than a zoological regard. They were superior animals, that was all. Walden was exhausted in two years. Then, for a time, he followed the family trade of pencil maker, writing in odd times most of his books and magazine articles. But his health soon gave way, and after a journey to Minnesota, the longest he ever took, this strange figure in American literary life died of consumption, at the early age of forty-five. His experience was necessarily limited, and his sympathies were New England and narrow. He knew little of America, and nothing of the Old World, and despised what he had read about it. A good garden wall he preferred to all the "vulgar grandeur" of Thebes; he had unmitigated contempt for the "ambitious booby" who degraded his species by building the Pyramids. Still, had he seen more, he might have been less interesting, for he would have been less original. He did admirable service in teaching his countrymen that there are higher ideals in life than dollars and trotting horses, and not the least striking of his sayings was one of his last:

when, as he lay on his deathbed, he replied, to an officious busybody who expressed the hope that "he had made his peace with God." Thoreau quietly replied, "Sir, I have never quarrelled with Him."

Standard, October 16, 1890.

[It is necessary to say, for English readers, that Curtis was not a matriculate of any university.]

[*"The Life of Henry David Thoreau." By H.S. Salt. London: Bentley and Co.*]

THOREAU'S LIFE

THOREAU'S aims were clear and simple,—he wished truly to live his own life according to his convictions. Yet no man, perhaps, has been the subject of more contradictory estimates. He has been called an "American Rousseau," a "Yankee Stoic," a "pistillate plant fertilised by Emersonian pollen," a "misanthropic recluse," "too nearly a stoico-epicurean adiaphorist[!] to discompose himself in party or even in national strife," a "*skulker*," a "mystico-transcendentalist realist," an "Anti-Slavery zealot,"—"that terrible Thoreau," a "morbid hermit," a "hybrid sentimentalist," an "American Diogenes," an "egotist in the guise of an indifferentist," a "modern St. Francis," a "cynico-humorous philanthropist," a "missionary of self-worship," and a "mystic preparer of the way for Darwinism." These terms suggest points of view sufficient to indicate something curiously vital, something difficult to diagnose or define, something at least puzzling, new, original, and suggestive. Mr. R. L. Stevenson wrote a brilliant essay, in which he declared that he, in reading the man through the books, found Thoreau crabbed and sour as the wild-fruits he delighted in; and then, under fuller knowledge of facts, which allowed him in some degree to read the books through the man, in a preface corrective of his points of view, really undid all that he had done. His text, like that of the Koran or the Vedas, was too sacred to be touched; but he wrote a preface which practically recalled and overshadowed it. To read that essay without the preface were to look at the landscape without regarding the figure in the foreground which imparted all the meaning to it. Mr. Salt writes on this matter very judiciously:—" 'A skulker' is the phrase in which Mr. R. L. Stevenson summed up Thoreau's character in his essay in *Men and Books*; but as he himself admits in the later written preface that he had quite misread Thoreau through lack of sufficient knowledge of his life, there is no reason why admirers of *Walden* should feel much disturbed at the bestowal of that singularly inappropriate appellation."

Notwithstanding that several Lives of Thoreau had been written prior to this of Mr. Salt, it could not be said that Thoreau had been altogether happy in his biographers. Emerson's sketch prefixed to the *Excursions* was slight— more the characterisation of a disciple by a master than a Life—loving and discerning, yet with a kind of egotistic colour suffusing it, like light through stained glass. Mr. Ellery Channing came next; his volume was disfigured by affectation and self-consciousness, and by too pronounced a vein of eulogy—too little attention to fact, and a lack of shading. Then came Mr. Page, who treated his subject, as it were, *at arm's-length* [*Dr. Jones's footnote reads, "The italics are the editor's. Pace 'Mr. Page.' "*], with sympathy, but rather vaguely in the biographic part, which was thin and meagre, though he should not be too harshly blamed for this, as he distinctly warned his readers that his little volume was a "study," and not a memoir. Next came Mr. Sanborn, full of facts, with access to the Thoreau family and to unpublished documents; but, alas! Mr. Sanborn had little or no artistic quality. His Life was the work of a Dryasdust, without perspective, colour, or elevation: correct, it may be, but hard, angular, sapless. If Mr. Page and Mr. Sanborn could only have been fused together, then a worthy memoir *might* have been the result.

It will thus be seen that ample room was left for a capable writer who could sympathise and yet discriminate, who would patiently search out details, and give unity by deep penetration to the springs of character and motive. It is not too much to say that Mr. Salt has done this. His perception of motive and tendency is as marked as are his complete command and skilful grouping of facts. And his reading of ethical purpose is self-consistent and interesting. Here Thoreau stands, fair and complete amid his proper surroundings, for Mr. Salt has found local colour and aptly used it. He has been as industrious as he is devoted, and has left no stone unturned. He not only understands his subject; he seems to have gained identity with him through some kindredship of interest, opinion, and thought. And he is careful to avoid painting too much in bright colours, and so incur the charge of white-washing! He seldom puts his points too strongly, and is concerned to let Thoreau, as far as possible, speak for himself. While he does not agree with Mr. R. L. Stevenson that Thoreau, in a cynically-humorous way, sought to impose on himself no less than on his readers, as in the essay on "Friendship," he is prudent enough to admit that light may be thrown on some of Thoreau's apparent paradoxes by perceiving that sometimes he half-humorously fenced his deepest thoughts, and only expressed them by asides.

It was inevitable that much in certain parts should bear a slightly polemic air. If Mr. Salt were at all to recognise the writings of such men as Mr. Lowell, Professor Nichol, and others, who sought to give colour to the idea that Thoreau was a morbid reactionary and nothing else, it could only be to rebut them by presenting a broader and more comprehensive view. This he has done as far as possible *indirectly*, letting his new facts and the lights they throw speak for themselves. Few persons of open minds, we should think, could read this volume, and not feel that something essential is wanting in the strictures referred to,—something which shall cover and include, without suggestion of strain or special pleading, Thoreau's constant, long-continued Anti-Slavery work and agitation, and his power, exhibited in the most effective manner, to keep a heart open for the individual while pleading for a race. Mr. Page, as Mr. Salt has pointed out, did not lose sight of this circumstance, and sought to bring *Thoreau's Anti-Slavery action into consistency with his retreat to the woods at Walden* [*Dr. Jones's footnote reads, "Again the editor has indulged in italics. Again,* Pace *'Mr. Page.' "*], which was, after all, confessedly and from the first, meant merely as an episode, an experiment to prepare the better for action in various lines afterwards. *Besides, we know now that Walden was a secret station for the "great underground railroad"* [*Again, Dr. Jones adds a footnote that reads, "Editor's italics. (By kind permission of the printer.)"*], which Thoreau made the means of helping more than one slave towards the North Star. His self-denials for the slaves, indeed, were many, and the thought of them should have given pause to much which has been written of Thoreau from the merely literary side. Thoreau, after all, would have looked askance at much which has been claimed for him by the high-flying literary critics; for, despite what has been called his "airs," expression with him was ever subordinate to experience, and he would far rather have been recognised as the writer of the *Plea for John Brown* or *Slavery in Massachusetts*, which some of the literary critics might sneer at, than be praised for the deftest sentences of description or of reflection.

It is worth noting that while justice is more and more being done to Thoreau as a true and tender-hearted man, an unaffected lover of his kind, in spite of expressions that sometimes, it must be confessed, bore an air of revolt, not against society, but against the evils that come in the train of artificial life, a higher and more distinguished place is claimed for him as a man of science which he himself hardly claimed to be. Listen to Mr. Grant Allen, who recently visited Concord and studied its natural history:—

"Like no one else, he knew the meaning of every note and movement of bird and beast and fish and insect. Born out of due time, just too early for the great change in men's views of nature which transferred all interest in outer life from the mere dead things one sees in museums to their native habits and modes of living, he was yet in some sort a vague and mystical anticipatory precursor of the modern school of functional biology. . . . Page after page of his diary notes facts about the pollen showers of pine-trees, the fertilisation of skunk-cabbages, the nesting of birds, the

preferences of minx, or musk-rat, the courtship of butter-
flies, all of a piece with those minute observations on which
naturalists nowadays build their most interesting theories." (*Fortnightly Review*, May, 1888.)

The St. Francis-like features in his character—his love and
care for the creatures of wood and wild—only come out the
more effectively when associated with this view of him as a
pioneer of scientific theory; only he would have claimed that
love, and all the finer instincts which it awakens and
strengthens, stand for more than any new principle of classification; and thus, though he sought for links of brotherhood
between man and brute, would hardly have proved a true
Darwinian, though perhaps he suggests the very elements
which future Darwins must fall back on to save them from the
master's fate,—loss of hold on poetry, beauty, and all that
these imply. But one thing is certain,—his significance grows
as we recede from him; he demands to be more and more
studied and recognised on many sides; and Mr. Salt's able
volume comes just in the nick of time to promote this object.
"The generation he [Thoreau] lectured so sharply," says Mr.
John Burroughs, "will not give the same heed to his words as
will the next and the next. The first effect of the reading of his
books upon many minds is irritation and disappointment; the
perception of their beauty and wisdom comes later."

[*Another review of the Salt biography, Bentley edition.*]

Spectator, October 18, 1890. [By Dr. A. H. Japp.]

THE

editor considers the above criticism, written by Dr. A. H. Japp,
the author of the first English Life of Thoreau, as, one of the
most sympathetic and of the truest and deepest insight of any

of the contributions that make up this compilation. It is equally just to Thoreau and to Mr. Salt. In it Thoreau is most assuredly in the hands of a friend.

Whilst the editor has for it only the heartiest commendation, he is under obligation to give a reason for interpolating his own italics into the text. Dr. Japp's review of Mr. Salt's Life of Thoreau was written in 1890, and in Lippincott's Magazine (August, 1891) there appeared a paper entitled *Thoreau and his Biographers*, the reading of which led Dr. Japp to publish the following:—

" 'What an odd thing criticism is!' we say once more. Here, in the current *Lippincott's Magazine*, is a Mr. Samuel Arthur Jones, who is determined to put Thoreau, the 'Walden Hermit,' to rights, despite his biographers. He is down on Mr. Sanborn for vilifying the 'old man' and the 'old woman;' and 'cums putty heavy,' as Artemas Ward would say, on Mr. H. A. Page. Though Mr. Page conspicuously warns his readers in the last paragraph of the preface to his sketch or study that '*it is not pretended this is a memoir*, or that I am able to present new or unpublished material: it professes to be a study only,' Mr. S. A. Jones insists that Mr. Page's little volume is a "Life" or "Memoir," and writes this in the high style: 'It was written at too great a distance from its subject and too near Thoreau's books to be of any other use than to whet the reader's curiosity and make him eager for a more extended knowledge of its hero.' That's good! To quarrel with a man in print for not doing what he never pretended to do, and then to say that he had done precisely all that he had attempted! 'To whet the reader's curiosity and make him eager for a more extended knowledge,' we should fancy, was all that Mr. Page aimed at; and how proud he should be of such a testimony fourteen years after the writing! To lead English readers who knew nothing of Thoreau—his exquisite style, his fine insights, and, above all, his wonderful intimacies with animals—to seek to know more of him, surely that was something.

"But that's not all—though one would fancy that's

enough. Mr. Page 'is the introducer and chief disseminator
of the figment that the shanty at Walden was a station of
the "underground railroad" (that is, was used to aid fugitive slaves to escape).' He infers this from a cursory statement of Channing's: 'Not one slave alone was expedited to
Canada by Thoreau's personal assistance.' There was no
need for Mr. Page to *infer as much as that* from a cursory
statement of Channing's. He had grounds more relative.
Here is Thoreau's own statement on page 165 of 'Walden'
(Boston edition of 1854): 'Men of almost every degree of wit
called on me in the migrating season. Some who had more
wits than they knew what to do with; runaway slaves with
plantation manners, who listened from time to time, like
the fox in the fable, as if they heard the hounds a-baying on
their track, and looked at me beseechingly, as much as to
say, "O Christian, will you send me back?" *One real runaway slave among the rest, whom I helped forward toward
the north star.*' Now this has reference only to one year's
work [Thoreau lived at Walden nearly two years and a half
—*Ed.*], and Thoreau was not likely to boast autobiograph-
ically of the good he had done in this way, and claim too
much: Mr. Page may have read there between the lines a
little something. Mr. S. A. Jones will have it that Thoreau
was a liar and a boaster. He surely may have his own way,
though 'tis very odd, very odd, when he's a great Thoreau
worshipper; or is it that he was too near the Thoreau stone
and lime, if not too near the Thoreaus, and too far from the
books when *he* wrote?"

Dr. Japp, masquerading under an anonym, says Mr. Page
"treated his subject, as it were, at arm's length;" the critic in
Lippincott's Magazine said that Mr. Page's Memoir "was
written at too great a distance from its subject." At the worst,
he simply overestimated the length of Dr. Japp's arm, ascrib-
ing to him a greater reach, it seems, than the Doctor's stature
justifies. And for this complimentary error, to be stripped of
his doctorate and reduced to "a Mr."—by an irate author

whose doctorate, an L.L.D., is like the curl in a pig's tail: an accident more ornamental than useful and adding not an iota to the quality of the pork!

Forgetting that he who excuses accuses, Dr. Japp invented a *raison d' être* for Thoreau's shanty life at Walden. That episode, he says, was designed "to bring Thoreau's Anti-Slavery action into consistency with his retreat to the woods at Walden," for, he reiterates, "we know now that Walden was a secret station for the 'great underground railroad'."

In the article which aroused the ire of Dr. Japp the unfortunate "a Mr." said: "The writer has made this [Dr. Japp's Walden figment] a matter of special investigation, and the truth is that there were specially-prepared houses in 'Old Concord' which afforded infinitely more secure resting- and hiding-places for the fugitive slave. Moreover, the survivors who had managed Concord 'station' declare that Thoreau's hut was not used for such a purpose." This was written after a six weeks' visit to Concord (whither the writer had gone to satisfy himself about many matters pertaining to Thoreau) and, as it seemed to him, after due and diligent enquiry of those who had intimately known Thoreau. He himself was satisfied, but upon reading Dr. Japp's "damnable iteration," he wrote to Mr. Edward Waldo Emerson making specific enquiries covering the whole ground of the question. With characteristic courtesy there promptly came the following in reply.

"Underground Railroad. Concord Station and Division.

"December 13th., 1891, I called on Mrs. Edwin Bigelow, widow of the blacksmith and friend of the slave. Mrs. Bigelow, be it said, knew Henry Thoreau from the time when he taught school in Concord until his death, and she values and honors his life and character.

"When asked about his connection with the Underground Railroad she said: The Thoreaus, in those days, lived in the Parkman House, where now the Library stands (a private tenement but bearing the name of its former owner, Deacon

Parkman, a relative of Parkman the historian). Squire Brooks and his wife lived next door, at the parting of the roads, and we (the Bigelows) just across the (Sudbury) street from them; so we were close together and all of us anti-slavery people, although Squire Brooks believed that it was his duty as a good citizen to obey the law.

"From the day of the passage of the Fugitive Slave Law the Underground R.R. was organized and active, and nearly every week some fugitive would be forwarded with the utmost secrecy to Concord to be harbored over night, and usually was sped on his way before daylight. They were escorted to West Fitchburg (near to Fitchburg, a large town), a small station, where they got aboard the Northbound train. Dr. Bartlett often drove them from Concord in his chaise with his swift horse. Sometimes they went by cars from Concord, and then Henry Thoreau went as escort probably more often than any other man. He would look after the tickets, etc., but in the cars he did not sit with the fugitive, and this so as not to attract attension to his companionship.

"The fugitives were harboured in Concord at Mrs. Rice's, Mrs. Thoreau's, Mrs. Bigelow's, and Miss Mary Rice's. This last lady lived in a little house in a field behind the old Hill Burying Ground. She had a little nook built by old Francis Butterick, the carpenter, in her attic, projecting over the eaves and ventilated by augur holes.

"While Henry Thoreau was in the woods the slaves were sometimes brought to him there, but, obviously, there was no possible concealment in his house. (H.D.T. built his house like Marcus Scaurus—into which all Rome could look); so he would look after them by day, and after nightfall—no street lamps in Concord in those days—get them to his mother's, or other house of hiding. He was always ready with service and didn't count the risk; and, also, though he had little money, always gave or advanced some to a slave who needed it. Sometimes this was repaid from the fund.

"It was no part of his plan in making the Walden hermitage to make there a refuge for fugitives—that was only incidental; but when they came to him there he acted more independently and by his own good judgment than while living in his mother's house: there she had sway and he took only a second place as helper.

"There never was any pursuit to Concord or domiciliary search. Shadrack, a slave who had been for some time at work in Boston, was identified by his master, and siezed by officers and handcuffed and carried to the U.S. Court early in the morning, before many officers or people were there. Word went abroad among the Abolitionists and in half an hour a crowd rushed in and surrounding him and the officers, took him out of their hands and brought him to the door (looking out on Court Square). There Mr. —— cried out to the crowd, 'For the love of Heaven, if you have any pity on this man, disperse in all directions!' So they shouted and put up their umbrellas and scattered. Mr. —— then, with Shadrack, slipped among the men, went through by-ways to the Cambridge bridge, crossed it (walking apart), but keeping within sight of each other, and so to the house of Mr. Lovejoy—brother of the Alton martyr—, where the handcuffs were removed, and from thence they proceeded to Concord. About three in the morning, a little before dawn, Shadrack was brought to Edwin Bigelow's house. Mrs. Bigelow was not well, so her husband made a fire in the air-tight stove in her room to get the slave and his rescuer some breakfast, and in the meantime went over to get Mrs. Brooks, a most ardent Abolitionist, saying that Mrs. Bigelow was sick and wanted her. At once the kind-hearted Squire Brooks said, 'But, if she is very sick, they may want me for something, so I'll go over with you.' Mr. Bigelow heard Squire Brooks's voice when he was talking to his wife, and when he got home he said, 'What shall we do now?' Mrs. Bigelow at once replied, 'There must be no concealment: let Squire Brooks and his wife come up.' The Squire and his wife entered Mrs. Bigelow's chamber and to

their surprise found there Mr. and Mrs. Bigelow, Mr. ——
and Shadrack the fugitive. Squire Brooks saw what was
going on at once, but here was an abstract matter hitherto
now presented to him in a most concrete form. They were
fitting Shadrack out with clothes: Mr. Bigelow's hat
wouldn't fit him, but the man of law straightly zealously
ran across the road to his own and fetched his own hat,
sheltered by which Shadrack departed for the North star,
driven by Mr. Bigelow, with a horse he got from the stable
near by, and the wagon of Lowell Fay, another near
neighbor.

"Next day, Mr. C., a Webster Whig, said sharply to Squire
Brooks: 'Shadrack was brought to Concord!' Which statement the Squire had to bluff off as best he might; but he was
now liable to fine and imprisonment for violating the law of
the land."

This succint and minutely circumstantial account by an
eye- and ear-witness should be satisfactory, but a passage in
Thoreau's *Walden* (a good example of his veiled meanings)
gave the editor pause. A "station" of the underground railroad
was also called by the initiated a "post," and on page 24 of the
first edition of Thoreau's best-known book he writes: "I have
thought that Walden Pond would be a good place for *business*,
not solely on account of the railroad and the ice trade; *it offers
advantages which it may not be good policy to divulge*; it is a
good *post* and a good foundation." The italics are our own, and
they show the grounds of our suspicion, which certainly give a
shade of probability to Dr. Japp's declaration.

This very year, through the courtesy of a book-loving friend,
the "a Mr." had in his hands Thoreau's own copy of *Walden*.
In it are some marginal corrections of errors of the press and
several foot notes. To the intense satisfaction of "a Mr.," page
24 has the perplexing word *"post"* stricken out, and on the
left hand margin is plainly written *"port."*

This, O patient reader, explains the interpolation of the
editor's italics into Dr. Japp's text. *Pace* "Mr. Page."

HENRY DAVID THOREAU

SAUL among the prophets was an amazing sight, but not more amazing than Mr. H. S. Salt disguised as a critic. Long ago we had given up hopes of hearing sense from him on the subject of Thoreau. His biography was a masterpiece of futility; his edition of the papers on Civil Government preached anarchism adulterated by a soft-saponaceous sentiment. But the little volume of *Selections from Thoreau* which he has just edited for Messrs. Macmillan is prefaced by a sane and weighty essay. Even Mr. Salt when he sifts the wheat from the chaff can find unity in this 'bundle of vain strivings, tied by a chance knot together,' and does not insist upon what one feels to be the absurd or over-acted elements of his hero's character. The selection could not have been better made. Nobody can read this volume without understanding Thoreau's immense and intense sincerity—a sincerity which was united to a wayward, fanciful and excessive habit of speech. We thank Mr. Salt heartily; as heartily as we have disagreed with him aforctime. He of course may regret that our thanks are due to his having refrained from connecting Thoreau with the Higher or Transcendental Anarchism. We can but urge that there is vitality in Thoreau apart from the anarchism which some writers see in him. Indeed this little book of Mr. Salt's has been to us like an excursion to Walden Pond. We cannot praise the new edition of *Walden* issued by Messrs. Walter Scott one half as highly. The binding is pretty enough, but the paper is ribbed and detestable, and the book seems to be intended for immediate consumption, not for use. The introduction is affected in style, nor are we assured that its writer has any view of Thoreau's character and aim— always assuming that Thoreau had an aim. One is never certain that he cared to make converts.

In reading his works it is difficult to disengage the prophet from the prig. Probably he could not have done it for himself. One must never forget that the acutest of his remarkably acute senses was the sense of his own identity. For him the world was Henry David Thoreau and Henry David Thoreau was the world. He condescended to preach or to rail: but his voice was always the voice of one crying in the wilderness; not so much because he spoke a strange tongue, as because he missed no chance of picturesqueness. He was a rebel—not against society but—against superimposed conventions which once had some purpose, though they lost their purpose in later times. But he gaily attacked society and civilisation, confusing the issues. Witness the following sentence: 'Undoubtedly, all men are not equally fit subjects for civilisation; and because the majority, like dogs and sheep, are tame by inherited disposition, this is no reason why the others should have their natures broken that they may be reduced to the same level.' That is not, and is not meant to be, an argument against civilisation: it is a capital argument against the democratic fallacy; which leaves civilisation where it stood, for civilisation never yet broke any man's nature. Thoreau was a highly civilised man himself, despite a faulty education, and he never scrupled to use what Society offered. Indeed one fault of his philosophy is that it demands all, or rather a selection of the best, for himself, while he offers nothing in return but advice, sometimes reckless, sometimes random in effect, and always delightfully impertinent in manner. Thoreau lived on and by himself, he wrote, as he might have said, epistles from himself to himself. He was immersed like a Buddhist fakir in the contemplation of his own navel, which he took to symbolise or to be the wheel of the universe.

'This is not meat for little people or for fools,' says Mr. Meredith, and the words apply to this little selection from Thoreau. You can imagine the philosopher scorning his lack of logic, and the stockbroker sneering at his zeal for the cultivation of beans and the spirit. He was no shirker, as Mr. Stevenson too hastily supposed: 'The student who secures his coveted leisure and retirement by systematically shirking any labour necessary to man obtains but an ignoble and unprofitable leisure, defrauding himself of the experience which alone can make leisure fruitful.' Nor was he a hermit by instinct. There can be no doubt that at the age of twenty-eight, he found his life to be something of a failure: 'I went to the woods because I wished to live deliberately, to front only the essential facts of life, and see if I could not learn what it had to teach . . . I left the woods for as good a reason as I went there. Perhaps it seemed to me that I had several more lives to live and could not spare any more time for that one.' Whatever else he learned at Walden, he learned the philosophy of rejection, that philosophy which made Thomas à Kempis say, 'Choose thou to have rather less than more.' He had no creed— on this he insists, and indeed his whole life was empirical— but experiment taught him how much one can do without. 'It makes but little differcnce,' he says, 'whether you are committed to a farm or a gaol.' Again: 'The cost of a thing is the amount of what I will call life which is required to be exchanged for it immediately or in the long run.' Thoreau found that he could only live deliberately by what the orientals call 'contemplation and the abandonment of works.' By a just measurement of cause and effect he discovered that half, or more than half, the works he had abandoned were of no practical benefit to himself or to Society; and he found that contemplation gave his spirit an opportunity of self-assertion. He did not wish that any one should imitate his way of life: 'I would have each one be very careful to find out and pursue his own way, and not his father's or his mother's or his neighbor's instead.' The great lesson of the Walden sojourn was 'that if one advances confidently in the direction of his dreams, and endeavours to live the life which he has imagined, he will meet with a success unexpected in common hours.' To live deliberately, to front the essential facts of life and to advance confidently in the direction of one's dreams. This is Thoreau's system. But the dreams must be one's own—'No way of thinking or doing, however ancient, can be trusted without proof'—and it is because man cannot dream in a crowded city, that 'the thoughtful soul to solitude retires.' Thoreau's message indeed is more important now than it was at the date of its delivery, for we are too busy to live deliberately, and instead of our confronting the essential facts of life a million accidents confront us, and we never dream; 'getting and spending we lay waste our powers.' Thoreau, transcendental egoist as he was, hit upon the true remedy, which is to cut down luxuries and hoe beans—or play golf.

National Observer XIV (June 1, 1895), pp. 75-76. [By W. E. Henley.]

An

esurient Philistine, seeking only the Port and Plum-pudding of Life, and as evidently one of the "mob of gentlemen who write with ease" and a reckless disregard for what is written. "Nor are we assured that the writer has any view of Thoreau's character and aim—*always assuming that Thoreau had had an aim*," is his flippant pronouncement, and hardly is the ink dry which records it than he tells us that Thoreau "went to the woods because he wished to live deliberately, to front only the essential facts of life." So certain is he of *this* that he himself assures us: "To live deliberately, to front the essential facts of life and to advance confidently in the direction of one's dreams: This is Thoreau's system." How significant it is that this species of critic should curtail Thoreau's *aim* of its keystone—"to front ONLY the essential facts of life."

Despite his inevitable limitations he now and then "saddens into sense," as when he reproves Stevenson for the shallow insight that deemed Thoreau "a skulker."

On the whole, the critic of the *National Observer* has given us a capital instance of the mental phenomenon that Professor Carpenter aptly termed *unconscious cerebration.* At his best he is only *semi*-conscious; otherwise he would have seen how infinitely superior is "a Buddhist fakir in the contemplation of his own navel" to a featherless biped who lives and moves and has his being only for the sake of the provender that he can put behind it.

LITERATURE

["THOREAU"]

EXCEPTING one small circle Thoreau, during his lifetime, was a prophet without honour either in his own
country or elsewhere. All that was generally known of him—
and it was not much—seemed to show him to be a person of
peculiar and impracticable ideas, and of unfriendly if not
actually morose disposition. The notion was inaccurate
enough, but those who held it were not without excuse. Connected with what has been termed the Transcendental
Revival of New England were several queer apostles of indi-
vidualism, but none on the surface more queer or underneath
the surface more solid than the subject of the works now under
review. He impressed his own small circle with the conviction
that he was a man of genius, but it was not for some time after
his death that he became known to the world at large. In 1862,
when he died, it would have been easy to predict that he and
his works would soon be forgotten.

It is now seen that the impression Thoreau made on his
friends was the right one; and he was not well appreciated by
the world outside, simply because he was not well known. A
change has taken place. The voice which thirty years ago was
crying in the wilderness is now listened to with respectful
attention in the drawing-room, and, what is more important,
in the study. It said to society—make straight your paths. The
paths of society were crooked then and they are crooked still,
while measures, far different from Thoreau's, intended to
improve them, are in favour at present. Yet Thoreau is not

unheeded; and, when the honest but mistaken attempt of Socialism to save society in the mass has proved to be ineffectual, Thoreau's appeal to the individual is likely to be better understood and approved.

Of Thoreau's critics a few have estimated him justly, while others of whom better things were to be expected have misapprehended him. Emerson recognised him early, and never faltered in his admiration. Emerson found it "a pleasure and a privilege to walk with him," and described him to Carlyle as "a noble, manly youth, full of melodies and inventions." Alcott's testimony was equally emphatic. Mr. Sanborn and Mr. Ellery Channing have written their reminiscences at length, while Mr. Blake has prefixed a few significant words to the volume called *Early Spring in Massachusetts*, which he edited. Hawthorne, a man not easy of access, made a friend of Thoreau. On the other hand, Mr. James Russell Lowell failed to admire him; for the reason, according to Emerson, that Mr. Lowell had a great deal of self-consciousness, and never forgave Thoreau for wounding it. Beyond this circle we have the enthusiastic estimate of Mr. H. A. Page, an essay which does not enlighten by Mr. Robert Louis Stevenson, miscellaneous magazine articles, and not much besides.

There is, therefore, ample room for Mr. Salt's biography, and it is timely. It is not a great critical study, nor is it such a revelation of the inner man as a discreet disciple could give. I should say Mr. Salt has been neither a profound student nor a disciple of Thoreau, but has considered him and learned what he knows about him mainly for the purposes of this biography. He has taken pains to make his work complete and accurate, and the mistakes are few and not important. He gives the details of Thoreau's career, describes his person, his habits, his work, and his opinions. He provides just the book on the subject that is needed at the present time. It enables the reader to know all about Thoreau, the necessary preliminary to knowing the man himself. I am glad this book is free from the slightly patronising tone that Mr. Salt adopted when he gave an account of James Thomson (B.V.); but who could patronise Thoreau, even in a book?

It does not detract from the merit of the work that Mr. Salt has little to tell that is new to persons who have already interested themselves in Thoreau. The sources of information which were open to him had been, for the most part, open to them. His communications with personal friends of Thoreau have enabled him in some cases to amplify certain incidents and characteristics; but Thoreau's best friend, Emerson, long since gave the pith of the subject in the biographical sketch which he prefixed to Thoreau's collected works. Elsewhere in H. A. Page's pleasant volume, or scattered up and down in magazines and books, or gathered together in disorder that rivals Teufelsdröckh's paper bags, by Mr. Ellery Channing and Mr. Sanborn, were fuller particulars. Lastly, there were Thoreau's writings to furnish the key to his actions and character. All these Mr. Salt has handled with patience and skill, producing now, for the first time, a clear, systematic story of Thoreau's remarkable career.

Mr. Ellery Channing—the poet, Thoreau's intimate friend—has named Thoreau a "poet-naturalist." It is a good name in its way, has a pleasant sound, and is likely to be used on that account. There is much to justify it; but it does not by any means cover the whole nature of the man, or even indicate his leading characteristic. Primarily, Thoreau was not a poet or a naturalist, or both in one; but a critic of society. White of Selborne was a poet-naturalist; or, coming to our own times, Richard Jefferies might be correctly described as such. But while neither White of Selborne nor Richard Jefferies was a closer or more interested observer of nature than Thoreau, this, to them, was an end in itself, whereas to him nature always had a human aspect and relation. In the case of White, who was a clergyman, more than in that of Jefferies or of Thoreau, we might fairly expect to find the human application of "moral" to his observations. But it is not there. The habits of martens, rooks, and rats interested him as such, and not because of any analogy between them and human habits or any influence they might exercise over human interests. Much the same is true of Jefferies. But Thoreau declared that

"nature must be viewed humanly to be viewed at all; that is, her scenes must be associated with human affections, such as are associated with one's native place, for instance. She is most significant to a lover. If I have no friend, what is nature to me? She ceases to be morally significant."

He comes "to the hill to see the sun go down, to recover sanity" by putting himself "in relation with nature." To him "nature is fair in proportion as the youth is pure." In the sky he discerns the symbol of his own infinity. "If we go solitary to streams and mountains," he says, "it is to meet man there, where he is more than ever man." He was a critic of society and student of mankind, who found the symbol of a purer society in the woods and fields.

Occasionally Thoreau preferred to give some direct and immediate application of his principles to a topic of the hour. This was notably the case in connexion with John Brown's arrest after his attack at Harper's Ferry. Thoreau's was the first voice publicly raised in behalf of the hero. Mr. Salt has done well to collect, in the volume of *Anti-Slavery and Reform Papers*, the several utterances of this description. That he should expressly choose these from all Thoreau's writings for separate publication, and yet maintain, as he does, in the Introductory Note, that "Thoreau considered the real business of his life" to be "the study of wild nature," is certainly curious. Thoreau was a social critic and reformer none the less because his method of reform was not by invoking mechanical contrivances but by example. His sojourn at Walden Pond was not for the purpose of studying "wild nature"; but for the purpose of protesting against chaotic society, and proving, first to himself and afterwards to others, how exceedingly simple human life might be. "I wished to live deliberately," he explained, "to front only the essential facts of life, and see if I could not learn what it had to teach, and not when I came to die discover that I had not lived." His experiment served to teach him that a man may use as simple a diet as the animals and yet retain health and strength. After leaving Walden he continued to live simply. For more than five years, during which he maintained himself by the labour of his hands, he found he could meet all the expenses of living by working for about six weeks in each year.

Such an arrangement harmonised well with Thoreau's peculiar notions about labour. He was no "skulker," as Mr. Stevenson has called him, but, on the contrary, an unusually energetic and hardworking man. But he believed that labour was sanctified only when it was in the direction of a man's life. It was valuable just so far as it contributed to develop the labourer. The incident of the pencil has been often quoted. He made one so excellent that people said there was a fortune in it. But it had already yielded him all he desired. He would not do the same thing again and again, as though he were a machine. Having the education he did not want the commodity. Yet he was the last man to shirk labour by transferring it to others. He never accepted leisure or convenience on such terms as these, for in his opinion

> "the student who secures his coveted leisure and retirement by systematically shirking any labour necessary to man, obtains but an ignoble and unprofitable leisure, defrauding himself of the experience which alone can make leisure fruitful."

He complained that because he walked in the woods for love of them he was in danger of being regarded as a loafer, while men who esteemed the forests only for their timber were considered to be industrious and enterprising citizens—"as if a town had no interest in its forests but to cut them down." Yet a time came when his family needed the labour of his hands for their support, and he was not found wanting. His purpose was neither to shirk labour nor to do it, for labour was not an end in itself. But he was thrifty, and would not waste life on anything that was useless. Herein he believed he served the Supreme Being best; and so when he was dying, and someone asked him, "Have you made your peace with God?" he was justified in replying that "he had never quarrelled with Him."

That, with all this, Thoreau was still a profoundly interested nature-lover is not to be disputed. Had he not been so he would have emphasised his protest against society in some other way than by retiring to the woods. The creatures of the woods and even the very trees were, in his eyes, his friends. He loved every season and every aspect. His senses were peculiarly acute, so in this way he was physically well adapted to the life he chose. If every sight and sound in nature yielded also a spiritual meaning to his mind, so much the greater was the gain. It made him a "poet-naturalist," and something more.

When the reader has learned all he can about Thoreau, if he wants to understand Thoreau himself he must turn to his writings. Of these probably the most interesting is *Walden*, which contains, in addition to a careful account of his experiment, much philosophical musing on men and things. He is, however, at his best in the journals which he wrote so diligently and from which Mr. H. G. O. Blake has published copious selections. These journals have none of the elaboration and not much of the bitterness to be found in the writings he prepared for publication. Yet such essays as "A Winter's Walk" and "Autumnal Tints" are marked by unvarying serenity and much poetic power. Thoreau may fairly be described as a poet, but he was not a singer. His verses stumble and halt. There is more of the tone and grace of poetry in some of his prose passages than in them.

Academy, October 25, 1890.

The Life of Henry David Thoreau. By H. S. Salt. (Bentley, 1890).

Anti-Slavery and Reform Papers. By Henry David Thoreau, Selected and Edited by H. S. Salt. (Sonnenschein.)

THE LIFE OF THOREAU

IT is an axiom of latter-day culture that you must know something about Thoreau. He has become the subject of periodic dissertation for the elegant reviewer in the magazines and in the daily press. Mr. Henry James, whose antagonism to a man of Thoreau's type may be regarded as temperamental, has gracefully alluded to him somewhere as "Emerson's moral man made flesh, living for the ages and not for Saturday and Sunday; ̇but Thoreau's name has of late years become more and more prominent, until now the reputation of Emerson's moral man almost predominates over that of Emerson himself. He was not without recognition in his own day, but of the two works which he published during his lifetime, "Walden" and "A Week on the Concord and Merrimac Rivers," the latter fell stillborn from the press. "Walden" has now innumerable readers; the "Week" has since run through seven editions in America, and a cheap edition of it recently appeared among Mr. Walter Scott's well-known "Camelot" volumes, the success of "Walden," which had previously appeared in the same series, having induced that publisher to issue the "Week." And since Thoreau's death, nearly thirty years ago, eight additional volumes have been made up from his occasional essays, and from the journals which he always so assiduously kept. Now, as the crown and apex of what has gone before, appears Mr. Salt's elaborate and scholarly volume. One may at once admit that this is for the most part a capital book, excellent both as a biographical record and as a piece of criticism—conscientious, discerning, discriminative, and instructive. Mr. Salt has had at least three precursors in the same field, three writers who have written monographs on the subject of Thoreau which have extended to the dimensions of volumes. The work by Ellery Channing (son of the better-known Dr. W.

160

E. Channing) is not without value; it is a wildish composition informed by a certain poetic feeling, but is often marred by the introduction of extracts from Thoreau of a quality which the world would willingly let die, as, for instance, his esoteric musings on a telegraph post. In "Thoreau: His Life and Times," a gentleman who writes under the name of H. A. Page discovers a special importance in the study of Thoreau, in that it will probably enable the pious to distinguish better between fact and fiction as recorded of the miraculous doings with animals of St. Francis of Assisi—undoubtedly a notable moral to arrive at! Mr. Sanborn's "Life of Thoreau" in the American Men of Letters is an amiable but puzzling book; exhaustive in its information about Thoreau's relatives, friends, and acquaintances, one may almost say that it sheds vivid enlightenment on everything but the subject of Thoreau himself. Mr. Salt's book is different; it does deal pertinently and actually with the man.

So far as external events go Thoreau's life affords but inadequate material for the biographer. Born in 1817 in Concord, Massachusetts, he there passed the main portion of his days. His most distant expedition was to Canada [Minnesota. Editor.]. He graduated at Harvard when about twenty; he became a schoolmaster, a pencil-maker, a surveyor, a gardener, a lecturer, and was equally efficient in all callings, and turned to each with equal facility when occasion came. "Apollo must serve Admetus," he was fond of saying, and Admetus, according to Mr. Robert Stevenson, who had an eye on the enormous amount of loafing Thoreau was able to accomplish, notwithstanding his proficiency as a jack-of-all-trades, never got less work out of any mortal since the world began. Thoreau's Walden exploit is the greatest external event of his career. Walden is a small lake in the woods, two miles out of Concord. Thoreau was hard up; he wanted to live cheap and do some thinking; he had a great love for the open air, and it occurred to him that he might most effectually attain his object by constructing a hut in the woods, growing his own provisions, and simplifying the conventions generally. Given Thoreau's temperament and out-of-door habits, a little camping out was the easiest and most natural thing he could do, and before so much attention directed itself upon his very simple expedient, it no doubt never occurred to him that he was doing anything unusual. However, out of this episode grew the book "Walden," one of his most popular and characteristic pieces of writing, though the "Week"—"a kind of missal and psalter of nature worship for each of the seven days," as it has been called—contains finer passages. He was "a Protestant *à l'outrance*," as Emerson says; "he was bred to no profession; he never married; he lived alone; he never went to church; he never voted; he refused to pay a tax to the State; he ate no flesh, he drank no wine, he never knew the use of tobacco; and, though a naturalist, he used neither trap nor gun." Of such were his practical negations, all highly characteristic of the man and his theories. If he was an unparalleled stoic, he was also a shameless epicurean of fine sensations—of the moral and intellectual kind. A naturalist all his life, he stood far apart from the "skin and bone mongers" whom Mr. Ruskin has so choicely vituperated; he was surely very much akin to the pattern naturalist which that gentleman has set up for our admiration. He was nothing of an anatomist; what he sought for in the woods and fields was the "fine effluence" of things; his particular genius lay in giving expression to the "poetry of natural history," as Mr. Salt, who lays considerable stress on Thoreau as a naturalist, happily puts it. In this his nearest English exemplar is Richard Jefferies. One of the most remarkable things about Thoreau is the wit which is constantly present in his writings; and it is fair to attribute some of its qualities—its buoyancy, its Celtic elusiveness—to the foreign strain (he was the descendant of a French family) that was in him. To find both a wit and a mystic in the same person seems an excessive anomaly, yet such an anomaly does Thoreau present. Above all things it is the transcendentalism of Thoreau that is vitally characteristic of the man. It is this very transcendentalism to which Mr. Salt gives least attention, and we cannot help regarding the omission as a serious blemish in a work otherwise so excellent. It surely lay within Mr. Salt's scope to give some account of the transcendentalism of the New England of the forties, to sketch its relation to previous movements of thought, and to indicate its special characteristics. Thoreau is certainly not understood without one grasps to some extent the meaning of that phase of transcendentalism which swayed him throughout his career—that feeling of the infinite, the universal, the endeavour to regard life imaginatively from the standpoint of all time—the feeling which, with him, living constantly in contact and intimacy with nature, was accompanied by so fine a poetic pantheism, the expression of which recurs so frequently throughout his work. The transcendental criticism of life has little practical value; its significance is for men's intellect and imagination—it displays the world and its doings in a new perspective. But Thoreau brought more than a transcendental criticism, useful as that is, to bear upon life; if he lived for the ages and not for Saturday and Sunday he had anyhow an astonishingly good idea as to how a man should conduct himself both on those and other days of the week. His undeviating belief in the life of the spirit—that is his gospel so far as his practical ethics are concerned; and he has delivered this gospel with such mastery of words, with such delicate ethical intuition, with so much excellent derision of that materialism which is antagonistic to it, with so caustic a wit, such illimitable genius of paradox, and withal out of so lofty and sincere a spirit, that an erring world is not likely to allow soon to drop into oblivion a missionary so eloquent for its correction.

It is ungracious, but before leaving Mr. Salt's book one would like to make a slight but quite indubitable protest, if only to a footnote, in which Mr. Salt makes comparison to "Walden" of a volume entitled, "England's Ideal," by a Mr. Edward Carpenter; a volume surely in which it were difficult for the judicious to discern either literature or wit, or anything but a talent for triviality remarkable for its ineptitude.   D.

Newcastle *Daily Leader*, November 25, 1890. [By W. H. Dircks.]

THOREAU

WHEN it was announced that Mr. H. S. Salt had a "Life of Thoreau" in the press we were much interested, anticipating not unreasonably that the writer of another biography of the "Poet-Naturalist" should have something fresh to communicate with regard to the life-history of his subject. Thoreau cannot be called a popular author—an author whose very popularity demands a multiplicity of "lives" and "memoirs." His story has already been more or less adequately told by his friends Emerson, Ellery Channing, and F. B. Sanborn in America, and by H. A. Page (Dr. A. H. Japp) in this country; and it therefore immediately suggested itself that the writer of a new life of Thoreau must have some fresh materials to further interest those already interested in his subject, or he must have hit upon a method of writing the life of an unpopular author in a manner specially calculated to recommend it to the mass of readers. Mr. H. S. Salt has done neither of these things. Probably all that there is to tell of Thoreau's uneventful life has been told; while of his works, and of what manner of man he was, it is scarcely necessary to say much—for there are his works themselves; and we have always held that Thoreau will be more easily and better understood by the extended publication of his work here than by the multiplication of any number of "lives," and expositions of his "aims." Indeed, we have no hesitation in hazarding the suggestion that where Mr. Salt's "Life" will gain one admirer for Thoreau, a book such as the one noticed below will win half a dozen. Such persons as have Sanborn's "Life of Thoreau" ("American Men of Letters Series") already on their shelves, will have but little reason for adding this new volume to their library, while anyone purchasing a life of the Hermit of Walden for the first time would, we think, if given an opportunity of comparing the works beforehand, unhesitatingly

164

purchase the earlier and (for such considerations will creep in) far cheaper one.

Not often, perhaps, has an author been so widely, so persistently, and so ridiculously misunderstood as has Thoreau. Here was a man who not only had an ideal, which is perhaps a sufficiently common phenomenon, but who steadfastly attempted so far as his own life was concerned to live up to that ideal. We hear a great deal said in favour of plain living and high thinking, yet when a man makes that rule the leading article of his creed and acts up to it, hard words are hurled at him—he is a "skulker" (*vide* Robert Louis Stevenson), a "cynic," a "man without a healthy mind" *vide* James Robert Lowell); he is, forsooth, a "stoic-epicurean-adiaphorist" (*vide* Professor Nichol). Such and similar are the expressions levelled at this man—one of the most original geniuses that America has produced—levelled at him, too, by men whose position in the literary world clothes their words with some authority, and whose *obiter dicta* are accepted as final by many persons too lazy to form opinions for themselves.

Mr. Salt, as has been said, gives us little that is new with regard to Thoreau's life and ethical teaching; his book is largely made up of passages from Thoreau's works and letters, and from other letters which throw more or less light on the life and work of Thoreau; though he is an appreciative student of the poet-naturalist, he maintains a fairly judicial attitude, and we welcome his book as we should always welcome any work that tends to set right a sadly mistaken view of any man, such as is that which obtains with regard to Thoreau. Mr. Salt has certainly added to the value of his book by an extremely useful bibliography.

The Anti-Slavery and Reform Papers of Thoreau form one of the latest volumes of Messrs. Swan Sonnenschein's useful "Social Science Series." The volume contains five papers, on "Civil Disobedience" two upon Captain John Brown, "Paradise (to be) Regained," "Life without Principle," and an introduction by Mr. Salt. Readers who know Thoreau only by such of his writings as "Walden" and "The Week" will meet him here, if not in a new light, at any rate amplifying on practical questions that are but casually touched upon in the books named. The paper on "Civil Disobedience" is mainly an attempt at justifying a man in refusing to support a Government (even to the extent of being imprisoned by it!) whose actions he cannot but condemn. "I think," he says—and surely, well says—"that we should be men first, and subjects afterwards." On hearing of the arrest of Captain John Brown (of Harper's Ferry fame) Thoreau sent round among the inhabitants of Concord saying that he would speak on the subject on the following Sunday. The Abolition Committee intimated that it would be ill-timed and unadvisable. "I did not send to you for advice," he characteristically replied, "but to announce that I am to speak." The result was the "Plea for John Brown," the most eloquent and impassioned of Thoreau's works. The last essay in this volume—that on "Life without Principle"—immediately brings to mind, as indeed does any consideration of Thoreau's life and work, that beautiful sonnet of Wordsworth's:—

> "The world is too much with us; late and soon,
> Getting and spending, we lay waste our powers:
>
> . . . . . .
> Great God! I'd rather be
> A pagan suckled in a creed outworn;
> So might I, standing on this pleasant lea,
> Have glimpses that would make me less forlorn,
> Have sight of Proteus coming from the sea,
> Or hear old Triton blow his wreathed horn."

Speaker, November 8, 1890.

The Life of Henry David Thoreau. By H. S. Salt. London: Richard Bentley & Sons. 1890.

Anti-Slavery and Reform Papers. By Henry D. Thoreau. Selected and Edited by H. S. Salt. London: Swan Sonnenschein. 1890.

HENRY DAVID THOREAU

To the majority of English readers Thoreau's works are probably but little known—still less perhaps is known of the character of the writer. It has, therefore, appeared to Mr. Salt that a comprehensive account of his life, and an endeavour to form a clear estimate of his ethical teaching may supply a real want to readers on this side of the Atlantic. Whether such a want as the author supposes really existed is open to doubt, but in any case Mr. Salt's labour has not been in vain, for it enables one to obtain an insight into the character of a man of no ordinary stamp. To plain matter-of-fact people, the story of Thoreau's life will appear very much like a romance—there is a vein of unreality about it that irritates whilst it interests; and although the author of this biography has been at some pains to portray the man as he appeared to his friends and admirers, still a knowledge of at least one of Thoreau's works, notably "Walden; or, Life in the Woods," which contains an account of his mode of life during his period of retirement from the world, is necessary to enable one to appreciate the peculiar bent of mind of this latter-day Diogenes. It is not surprising to hear that from his childhood Thoreau had been a keen lover of nature, that this feeling grew with his growth, so that after finishing his college career he determined to devote the rest of his life to the study of wild nature, to become, as he called it, a professional walker or saunterer, "to spend at least one half of each day in the open air, to watch the dawns and sunsets, to carry express what was in the wind, to secure the latest news from forest and hill-top, and to be a self-appointed inspector of snowstorms and rainstorms." It is no wonder that with his intense ideality of temperament the movement known as Transcendentalism, which had for some years been gathering force in America, should powerfully have affected Thoreau's mind, or that he should have aided the propagation of this new faith with all his powers. His adherence to the Transcendental creed marks the most important epoch in his life. By reason of it he seceded from the religion in which he was brought up, and henceforth held and practised a religion which, as Mr. Salt says, may perhaps be best described as Pantheism. "Formerly," Thoreau wrote, "methought Nature developed as I developed, and grew up with me. My life was ecstasy. In youth, before I lost any of my senses, I can remember I was all alive, and inhabited my body with inexpressible satisfaction; both its weariness and refreshment were sweet to me. This earth was the most glorious musical instrument, and I was audience to its strains. I said to myself, I said to others, there comes into my mind such an indescribable, infinite, all-absorbing, divine heavenly pleasure; a sense of salvation and expansion. And I have nought to do with it; I perceive that I am dealt with by superior powers. By all manner of bounds and traps threatening the extreme penalty of the divine law, it behooves us to preserve the purity and sanctity of the mind. That I am innocent to myself, that I love and reverence my life." It seems highly probable that Thoreau drew not a few of his social and ethical opinions from Emerson, with whom he formed a close friendship; indeed, so great was the influence exercised over him by that teacher that it has been said "that in his manners, in the tones of his voice, in his modes of expression, even in the hesitations and pauses of his speech," he became the counterpart of Emerson. His acquaintance with Nathaniel Hawthorne, a mystic of even a gloomier type than himself, never became very cordial, but his reference to Thoreau in his journal is of some interest. He thus describes him:—"He is a singular character—a young man with much of wild original nature still remaining in him; and so far as he is unsophisticated, it is in a way and method of his own. He is as ugly as sin, long-nosed, queer mouthed, and with uncouth and somewhat rustic though courteous manners, corresponding very well with such an exterior. But his ugliness is of an honest and agreeable fashion, and becomes him much better than beauty." By nature he was un-

social, and, in a degree, unsympathetic, and his dislike to
society in the ordinary sense of the word was intense. In the
drawing-room he was by no means at his best, the convention-
alities irritated him, and he became contradictory and pug-
nacious. "His mental appearance," says Channing, who
knew him well, "at times almost betrayed irritability; his
words were like quills on the fretful porcupine. Like a cat he
would curl up his spine and spit at a fop or monkey, and
despised those who were running well downhill to damna-
tion." His external coldness is well illustrated by another of
his friends, who said, "I love Henry, but I cannot like him, and
as for taking his arm, I should as soon think of taking the arm
of an elm-tree." Yet he had a great liking for children, amongst
whom he was a hero, and would amuse them by the hour
telling stories, singing to them, or playing on his flute, at
which he was an adept. It was in the huckleberry expeditions,
however, that his services were in the greatest request, for his
presence ensured finding acres of bushes laden with this fruit.
The most characteristic episode in Thoreau's career, and the
one that has been most freely criticised, was undoubtedly
when he put into practice an idea that had long been maturing
in his mind—to withdraw from the society of his fellow-men
for a season, and to live such a life in such a manner as might
be most conducive to his intellectual and spiritual advantage.
His reasons for taking such a step are best given in his own
words:—

"I went to the woods," he says, "because I wished to live
deliberately, to front only the essential facts of life, and see
if I could not learn what it had to teach, and not, when I
came to die, discover that I had not lived. I did not wish to
live what was not life, living is so dear; nor did I wish to
practise resignation unless it was quite necessary. I wanted
to live deep, and suck out all the marrow of life; to live so
sturdily and Spartan-like as to put to rout all that was not
life, to cut a broad swath and shave close, to drive life into a
corner, and reduce it to its lowest terms, and if it proved to

be mean, why then to get the whole and genuine meanness of it, and publish its meanness to the world; or if it were sublime, to know it by experience, and be able to give a true account of it in my next excursion."

His period of retirement lasted two years, during which, says his biographer, he learnt two great lessons, viz., that it is not a hardship, but a pastime, to maintain one's self on this earth if we live simply and wisely—which may be taken to mean not living at all, but simply existing; and that in proportion as one simplifies his life, the laws of the universe will appear less complex—doctrines which have been taught for ages, so that they can hardly be considered either original or novel. As Mr. Lowell truly said, "His shanty life was a mere impossibility, so far as his conception of it goes, as an entire independency of mankind. The tub of Diogenes had a sounder bottom." Upon his return to the world in 1847 he gave himself up to literature and lecturing. His first book, however, proved a sad failure, and seven hundred volumes of it—a thousand copies were printed—were thrown on his hands. His second venture, "Walden," proved more successful, notwithstanding that it met with a good deal of ridicule and not a little hostile criticism. This was the most important work that Thoreau wrote, as it contains the sum and essence of his ideal and ethical philosophy, and whilst it increased his repute as a writer, the author was considered by at least a portion of his countrymen as a humbug. As a lecturer he was not always happy, his uncompromising character occasionally straining the relations between himself and his audience. "I take it for granted," he wrote, "when I am invited to lecture anywhere . . . there is a desire to hear what I think on some subject, though I may be the greatest fool in the country, and not that I should say pleasant things merely, or such as the audience will assent to; and I resolve accordingly that I will give them a strong dose of myself. They have sent for me and engaged to pay me, and I am determined they have me, though I bore them beyond all precedent." Thoreau has been well-termed "a Yankee Stoic," and the essence of his practical philosophy Mr. Salt sums up in these words:—"To waste no time in brooding over the past, but to live in the present and nourish unbounded confidence in the future; and for support in this creed, and refreshment in the weaker moments of life, he looked to the unfailing health and beneficence, as he considered it, of wild nature." He was an extraordinary man, and as such his life is of considerable interest.

London *Evening Post*, January 9, 1891.

[*Another review of the Salt biography, Bentley edition.*]

THOREAU

I<small>T</small> is only after death that many men become citizens of the world. They then cease to be provincial, and come to belong to all mankind. This has been eminently the case with Thoreau. Twenty-five years ago we heard of him, anon and anon, but as of a man who had no connecting links with life in him. From what could be gathered, he seemed a supremely cultured woodman, who cared a great deal more for trees than he did for men; who spent a solitary life in the forests, abjuring most society, but yet one who had chosen friends in great spirits. Was he a man who merely affected the life which the American novelist has made so popular—a nineteenth-century Massachusetts Natty Bumpo? Or was he a genius, who simply wanted time to show himself to men, and speak his own words to the universe?

To many of his old neighbours in Concord, where he lived and died, and which he seldom left, and never for long absences, he was simply a queer and incomprehensible character, full of odd whimseys, going cheerfully to jail rather than pay taxes, and living alone in a hut by a pond near the village. To many others—men of education and literary taste, who had known him at college, and who knew his writings—he was merely an extravagant imitator of Emerson, copying his tone of thought, his style, and even his personal manner and expression. This class was more impatient of him than his neighbours, and was secretly inclined to think of him, in plain speech, only as a lazy humbug.

Yet, in fact, Thoreau was one of a group of remarkable men that appeared in New England during the first half of this century, all of whom were by no means the children of transcendentalism, but whose combined names largely compose the chief glory of American literature. Notwithstanding peculiarities which dwarfed him to the sight of ordinary men, he was a man of great stature and beauty of mind, and especially a man who could read, as few can, or have ever been able to do, the secrets of the nature surrounding him. In the presence of nature most of us are silent. We are so, because she is talking to us in a language which we do not understand, or only half understand. Now and then we seem to hear a voice, but as the pages of our marvellous nineteenth century history. If a man wishes to see on how little, or with how little one can live, let him read "Walden." If he believes that all which is commonly regarded as belonging to the necessaries of life is really indispensable, Thoreau's experience will dispel the illusion. The solitary of the woods at Walden, unquestionably one of the greatest and most remarkable, has become one of the best known characters of our age; and we believe Mr. Salt is right in his prophecy, that "when time has softened down the friction caused by superficial blemishes and misunderstandings, the world will realise that it was no mere Emersonian disciple, but a master-mind and heart of hearts, who left that burning message to his fellow men." S.F.W.

London *Inquirer*, July 18, 1896.

[*"Life of Thoreau. By Henry S. Salt. London: Walter Scott. 1s. 6d.*]

THOREAU'S POEMS

NOTHING is more curious in literary art than the line which divides the poet usually so called—that is the verse-poet—from the prose poet. Of course there have been poets who could write prose and prose-writers who could write verse—but their names were not Tennyson or Carlyle. Shakespeare and Milton are the greatest examples of the rare union of the two arts—or rather two branches of the same art. In our own time Matthew Arnold succeeded so equally with both that one is at a loss to say under which head one should place him as most eminent—as who shall say which is the greater, Rossetti the painter or Rossetti the poet? And then, of course, there was Heine. It must be confessed that for the most part the verse-poets turning to prose have the greater average of success than the prose-poets turning to verse. When Keats and Shelley and Burns took to prose they didn't fall far short of the professional prose-man—made no such grotesque fiasco of it as, for example, Carlyle taking to verse. But no doubt the distinction between verse-poets and prose-poets is a distinctly arbitrary one—as it would be arbitrary to draw a line between verse-poets who can write sonnets and those who cannot. Tennyson, for example, "mighty-mouthed inventor of harmonies" as he was, could never write a good sonnet—other poets there have been who could write nothing else. Then there are poets who can write blank-verse, poets who can write hexameters, and there are poets who seldom succeed with any form more complicated than the lyric in four-line stanzas. Perhaps the classification fairest to the prose-poet would be one that would include the rhythm of prose among the accepted poetical metres, as blank verse is included. After all, the laws regulating blank verse, outside the law that its lines shall not exceed ten syllables, are hardly less breakable, less ductible by temperament, than the unwritten laws of prose. One has only to compare the blank verse of Shakespeare, Milton, and Tennyson to see that the form in their hands is hardly less variable than the form of prose in the hands, say, of a Gibbon, a Lamb, a Carlyle, and a Stevenson. And there is this much to be said for the prose-writer—that the metre he manages best, when he turns to verse, is—blank verse, which is usually regarded as the most severe test of the verse-poet himself!

* * * * *

Thoreau, a collection of whose verses, edited by Mr. Salt (Lane), is the occasion of these remarks, is a case in point. That Thoreau was a poet is undeniable, not merely by virtue of his lofty mystical vision of human life, and other such "essentials" of poetry, but also by virtue of his expression—the medium of his grave, impassioned prose. Accustomed to the great rhythms of prose, with lines like the lines of mountain ranges, it was apparently next to impossible for him to adapt himself to the jigging measures, the childish verse-patterns of the "poet" proper—as it would have puzzled Michael Angelo to paint fans or dress dolls, or some of the greatest humorists to hold their own with a Cockney bus conductor. The greatest art, like the greatest wit, is not necessarily the nimblest. It is undeniable that Thoreau moves in verse, like a captive, with a rattle of chains. He rhymes "dawn" and "adorn," and is capable of a verse such as this—

> But now there comes unsought, unseen,
>   Some clear divine elect*uary*,
> And I, who had but sensual been,
>   Grow sensible, and as God is, *am wary*—

and yet he is a much greater poet than Mr. ____, who shall we say? He made the best excuse for such verse when he said—

> My life has been the poem I would have writ,
> But I could not both live and utter it.

Yet, of course, he did utter it as well. He uttered it best, it is obvious, in his prose. Prose was the metre best suited to his poetic impulse. To realise this one has but to come across such a fragment of it as this which Mr. Salt quotes in his preface: "Great prose," he thinks, crying his own fresh fish like any wise man, "commands our respect more than great verse, since it implies a more permanent and level height, a life more pervaded with the grandeur of the thought. The poet only makes an irruption, like a Parthian, and is off again, shooting while he retreats, but the prose writer has conquered, like a Roman, and settled colonies."

*   *   *   *   *

Nevertheless, Mr. Salt has done well to collect these verses, although Emerson, whose influence in so many ways was repressive of Thoreau's perhaps more significant individuality, thought but little of them. In some respects they resemble Emerson's own verses, being often poetic epigrams, gnomic compressions of philosophy, and "sibylline leaves" of thought rather than "poems." But the earnest gold-seeker is not impatient of quartz, and, after all, the proportion of gold in Thoreau's poems is as large as that, say, in the poetry of Wordsworth or Coleridge—though, of course, the quality of it is another matter. Yet if it be not of the finest gold, gold it is, and it resembles Wordsworth in that it is nearest poetry when it is nearest nature. Take this picture of "Mist," which compares favorably with its companions, perhaps for the very reason that it is free of rhyme:—

> Low-anchored cloud,
> Newfoundland air,
> Fountain-head and source of rivers,
> Dew-cloth, dream-drapery,
> And napkin spread by fays;
> Drifting meadow of the air,
> Where bloom the daisied banks and violets,
> And in whose fenny labyrinth
> The bittern booms and heron wades;

Spirit of lakes and seas and rivers,—
Bear only perfumes and the scent
Of healing herbs to just men's fields.

Coleridge, somebody said, reversed the miracle of Antaeus, and lost his strength as he touched the earth. With Thoreau it was just the reverse. With him it was always nature first and books afterwards. Homer and Shakespeare interest him so long as there is no battle between the red and black ants to umpire:

Bid Homer wait till I the issue learn,
    If red or black the gods will favor most,
Or yonder Ajax will the phalanx turn,
    Struggling to heave some rock against the
        host.

Tell Shakespeare to attend some leisure hour.
    For now I've business with this drop of dew,
And see you not, the clouds prepare a
        shower—
    I'll meet him shortly when the sky is blue.

One notes for remembrance many a fine line, couplet, and quatrain, such as—

Sometimes a late autumnal thought
Has crossed my mind in green July.

Or—

Give me simple laboring folk,
Who love their work,
Whose virtue is a song
To cheer God along.

Or this, how characteristic of Thoreau!—

The life that I aspire to live,
   No man proposeth me;
No trade upon the street
   Wears its emblazonry.

Or again the concluding prayer "that I may not disappoint myself," and "that I may greatly disappoint my friends"! But though Thoreau's verse is thus seen at its best in snatches and extracts, he sometimes comes near to writing a perfect lyric, as in the poem on "Free Love"—which has nothing to do with the New Hedonism, and which contains this memorable verse:

I cannot leave my sky
   For thy caprice,
True love would soar as high
   As heaven is.

A final word of thanks to Mr. Salt for his interesting and temperate introduction. Mr. Salt is under no illusion in regard to Thoreau's verse, but he is quite right in thinking that it will be of interest to those who value the greater poetry of his prose.
   Richard Le Gallienne, London *Star*, January 23, 1896

I N

writing verse there is something artificial, the "mechanic exercise," as Tennyson calls it. Thoreau was too earnest to copy "the childish verse-patterns of the 'poet' proper." As the lyric is a spontaneous outburst of feeling and not "premeditated art," it is the form in which we should expect him—despite his seemingly stoical nature—to be most happy. From this standpoint he can be best judged by the short poem,—

PILGRIMS

Have you not seen
   In ancient times
Pilgrims pass by
   Toward other climes?
With shining faces,
   Youthful and strong,
Mounting this hill
   With speech and with song?

Ah, my good sir,
   I know not those ways:
Little my knowledge,
   Tho' many my days.
When I have slumbered,
   I have heard sounds
As of travellers passing
   These my grounds.

'Twas a sweet music
   Wafted them by,
I could not tell
   If afar off or nigh.

Unless I dreamed it,
   This was of yore:
I never told it
   To mortal before.

Never remember
   But in my dreams,
What to me waking
   A miracle seems.

This and the unrhymed poem, *Smoke*, reveal the heart pregnant with celestial fire.

Light-winged Smoke, Icarian bird,
Melting thy pinions in thy upward flight;
Lark without song, and messenger of dawn,
Circling above the hamlets as thy nest;
Or else, departing dream, and shadowy form
Of midnight vision, gathering up thy skirts;
By night star-veiling, and by day
Darkening the light and blotting out the sun;
Go thou, my incense, upward from this hearth,
And ask the gods to pardon this clear flame.

The quotable felicities that enter into a language and become "household words" are not within Thoreau's range; but he never aspired to the proprietorship of a place on Parnassus. He would be

"Only a zephyr that may blow
Among the reeds by the river low."

His view of the poetic character is marked by the clear sanity of genius: "A true poem," he writes, "is distinguished not so much by a felicitous expression or any thought it suggests, as by the atmosphere which surrounds it. There are two classes of men called poets. The one cultivates life, the other art: one seeks food for nutriment, the other for flavor; one satisfies hunger, the other gratifies the palate." Evidently, the "jigging measures and the verse-patterns of the 'poet' proper" could not possibly enter into his conception of poetry.

In his most appropriate *Introduction* Mr. Salt writes: "Thoreau's poetry, whatever its intrinsic value may be, is full of personal significance; in fact, as Emerson remarked, 'his biography is in his verses.' Thus, many of his poems will be found to throw light on certain passages of his life. 'Inspiration,' for example, is the record of his soul's awakening to the new impulse of transcendentalism; the stanzas on 'Sympathy' perhaps contain in a thinly-disguised form the story of his youthful love and the sacrifice which he imposed upon himself to avoid rivalry with his brother." And in a foot-note to the poem he says: "The explanation of this poem, given on Emerson's authority, but necessarily somewhat conjectural, is that a reference is made, under the character of the 'gentle boy' to the girl with whom both Henry and John Thoreau were in love." Mr. Salt and the editor have had much correspondence anent the proper interpretation of this poem in the light of Emerson's "explanation" of its veiled meaning. After trying all manner of literary legerdemain with the text and the punctuation we were as far as ever from the solution.

At last, by the death of one of Thoreau's correspondents, the editor came into possession of his collection of Thoreau's published works, and in the copy of the 1868 edition—the real "second edition"—of *A Week on the Concord and Merrimack Rivers*, a pencilled note by the original owner of the book settles the whole question. On page 276 the poem called *Sympathy* is printed, and at the end of the first line, "Lately, alas, I knew a gentle boy." and at the end of the line is an asterisk. At the bottom of the page is written,—"His brother *John*. The sister told me. G.".

So that perplexing stanza,

> "Eternity may not the chance repeat;
>   But I must tread my single way alone,
> In sad remembrance that we once did meet,
>   And know that bliss irrevocably gone."—

"darkening the light," may no longer vex the thoughtful reader of Thoreau.

GLIMPSES OF FORCE

THOREAU AND ALCOTT

By Rose Hawthorne Lathrop.

I WAS about 9 years old and coming sternly to realize that I had been transferred from English homelikeness to American sandbanks, when, a little above the garden path, I beheld two enormous eyes not far from each other. They moved toward me. I melted away. Thoreau had come to call at the house.

The horrible effect of the great eyes, grey as autumn pools lit by a rift in the clouds, upon a mind pining for luxurious verdure and gem-like blue heavens, created a thirst in me for the dreadful. I hung about the garden (it was a grim failure of a garden) until the strange being, native to harsh America, should again emerge for departure. Stationed in a more retired spot I watched for him, and by and by he came. I noticed with transfixed pulses that he strode, clothed in exaggerated dignity, with long steps, placing one foot exactly before the other according to the Indian fashion, which in Thoreau's case was a downright marvel, since his feet seemed interminable. I next became conscious of a vaguely large nose that finally curved to his chin, and then I realized that this being was looking at me—the huge eyes at a slight oblique angle; and he passed so close to me, in consequence of a roguish turn of the path, that I found his grey-brown irises were bordered by heavy dark lines, like a wild animals. For years this vision really distressed me in remembrance, and appeared to have a harmonious connection with my bitter lot in being an exile from British daisies and robins. And yet the time came when both Thoreau and America were revealed to me!

182

The first thing which Thoreau did to soften my heart toward him was to fall desperately ill. My mother sent him our sweet old musicbox, which softly dreamed forth its tunes, and he enjoyed its gentle strains as he lay perishing. I had heard a great deal of his poetic nature and instructive genius, and when he died it seemed as if an anemone, more lovely than any other, had been carried from the borders of a wood, and dropped, fading, in its depths. I never crossed a hill or a field in Concord, or gathered a cardinal-flower or any other rare bloom, without thinking of Thoreau as a companion of delicacy, though also a brother of the Indian. However, I never quite forgave him the steady stare of those unhuman eyes when I was a disheartened child. And I think I was right, for I do not doubt that his peculiar step, the stride adopted, was a sign of affectation; and that his intense gaze was the result of an abnormal self-consciousness. As a child the superficial faults which I noticed stood for the man himself; but to-day I judge that of all affectations that ever were, perhaps his of a new outward bearing and manner of thought, to distinguish him severely from futile mortals, was the least culpable. He had so much provocation on his side! He longed to herald the fact that he was not one of the triflers, even at the risk of resembling a savage. Walden woods rustled the name of Thoreau whenever I walked in them; and the lovely pond looked always so beautiful as amply to excuse his odd retirement to its margin. Not a theory, so much as the enchantment of Walden, was the cause of his living for so long principally on his mother's bread. He thought he fed upon almost anything else not alienated from nature; but we, who are free from the intoxicating love of air and branches, we who stay calmly at home and eat strange food, know that but for Mrs. Thoreau's loaves of bread, faithfully supplied, Philosophy and Superiority would have held a council of war and have capitulated to smiling Conventionality.

A little cairn of shabby stones upon the pond's brink, added to by every thoughtful visitor, commemorated Thoreau's stay there. It may be very fitting to do one's best in his honor from the material nearest at hand; but such a cairn seems to some of us like a childish notion and casts a humorous ray upon the hero of it, making the regret sadder and longer that so fair a soul should have masqueraded at all as one set apart from his fellow men, and should have taken a queer flight into the neighborly, uncriticising solitude of Walden woods. Standing beside the cairn, it perhaps seems to the visitor that the people who snap their fingers at the route of their race, and swerve aside to better themselves intellectually, were the sport of great forces in moments of relaxation; while the despised herd—the race—looks at these seceders with a large tolerance from the vantage ground of co-operative work. But glancing off over Walden's beautiful dark stillness, crossed here and there with lines of light, one believes with all one's heart that the few men who see largely and think reverently away from the daily shams to the vast realities, are guides to the Eternal City. They may be quaint, but they are honest and unweary-ing, and their mission is divine. Thoreau! The very word has come to mean for me—notwithstanding his half humorous angers—force at peace; wisdom forgiving.

He had an uncanny, subordinate resemblance to Emerson. There were deep fissures from the nostrils along the cheeks, which were similar to those marking Emerson's smile. But his countenance had an April pensiveness about it, and the slight peculiar kinship of physiognomy between the two friends merely emphasized their essential difference.

* * * * *

It was never so well understood at the Wayside that my father had somewhat reclusive habits, as when Alcott was reported to be approaching along the Larch Path. Yet I never was aware that the seer failed to gain admittance—one cause, perhaps, for the awe in which his visits were held. I know that my observation was attracted to him from the fact that my mother's eyes grew a darker grey at his advents, and because she spoke of a long manuscript poem which he had once brought and read aloud to her and to my father. The impres-sion I gathered from the mention of the poem was of a moonlit expanse, quiet, somnolent, cool. I fancy that Alcott's charm needed the stimulus of a rather large audience, of which he might be the recognized prophet. It seems to have been concluded that his "conversations" (monologues) were infinitely above his writing, and most delightful. The Concord school of philosophy, although Alcott established it toward the close of his life, gave many persons an opportunity to observe the fervor of his speech when surrounded by a group of eager minds. Even if some of us imagined that his matter was singularly like nonsense, still his manner was exquisitely inspired. Rapture, conviction, tenderness glowed about his features and trembled in his voice, until his tall person shone transfigured, and he blushed, smiled, was positively beautiful. It was most interesting to learn that Alcott's genius did not delay for a genuine or transient idea. He was so replete with the energy of philosophic devotion that his windmills were themes of sublime account, and he wrestled with them as with principles real and progressive. And it struck me that his enthusiasm transmuted any subject which might already be under discussion into a phantasm of his own brain, until its resemblance to what had been propounded was no more than that of a "Castle in the air" to the "house of the understanding." We are apt to take pleasure in anything spontaneous; we are tired of calculated effects and defenses; and a very poor speech goes far if there are no written notes for it. Therefore Alcott's triumph was dazzling; he not only spoke extemporaneously, but enticingly and superbly. I believe he was never once wholly startled from the dream of illusion, which pictured to him all high aims as possible of realization through talk; and which unfailingly gave him either an opinion of his own to aid these ends, or some one else's truth defined with a difference. And this illusion endowed him to the last with the expression of a boy who was only half mischievous, and for the rest happy, hopeful, inexperienced. When I think of Alcott I always see a fresh, rosy-cheeked face; long, but not dolorous. Yet I often saw him pale and dolorous enough. But that was not in character; and he seemed, when sad, thin, forlorn, like a lamb in chains. At the time Miss Alcott was upon the verge of her fame and fortune her father might have been taken for a centenarian when I beheld him one day slowly and pathetically constructing a pretty rustic fence before his gabled brown house, as if at the unreasonable command of some latter day Pharaoh. Ten years afterward he was, on the contrary, a Titan; gay, silvery-locked, elegant, ready to begin his life over again.

Alcott represented to me a fairy element in the up-country region in which I so often saw him. I heard that he walked the woods for the purpose of finding odd coils of tree roots and branches, which would on the instant suggest to him an ingenious use in his art of rustic building. It was rumored that nobody's outlying curios in this line were safe under his eye, and that if you possessed an eccentric tree for a time, it was fated to close its existence in the keeping of Alcott. I imagined his slightly stooping, yet tall and well-grown figure, clothed in black, and with a picturesque straw hat, twining itself in and out of forest aisles, or craftily returning home with gargoyle-like stems over his shoulders. The magic of his pursuit was emphasized by the notorious fact that his handiwork fell together in the middle, faded like shadows from bronze to hoary pallor; its longevity was a protracted death. In short, his arbors broke under the weight of a purpose, as poems become doggerel in the service of a theorist. Truly, Alcott was completely at the beck of illusion; and he was always safer alone with it than near the hard uses of adverse reality. I well remember my astonishment when I was told that he had set forth to go into the jaws of the rebellion after Louisa, his daughter, who had succumbed to typhus fever while nursing the soldiers. His object was to bring her home; but it was difficult to believe that he would be successful in entering the field of misery and uproar. I never expected to see him again. Almost the only point at which he normally met this world was in his worship of apple trees. Here, in his orchard, he was an all admirable human being and lovely to observe. As he looked upon the undulating arms or piled the excellent apples, red and russet, which seemed to shine and shimmer at his glance, his figure became supple, his countenance beamed with a rose and gold related to the fruit. Apples were his one revenue of quantity, and he appreciated their source and them, and with kingly liberality filled the hands of friends with choice favorites. In his orchard by the high road, with its trees rising to a great height from a basin-shaped side lawn (which may originally have been marshy ground) he seemed to me a perfect soul. No doubt the garden of children at the beginning of his career inspired him likewise; and in it he must have shown the same tender solicitude and benevolence. No doubt he beamed upon his young scholars with a love which exquisiteley tempered his fantastical suppositions and his self-complacency. Certainly he reverenced childhood, whose instincts and desires and powers he so beautifully defended and developed, too much to drink deeply in its presence of the strong wine of speculative license, or to look down upon it from the dizzying arrogance of philosophical conceit. With children his eccentricities must have wholly given place to his inoffensive daemon of unpractical confidence. But Alcott was unmistakably vain among his compeers. He often spoke humbly, but he never let people think he was humble. His foibles appeared to me ridiculous, and provoked me exceedingly—the brave cat of the proverb must be my excuse—but I awakened to the eternal verity that some such husks are rather natural to persons of purely distinctive minds, perhaps shielding them. And I think one comes to particularly value a bent blessed with earnest unconsciousness; a not too clever Argus vision; a childlike gullibility and spontaneity. This untarnished gullibility and gentle confidence, for all his self-laudations and trivial insincerities, Alcott eminently harbored; and when he did not emerge either from his apple orchard or his inspirations he was essentially wholesome, full of an ardent simplicity, and a happy faith in the capacities given him by his Creator. So that his outline is one of much dignity, in spite of the somewhat capricious coloring of his character; the latter being not unlike the efforts of a nursery artist upon a print of "The Father of His Country," for whom, as he stands proudly upon the page, a green coat and purple pantaloons were not intended, and are only minor incidents of destiny.

Weekly Inter-Ocean, July 7, 1891

Is

there a fatality attending the *H's*? Mr. Hiram Adolphus Hawkins "spoke blank verse in the bosom of his family"—and he became "a pyramid of mind on the dark desert of despair": undoubtedly as a warning.

Another of the *H's*, at the tender age of nine, is subject to "transfixed pulses"—and she became a contributor to the *Inter-Ocean*!

This frail creature of the *transfixed pulses*, American born but exported to England in recognition of a prostitution of the paternal pen is, by a veering of the political pen "transferred from English homelikeness to American sandbanks;" but she absolutely can not become reconciled to the exchange of "British daisies and robins" for American golden-rod and Bobolinks. Fresh from the fogs of Liverpool, she brings to her native land "a mind pining for gem-like blue heavens": British skies being so much "bluer." Is there a Nemesis that harries the *H's*?

Long after the time when ordinary folk have reached the years of discretion, this creature of curious pulses becomes tempted of the Devil to let the readers of the *Inter-Ocean* know her estimate of Henry D. Thoreau. With the very eyes that a Liverpool fog failed to faze, she detects in him "an affectation of a new outward bearing and manner of thought." Surely, it is the reader now who has the "transfixed pulses." She also assures us that "Not a theory, so much as the enchantment of Walden, was the cause of his living so long on his mother's bread."

What detestable bread Mrs. Thoreau must have baked! However, as her son withstood this diet for more than two years, it is evident that "the enchantment of Walden" is actually "too many" for the soggiest loaf—thus doth Nature provide her kindly compensations!

But one unhappy day this *Inter-Ocean* correspondent was filled (from back-comb to shoe buttons) with "a regret sadder and longer [than one of Mrs. Thoreau's loaves?] that so fair a soul should have masqueraded at all as one set apart from his fellow men." One can but share her loaf-long regret: still, isn't it quite likely that poor Thoreau felt the need for a "masquerade" after *that* bread? Besides, as man can't live on bread alone, what is the matter with a "masquerade" by way of variety?

At last, this lark of the pranksome pulses soars far away from "daisies and robins" to the cloud-capped Pisgah of Political Economy to chirrup this Benthamitish psalm: "Perhaps the people who snap their fingers at the route of their race, and swerve aside to better themselves intellec- tually, were the sport of great forces in moments of relaxation; while the despised herd—the race—looks at these seceders from the vantage ground of co-operative work."

What a nice "derangement of epitaphs"! And yet even she has transient glimmerings of sanity: "Thoreau! The very word has come to mean to me . . . wisdom *forgiving*." Let us hope that according to the law of the market-place the demand determines the supply. How about those "who swerve aside to better themselves" pecuniarily? Swerving smoothly and receiving the sop of a consulate as the recompense! Such swervings have been known, "but the pity of it, Iago, the pity of it!" In Sleepy Hollow and within a stone's throw from one grave there is another and sleeping serenely in it—one whom not the universe could "swerve,"

"He nothing common did, nor mean.
In his life's memorable scene."

GLIMPSES OF

FOOLISHNESS BY THE

SON OF HIS FATHER

Henry David Thoreau (1817-1862) had the initial distinction of being born in Concord, though that village was then nothing but a pretty hamlet, lying between level meadows and low hills, on the banks of a loitering stream. Here, it is true, the first blood of the Revolution had been shed, more than forty years before; but that fact might have lapsed into oblivion had not Emerson's "Hymn," recited on the site of the conflict, in 1836, put a life into the event that is still vigorous.

Thoreau was, remotely, of French extraction, and he had a swarthy, Norman cast of features. but his ancestors had become English before they became American, and the genuine New England farmer blood beat in his veins. Personally, he was odd, in all senses of the term. He was bilious in constitution and in temper, with a disposition somewhat prone to suspicion and jealousy, and defiant, rather than truly independent, in spirit. He had a searching, watchful, unconciliating eye, a long, stealthy tread and an alert but not graceful figure. His heart was neither warm nor large, and he certainly did not share that "enthusiasm for humanity" which was the fashionable profession in his day. His habits were solitary and unsocial; yet secretly he was highly sensitive to the opinion of his fellow-men, and would perhaps have mingled more freely with them, but for a perception that there was no vehement demand for his company. The art of pleasing was not innate in him, and he was too proud to cultivate it. Rather than have it appear that society could do without him, he resolved to make haste and banish society; for a couple of years he actually lived alone in a hut built by himself, on the shores of Walden Pond, near Concord: all his life he kept out of people's way,—you were more apt to see his disappearing coat-tails than his face,—and he was most at ease in his walks through the woods and fields surrounding Concord, and on his exploring tramps to Canada, to Maine, to Cape Cod and along the Merrimac River. Thus thrown back upon himself, his egotism and self-consciousness could not but become emphasized: and since he might not shine in society, he determined to be king in the wilderness. He asserted, and perhaps brought himself to believe, that all that was worthy in this world lay within the compass of a walk from his own door-step; and we might add that he came to regard the owner of that doorstep as the centre of all this world's worth. Existing in space, as it were, with nothing to measure himself by, he seemed to himself colossal.

Had Thoreau been nothing more than has been indicated, the world would not have been likely to hear of him. But there was more in him than this, and more still was added by education and by the influence of certain of his contemporaries, and of their opinions. His father was able to send him to school and to Harvard College: after graduating he taught school, and finally learned surveying. This trade, and a little money that he had, sufficed to support one of habits so economical as his. He was endowed with some imagination, and it partly found expression in poetry—moralized descriptions of nature, a little rough in form, and anything but ardent in feeling, but individual and masculine. Several of these poems, written soon after Thoreau left college, were published in "The Dial," and also some essays on the natural history of Massachusetts. Emerson was the medium of this early literary recognition, and his contact with the odd and

whimsical young man who had so few intimates inevitably
had an effect upon Thoreau's development, both literary and
philosophical. He did not want to imitate anybody, and he did
his best to digest Emerson, so that his own work and cast of
thought should not betray the contagion. Measurably, but not
completely, he succeeded. His writings are thinly overspread
with Thoreau, but here and there the coating has worn off, and
the Emersonian basis shows through. It is quite open to question whether this has not done the writings more harm than
good. The nectar and ambrosia of Emerson does not assimi-
late kindly with Thoreau's harsh and rather acrid substance.
Thoreau was a humorist,—in the old, not in the new sense,—
and it is indispensable to the prosperity of the humorist that
he be himself. He was no optimist, and he cared nothing for
the welfare of mankind, or the progress of civilization. When,
therefore, he ornaments his records of the facts of nature with
interpretations of their moral and spiritual significance, we
feel a sense of incongruity. The interpretations have not the
air of developing spontaneously from the interior of the
writer's thought; they are deliberately fitted on from the outside, and the marks of juncture smoothed off. On the other
hand, it did come naturally to Thoreau to fall into a vein of
talking about natural objects—plants, animals and meteor-
ology—as if they were human creatures, and to credit them
with likes, dislikes, thoughts and personalities. When he does
this, he is entertaining and attractive, and it is a pity he did
not develop a vein so proper to him, rather than snatch with
his earthly hands at the Empyrean.

His poems of observation were good, and, like a pointer-dog,
he could fix his gaze upon an object for a long time at a stretch.
Nevertheless, he cannot be considered an especially objective
writer. He reverts continually to himself, and examines his
own attitude and impressions in regard to the thing even more
solicitously than the thing itself. The poet in him helps the
naturalist, but the philosopher sophisticates him. Now and
then, in the midst of the pathless woods, we are aware of a
queer bookish flavor in the air. The literary artist arranges his

little scene, pleasing in its way, and well done; only it was not just the kind of pleasure we were looking for. Other and greater artists can do that better: what we want of Thoreau is his own peculiar service, and nothing else.

In truth, he was not free from affectations; he was radically provincial; and often (as children complain of one another) he was "disagreeable." But he had deep and true thoughts, he was of pure and upright life and he made a real and lasting impression. He deserves the reputation that he has with the average reader, though not the violent panegyrics of his thick-and-thin admirers. He assumed the stoicism and some of the habits of the Indian, and his physical senses were approximately as acute as theirs; but he was really a civilized man who never found a home in civilization. One leaves him with a feeling of unmixed kindliness; and in his "Walden," his "Week on the Concord and Merrimac," his "Cape Cod" and other books, will be found many passages worthy of preservation, which only he could have written.

From Julian Hawthorne and Leonard Lemmon, *American Literature: A Text-Book for the Use of Schools and Colleges* (Boston: D.C. Heath & Co., 1892), pp. 145-148.

REMINISCENCES OF

THOREAU

MORE than forty years ago half a dozen boys were on the east bank of the Assabet river taking a sun bath after their swim in the stream. They were talking about the conical heaps of stones in the river, and wishing that they knew what built them. There were about as many theories as there were boys, and no conclusion had been arrived at, when one of the boys said "here comes Henry Thoreau, let us ask him." So when he came near, one of the boys asked him "what made those heaps of stones in the river." "I asked a Penobscot Indian that question" said Thoreau "and he said 'the musquash did,' but I told him that I was a better Indian than he, for I knew and he did not," and with that reply he walked off. John — said, "that is just like him, he never will tell a fellow anything unless it is in his lectures, darn his old lectures about chipmunks and Injuns, I wont go to hear him," and the unanimous conclusion of the boys was, that when they got left again, another man would do it. The boys could not understand Thoreau, and he did not understand boys, and both were losers by it.

While looking over Thoreau's "Autumn" lately, the writer was reminded of the time when Thoreau and the writer's father spent some two or three weeks running anew the boundary lines in Sudbury woods. I think it was in 1851, and there were grave disputes, and law suits seemed probable but after a while these two men were selected to fix the bounds. The real trouble was owing to the variation of the compass, the old lines having been run some 200 years before; but Thoreau understood his business thoroughly and settled the boundary question so that peace was declared. Thoreau's companion was an old lumberman and woodchopper and a close observer of natural objects: but he said that Thoreau was the best man he had ever known in the woods. He would climb a tree like a squirrel, knew every plant and shrub and really seemed to have been born in the forest. Thoreau asked many questions; one of them was, "Do you know where there is a white grape, which grows on high land, which bears every year and is of superior quality?" "Yes," was the reply. "It is a little north of Deacon Dakins' rye field and when the grapes are ripe if you are not on the windward side your nose will tell you where they are." Thoreau laughed and appeared satisfied.

About this time Thoreau went to a party in Concord, and he says in his journal or diary, that he would rather eat crackers and cheese with his old companion in the woods.

It is a great mistake to suppose that Thoreau was a solitary student of natural history in Concord and vicinity at that time. He was better equipped for his work, and could record his observations and discoveries better than his fellow students and this was enough to make him famous in later years.

There was a young man who worked on a farm one year, and saved his money like a miser, to spend it the next year in travel and the study of natural history. This was done for several years or so long as the writer knew him. Another deliberately chose a hunter's and trapper's life in the wild, northwestern section of our great country, and he had the nerve and determination to stick to his wild, dangerous pursuit. There was a man in Burlington, Mass., 70 years old who would be in the woods and fields as early as 3 o'clock during the summer months, and as soon as he could see in the winter, returning in time to do a full day's work at the shoe bench.

He was a most enthusiastic student, but he was a good business man as well. He supplied the city stables with skunk's oil at $2.00 per quart, sold woodcocks and partridges

in their season, and by his skilful administration of strych-
nine cleared the country of foxes and other pests, and put
many dollars in his pocket. On Sundays he would let his birds
and squirrels out of their cages, call in the dog and cat, and a
pet lamb, and then, the boys said, "father was in heaven." This
man's sons solved the problem which had never been solved
before; namely, "where is the other end of a squirrel's hole?"
and the name of Skelton is forever more associated with that
problem which had vexed the rustic minds for centuries. I was
much pleased with the reply which a Lynn shoemaker made
me when I asked him if he read Thoreau's books? He replied
that he only read them during the winter months, when he
could not go out and look for himself, and that they were a
good substitute for his out door rambles.

These unknown men are, and have been the branch lines,
the feeders of the Grand Trunk naturalists, and they have not
lived in vain.

There was a great intermediate class between Emerson and
the Canadian wood chopper who would have gladly aided
Thoreau if he had been a little more human in his dealings
with them. The modest, unpretending Concord farmers who
cultivated their fields, educated their children, paid their
taxes for the support of schools, churches, and their chosen
form of government, whose sons gave their lives for their
country in its years of peril, are not to be sneered at and
despised by men whose occupations and opinions differ from
theirs. In the language of Ruskin "let us think less of
peculiarity of employment and more of excellence of
achievement."

Crayon.

REMINISCENCES OF

THOREAU II.

THOREAU often visited the west park of Concord, passing along the east bank of the Assabet river from Derby's bridge up the stream, along the high banks which overlook the river to the land formerly owned by Timothy Shehan, and from there to the Ministerial swamp and vicinity where he first found the climbing fern. The writer saw him the day he found the rare plant while returning home with his prize. I never saw such a pleased, happy look on his face as he had that day. He took off his hat, in the crown of which the fern was coiled up, and showed me the dainty, graceful glory of the swamp. He said it had never been seen before in the New England states, outside of the botanical gardens in Cambridge, and he volunteered the information that it grew in a swamp between the place we were on and Sudbury.

Soon after, perhaps two weeks, two men, who said they came from Cambridge came to me and asked where the climbing fern grew. I did not tell them for many reasons, perhaps the best one was that which Thoreau gave while speaking of the pink lilies which grew on the Cape. In reply to my question whether he had seen the pink lilies which grew in Hayward's pond in Westvale, he said he had never seen them there or on the Concord rivers, but there was a place on the Cape, a sort of creek, where they had grown unnoticed by the inhabitants until Theodore Parker saw them one summer and gathered them, and "after that," said Thoreau, "the bumpkins grubbed them up root and branch, and almost exterminated them."

While passing over the route mentioned at the beginning of this article, Thoreau was only a gleaner after his father and mother, who together had been seen there more than once by the writer, years before Henry D. followed in their footsteps.

Let the young men and women of Concord who have a love for the study of botany and natural history not be afraid to glean after Thoreau, for he said "that he had much to report on this subject." Two ladies who spent a part of the last summer in Acton found many rare plants and flowers, and introduced the Acton people to their own near neighbors. Last year there were large bunches of the beautiful bloodroot flowers gathered the 14th of April. The yellow violets grow in North Acton, the white "huckleberry" grows in several places, the beaked hazel is abundant on the northern slopes of Nagog hill, and late in November the air in the woods is heavy with the odor of the witch hazel which puts forth and blossoms like love and generosity in some human beings only just before the winter of death.

Crayon

Concord *Enterprise*, April 13 and 22, 1893. [By Horace Hosmer]

The

writer of these *Reminiscences*—Horace R. Hosmer, of North Actio (*Ivit ad plures!*) was once a pupil of John and Henry D. Thoreau. There is shining in the editor's memory the recollection of a visit with him—alas, the only one!—and a note book of memoranda is a pleasant token of that interview.

He that we knew as Horace R. Hosmer was a man in whom chill penury did not repress

"— — — — — — the noble rage,
And freeze the genial current of the soul."

All his "schooling" was had from the Thoreau brothers, and this he supplemented by a most esurient reading. He had from Nature a fine discrimination, a broad and catholic charity and an undaunted courage of opinion. He bought the only copy of the third edition of *Leaves of Grass* that was sold in Concord, although an Emerson had written

"I am not blind to the wonderful gift of *Leaves of Grass*. I find it the most extraordinary piece of wit and wisdom that America has yet contributed. I am very happy in reading it, as great power makes us happy. It meets the demand I am always making of what seems the sterile and stingy Nature, as if too much handiwork or too much lymph in the temperament were making our Western wits fat and mean. I give you joy of your free and brave thought. I have great joy in it. I find incomparable things, said incomparably well, as they must be. I find the courage of treatment which so delights us, and which large perception only can inspire.

I greet you at the beginning of a great career which yet must have had a long foreground somewhere, for such a start. I rubbed my eyes a little, to see if this sunbeam were no illusion; but the solid trace of the book is a sober certainty. It has the best merits, namely, of fortifying and encouraging."

Despite this explicit and emphatic *imprimatur* for "the most extraordinary piece of wit and wisdom that America has yet contributed," *one* copy found in "Old Concord" *one* man broad-minded enough to buy it. Surely, a prophet is not without honor, save in his own country!

This very copy came to us after this solitary Concordian had passed from the mirage we call "Life" into the *lumen siccum* of Eternity. It is filled with his pencillings, showing that he had "read and inwardly digested" as your mere college-bred suckling can never do.

A distinguished librarian once said "The supreme question in regard to any book is, What has it done for any man's soul?" It is by this touchstone that we will try the Hosmer copy of *Leaves of Grass*.

Opening the pages almost at random, we find this marked:

> "I do not know what follows the death of my body,
> But I know full well that whatever it is, *it is best for me,*
> And I know that whatever is *really Me* shall live
>   just as much as before.

(The italics are his, and all that follow are the same.)

> "You are not thrown to the winds—you gather certainly
>   and safely around yourself,
> *Yourself*! *Yourself*! *Yourself*, forever and ever!
>
> It is not *to diffuse* you that you were born or your
>   mother and father—it is *to identify* you,
> It is not that you should be undecided, but that you
>   should be decided.
>
> **Something long preparing and formless is arrived and
>   formed in you,**
> You are therefore secure, whatever comes or goes.
>
> *The threads that were spun are gathered, the weft
>   crosses the warp, the pattern is systematic.
>
> The soul guest that was coming—he waited long, for
>   reasons—he is now housed,
> He is one of those who are beautiful and happy—
>   he is one of those that to look upon and be
>   with is enough.

I shall go with the rest,
We cannot be stopped at a given point—that is no
    satisfaction,
To show us a good thing, or a few good things, for a
    space of time—that is no satisfaction,
We must have the indestructible breed of the best,
    regardless of time.

Pleasantly and well-suited I walk,
Whither I walk I cannot define, but I know it is good,
The whole universe indicates that it is good,
The past and the present indicate that it is good.

I swear I think there is nothing but immortality!
That the exquisite scheme is for it, and the nebulous
    float is for it, and the cohering is for it!
And all preparation is for it! and identity is for it!
    and life and death are altogether for it!

Evidently, tried by the old librarian's test, this man found
the Emersonian *imprimatur* satisfactory to his soul, for the
book had proven itself "fortifying and encouraging."

When the keepsake came to us there was found in it a
clipping from the *Concord Enterprise*, faded and yellow with
age. As it belongs to the history of *Leaves of Grass*, it shall be
preserved in these pages from the accidents of a scrap-
book.

"How *Leaves of Grass* first came to the Concord People."

"In 1856 a gentleman residing in Woburn sent a copy of
Walt Whitman's *Leaves of Grass* to the writer, who was
then living in Burlington. To me it was certainly unlike
anything I had seen or read. I showed the book to some of
my friends and adverse criticisms were plentiful. Dr. Daniel
Parker of Bilerica had patients in Burlington, so one day he

carried the book home and at the end of a week he returned it, saying that it was a wonderful book, but he greatly regretted that some portions of it had not been omitted. However, he became so innoculated with the virus of the book that he was delivered of a poem in a similar style within a year, and readers of the *Lowell Journal* of that time and later may remember his "Concord River" and other pieces.

Of course my Concord friends must see the book, so to Concord it went and was passed from one hand to another, and to my great surprise, it was warmly commended. These men were mostly mechanics who read the *Atlantic Monthly* and some of the Reviews, and I considered them good judges.

The book was among the people, passing from hand to hand till one sad day it fell into the hands of a maidenlady, who was old enough to know better, was wealthy and charitable and claimed to know something about books; and she with a pencil erased or blackened all the (to her) objectionable words and phrases.

It was a trying time for me, and what I said was "neither brave, polite or wise." I sent the book to a bookbinder and ordered the best Russia leather cover that he could put on, and in this shape returned it to the owner.

When the new edition by Thayer and Eldridge, 1860-61, came out, I bought at Stacey's book store the only copy sold in Concord, and have it now, with criticisms by doctors, ministers and laymen, wise and otherwise—I mean the criticisms, of course.

I lent the book to a friendly Swede who returned it with a slip of paper in it on which was written the following lines:

'With Solomons wisdom, Samsons strength,
  wi meet quit many men.
Dog scarce wi meet the Sacred Truths
  this Leaves of Grass Contain.' "

Perhaps the untutored Swede's *imprimatur* is a truer testimonial than could possibly come from any Harvard graduate.

[*For a modern transcription of some of this material, see Appendix B of
   George Hendrick*, Remembrances of Concord and the Thoreaus,
   pp. 133-134.]

MEMORIES

OF THE THOREAUS

AND OF OTHER NOTABLE PEOPLE IN CONCORD

Mr. Irving Allen Gives His Memories of Hawthorne and A. B. Alcott—Thoreau a Delightful Talker—A Remarkable Group Under a New England Roof 43 Years Ago.

O F all the days of my student life at Harvard there are few connected with more delightful memories than those that recall friendships formed at old Concord. Especially do I remember in these later days a winter evening 43 years ago at the pleasant home of the Thoreaus.

It was some family anniversary—a birthday, I think—and late in a February day of 1851 our little party started on a sleigh-ride to the famous town.

It was one of those mild afternoons, toward the close of winter, that breathe promises of the coming spring; a day described by a classic poet as "nurse of the beautiful Halcyon." Under the influence of the February sun the snow was melting fast, and the sleighing between Cambridge and Concord was not of the best; but a merrier party of eight never journeyed together on runners or wheels, and the too-frequent "bare spots" were doubtless far more annoying to our tugging and toiling horses than to us.

Alas—of that jocund company but three are left. There was

the poet, some of whose songs are familiar the world over; the divinity student, whose best years were spent as a missionary under burning Indian skies; the student of law, who eleven years later exchanged the revised statutes for the sword, going to the war as second lieutenant in a Massachusetts colored regiment, and within two years becoming commander of the post of Key West, and a judge advocate-general in our army, to die years after the close of the war at the hands of a rebel assassin in a South-western city. But these things were of the future, and, happily, unknown to us.

At the period of which I write, the Thoreau family consisted of the father and mother, their now famous son—Henry David, a daughter, Sophia, and two maiden sisters of the elder Thoreau.

Mr. John Thoreau was in outward aspect and gesture, a typical Frenchman,—a little man with a charming simplicity and amiability both of face and manner. In his early days he had been a manufacturer of lead pencils; but as a business man was never a distinguished success. It has been said that he was too honest to compete with prevalent business methods, and it is certain that he was not a man of great energy or force of character.

As is true of so many eminent men, it was to his mother that Henry Thoreau was indebted for his intellectual preeminence, and whatever measure of genius he possessed, I shall always remember Mrs. Thoreau as one of the most remarkable and brilliant women I ever met. As a conversationalist, I never knew her equal, and the flashes of witty rejoinder from her lips ever keen and nimble as the play of a rapier in the hands of a practised swordsman—and not seldom, well-nigh as dangerous.

Mr. John Thoreau was an amiable and delightful old gentleman, who always seemed well satisfied to let his wife do most of the talking. He was, as I have said, a little man, apparently half a head shorter in stature than his wife, whose slender proportions gave her the appearance of unusual height.

Henry had neither the features nor the expression of his father, but greatly resembled his mother in many respects; his peculiar taciturnity, however, was by no means a maternal inheritance.

The daughter, Miss Sophia Thoreau, to whom we are indebted for the publication of her brother's letters, and more than one of the other volumes of his works, was at this time a woman of about 40, of strong and cultivated intellect, and lacking only the divine gift of expression to be herself a writer of note. The two maiden aunts were lovable and admirable old ladies, of whom I have pleasant and delightful memories.

It was a memorable occasion—that evening at Concord forty-three years ago. The company was such as will never again be gathered under a New England roof. There was Emerson—grave, severe, child-like—yet not unconscious of his greatness, nor of the love and reverence that compassed him on every side.

There was Hawthorne, on whom nature, prodigal of marvelous gifts, had bestowed not only genius of the loftiest type, but its outward presentment in face and form.

It was at this date, about two years since the publication of "The Scarlet Letter," and the fame of the author, which has since glowed with an ever brightening lustre, was even then becoming world-wide. It was the dream of my youth to meet the magician whose "Grandfather's Chair" had been the delight and marvel of my childhood, and to whom I owed—for the "Twice Told Tales"—my passport into the magic realms of genius and deep, poetic thought.

Hawthorne was then in the prime of life and at the acme of his transcendent intellectual powers. His resemblance at this period to the admirable engraving which is the frontispiece to Bridge's recently published "Reminiscences" was more striking than to Thompson's well-known portrait, the work of earlier years.

Well, I was at length in the very room with the object of my youthful idolatry; but I asked no introduction, and did not once venture to approach him throughout the evening.

Indeed, he seemed to me literally unapproachable; for I do not think he addressed a dozen words to a person present during the evening. He seemed apart from all the rest of that cheerful company; yet it was scarcely the shrinking from society of a man naturally shy and sensitive; but rather—as it seemed to me—that he existed in an atmosphere peculiarly his own.

I heard it said that he was more sociable and cheerful in company when his wife was present; on the evening of which I write, Mrs. Hawthorne was at the bedside of her father—Dr. Peabody—whose death occurred a few days later.

There too was the benignant face of that most unpractical of philosophers—A. Bronson Alcott, and one of his afterward distinguished daughters, which one I do not recollect; and there was Rockwood Hoar, a stern law-giver, and not always over gentle in his communion with his fellow men, but witty and genial, and kindly enough in social intercourse. There too was the judge's sister Elizabeth, lovely alike in person and character, whose epitaph in the sacred cemetery of Sleepy Hollow written it was said by Emerson—has been read and pondered by thousands of visitors to that Mecca among the burial places of New England.

I do not remember whether Mr. F. B. Sanborn, who still lives and writes, was a guest on that well-remembered evening; indeed, I may confess, perhaps to my shame, that a certain youthful prejudice against the honorable guild of school-masters—of which Mr. Sanborn was then a member—would have precluded any peculiar pleasure on my part in his company, this was, I think, about three years before that gentleman's temporary renown as the victim of an attempted political abduction.

Forty-three years ago Henry D. Thoreau was scarcely recognized in the ranks of American authors, though the Maine Woods sketches had been before the public several years; I forget whether it was before or after the publication of "Walden."

He was chiefly known to the good people of Concord as a shy and eccentric recluse; a man who preferred the society of birds and fishes and other wild living things to that of his fellow men; a citizen who, a few years earlier, had denied the State's right of personal taxation; and proved the sincerity of his convictions by peaceably allowing a constable to conduct him to Concord jail, from which he was released after a brief captivity on the interposition of dear old "Aunt Jane"—one of his father's maiden sisters—who insisted on paying the sum in dispute, much, however, against her nephew's wishes.

Anything in the way of a social gathering was exceedingly distasteful to Henry Thoreau; and as I was afterwards told—it was only at his mother's urgent request that he honored our little company with his presence; but however strongly he may have felt himself out of his element, there was no evidence of it in his conduct or manner.

Although by no means a free or ready conversationalist, Thoreau was at times a charming talker. It was delightful, when a sympathetic listener was at hand, to hear this instinctive naturalist—if I may use such a term—discourse of his innocent and interesting intimates of the woods and the lake. I remember how his eye kindled when he talked of his frequent discoveries in the Concord fields and meadows, of Indian relics. I think it is Hawthorne who somewhere speaks, perhaps in the marvelous introduction to the "Mosses," of this exceptional aptitude in Thoreau.

This is not the place, nor is mine the pen, to indite any estimate of Thoreau the man or the author. Like all self-centered men,—like, indeed, all men and women of any measure of true originality—Henry Thoreau was doubtless more or less of an egotist. It is no doubt true that he over-estimated in some directions his own powers. Thus, while a true poet in mind and heart, he was certainly sadly deficient in the gift of poetic expression. As Lowell says, in quoting some of his stanzas: *"Here is very bad verse and very good imagination,"* but that he was a most delightful and instructive companion with whom to spend a summer afternoon, especially out of doors, I can testify from personal and most pleasant experience.

At the date of which I speak, Margaret Fuller—then the Countess Ossoli—was living in Italy, and I think there was no member of her family present—, unless I may designate the husband of her younger sister—Wm. Ellery Channing; not unknown as a writer, but more distinguished as enjoying the friendship of Hawthorne and Thoreau.

The hours sped all too swiftly, and the end came to that evening of happy memory. As we passed the old First Parish meeting house, the sweet-toned bell in its quaint steeple struck the hour of eleven. Three times, in later years, I heard that solemn voice under very different circumstances; once, on the afternoon of an April day eleven years later, when all that was mortal of Henry Thoreau was borne to its resting-place in Sleepy Hollow beside father, brother and sister. Emerson's beautiful words on that funeral day of early spring were indeed prophetic of the fame which came too late to warm the heart of the gifted student and lover of nature:—

"Dead ere his prime, and hath not left his peer," in his own peculiar and most interesting department of letters.

Two years later, on the memorable 23d of May, 1864, the voice of the old bell summoned another great man to his grave under the whispering pines of Sleepy Hollow; he of whom James Russell Lowell truly says: "*The world may see another Shakespeare, but never another Hawthorne.*"

Who that was in the old church on that loveliest of summer days can ever forget the hour and the scene? The wild wayside flowers with which the walls, the communion-table and the pulpit were sweetly adorned; the coffin, bearing on its closed lid a wreath of apple-blooms from the Old Manse and the sadly significant manuscript of the unfinished tale of "Little Pansy"—called by Alexander Smith "the sweetest child in English literature;" the group of illustrious Americans—the like of which has, I believe, never again been gathered; Emerson and Whittier, Longfellow and Lowell, Stoddard and Steadman, Agassiz and Holmes, Geo. W. Curtis, Edwin P. Whipple, Benj. F. Thomas, Franklin Pierce—, and many besides of scarcely less note in the world of statesmanship, art and letters.

Almost twenty years later on in time, to the measured music of the same old bell, I followed the body of Emerson to its grave in famous Sleepy Hollow. Even then the ranks of the great associates who walked beside Hawthorne on that perfect day of May were sadly thinned; and today there are living, I believe, but three: Stoddard and Steadman, and the beloved and honored *Autocrat*, Dr. Holmes.

Forty-three years is a long space in a human life, and few of the friends assembled that February night of 1851 under the hospitable roof-tree of the Thoreaus are among the living of today. I spent the summer of 1869 with my family in Concord, and many were the pleasant hours passed that season with the two remaining members of the Thoreau family, Miss Sophia and her aged mother.

During the troubled years just preceeding the war, the prevailing sentiment in Concord, under the intellectual leadership of Emerson and the Hoar family, was very strongly anti-slavery; the feeling against the fugitive-slave law and its promoters was especially bitter; and the leaders of the abolition party had no warmer friends or more faithful adherents than in the famous centre of transcendental thought and culture. Every member of the Thoreau family was a sincere and consistent hater of the slave system—I may almost say, of the South itself. I think the only appearance of Henry in public as an orator was at a meeting of the townspeople on the evening of the day of Capt. Brown's execution, on which occasion he made an address almost revolutionary in the violence of its invective.

His sister Sophia was, as I have said, a woman of strong mind and independent thought, and fully sympathized with her brother in his loathing of human slavery.

At Hawthorne's funeral I sat with Miss Thoreau, in a pew of the old parish Meetinghouse, and in a brief conversation before the commencement of the service, I inquired if the family had known much of Hawthorne since his return from Europe. In reply she told me that they had seen but little of the great author "since his fall."

I naturally supposed that the expression referred to some accident of which I had not heard, but was presently made to understand by his "fall" the speaker intended to characterize his labor of love in writing the life of his classmate and life-long friend—Franklin Pierce!

It was thus that even the friends and neighbors of the immortal writer misjudged his disinterested and kindly effort in behalf of one to whom his soul was knit in the bonds of a friendship as rare as it was pure and unselfish.

But at the date of which I am writing now, the war was a dark memory of the past and our talk was no longer of battles and strange perils, but of old friends and scenes with which we had been familiar in other days.

Three years later—in 1872, on the 23d day of May, the anniversary of Hawthorne's burial day—I called at the old home on Main street, and for the last time spent a charming hour in conversation with the dear old lady. I call it a *conversation*,—it was in reality a monologue, for I do not think I found a chance to utter half a dozen consecutive words throughout the interview.

It was Mrs. Thoreau's 86th birthday; and never, during all the years of our acquaintance, do I remember her as more witty and vivacious, or fuller of life and youthful spirit than on that afternoon of her last earthly May.

So frail was her bodily aspect that she seemed, indeed, almost pure spirit: and her death, which occurred a few months later was but the quiet and painless entrance of the soul on its eternal home. It is the literal truth that she died with a song on her lips; if I remember rightly, it was Sarah Flower Adams' noble hymn, "Nearer, My God, to Thee."

On an afternoon of October, 1874, two friends—one a man not unknown to fame—stood together on the narrow path that divides the graves of Hawthorne and Thoreau in the sacred burial-place of old Concord. Presently a procession entered the cemetery, and slowly climbed the hill to the resting-place of the Thoreaus.

It was the funeral-train of the last of the name—Sophia—whose death had occurred a few days earlier in a distant city.

They rest together on the pine-clad slope in Sleepy Hollow—father and mother, sons and daughters; a family re-united in death; close beside them the grave of Hawthorne, and a little farther off that of Emerson.

It is probable that the fame of the singularly gifted son will outlive that of many a writer of loftier genius and nobler endowments of expression, for apart from intellectual power or skill of utterance, there was something in the personality of that sincere student and loving child of nature especially winning and attractive.

By those who can truly sympathize with the man rather than the author, who really knew him—personally or in his works—will his memory be kept green and fragrant.

Irving Allen.

Boston *Daily Advertiser*, April 23, 1894.

THE RIVERSIDE THOREAU

FIRST COMPLETE EDITION OF HIS WRITINGS

The merits of the Concord Naturalist Compared with Those of Emerson—His Books of Permanent Value—Reasons of the Growth of His Fame—One of Our Great Writers.

The complete edition of a man's writings, when made for the first time, marks the climax of his fame, and if his works continue to be called for in complete edition it shows that his fame is permanent. At the death of Thoreau, in 1862, only two of his books had been published, "Walden" and "Concord and Merrimac Rivers." These were two of his best and strongest works, but by neither of them was he assured that he could obtain rank as an American author. He wrote in a style that was new to American readers, and on subjects for which there did not exist a sufficient audience. His "Concord and Merrimac Rivers" sold hardly at all, and his "Walden" was a long time in paying the expenses of its publication. At his death he was regarded as a bright but eccentric man, whose individuality was so excessive that no one could get on with him, and who had no special message to the world. But hardly had the grass grown over his grave before his reputation began to increase, and it has grown steadily during the last 30 years up to that point where a complete edition of his writings has been called for, and we have at the Christmas holidays of 1893 for the first time the full Riverside Thoreau. It is an event of the first importance in American literature that so original, so unhackneyed, so fresh and so inspiring a writer as Henry D. Thoreau should have fought his way at this long interval after his death, on his merits alone, to the very front rank in American letters. Complete editions of other American authors were a matter of course. Irving, Bancroft and Cooper obtained a complete edition of their works at a comparatively early date, and Hawthorne, Emerson, Longfellow and Whittier received this honor as a tribute due to their memories and as a right which American readers claimed. Mr. Lowell had hardly passed away before a complete edition of his ritings was on the market, and an edition that was worthy of his fame and of his publishers. Nobody would have dreamed 30 years ago that Thoreau would ever attain the literary honor which his writings have at length commanded and received. This Riverside Thoreau is in some respects

THE PROUDEST ACHIEVEMENT

which has been secured in American letters. It has come without advertising, without any effort to draw attention to his writings, simply and only through the inherent strength and vitality of articles for which he could find no market while living.

A similar posthumous vitality was witnessed in the appreciation of the late Richard Jefferies, an English writer who had the same absorbing passion for outdoor life that Thoreau had, without his wonderfully keen and individual appreciation of the forces of nature, but it would have taken a dozen Richard Jefferies to make one Thoreau, and the time has come for a literary estimate of Henry D. Thoreau which should be as generous in its appreciation of his merits as his publishers have been in presenting his writings to the world in their complete and beautiful form. It is evident that Thoreau, like many other great writers, has created his audience, and that the people who appreciate him are those who believe in reality, and who like an author because he meets their needs and satisfies their aspirations. The time was when Thoreau was regarded as a second and tamer edition of Emerson, but that day has passed by. Emerson and Thoreau are like two stars of the first magnitude moving on parallel lines through the heavens. They borrow nothing from each other, but each draws his inspiration from the same central source, and each does his thinking under his own hat. Perhaps two sturdier Americans never lived, two men who were more indebted to books and intercourse with men for their culture, or less indebted than they were to the schools and letters for the originality and mental force which they employed in the work of thinking. Emerson may be the profounder man, but Thoreau gave an amount of thought and meditation to nature and the natural world which Emerson divided between nature and man. Both of these writers were men who wrote but one book. The 10 volumes of Thoreau and the 13 of Emerson are only different chapters in the same story, but Thoreau magnifies where Emerson reverences nature.

The first thought which impresses one in taking up Thoreau's writings is that he recognizes the natural world for all that it is worth. Here the

FORCES OF NATURE ARE STUDIED

by one who believes that they are as eternal as himself, and that all parts of creation are intimately related to one another, as elemental as himself, and parts of a great totality. The most remarkable thing about him was that he was born into this world with no partiality for traditions. He was free from the prejudices of other men, and grew up with a stern and emphatic protest against the subserviency of his own mind to the methods of education and belief which have been regarded by others as of supreme importance. He did not rebel against the pursuit of an education, and here he yielded to traditions in order to become a man of culture, but in religion, in politics, in the ordering of his social life he was a man by himself, separate from all others. "His soul was like a star and dwelt apart." In the ways in which other men depend upon the guidance of others he depended upon himself, but he had no sense of the continuity of things in practical life. His father was a manufacturer of lead pencils, and the son practised his father's art until he produced the best pencil that was ever made. He then gave up the making of pencils and could never be induced to prepare another. He had a complete disregard for the ordinary means by which people acquire wealth and obtain distinction, and nothing could turn him from his "other worldliness" to the ordinary pursuits of life. A man who could hold himself, in his capacity as an individual, thus apart from his fellows in an attitude of self-dependence, and who had infinite resources in himself, must have been endowed with original powers of a high order, and it was through these qualities that Thoreau from the first became a pronounced and original man.

This originality was seen in his study of nature. Probably all original observers have much the same feeling toward fundamental facts and experiences. Homer and Wordsworth and Emerson rejoiced alike in the bare facts which impressed their imaginations and gave them the sense of

BEAUTY IN THE EXTERNAL WORLD,

but, though the contact with nature was a great part of their lives, it was not, as in the case of Thoreau, nearly the whole of life. Here was a man to whom the facts of the external world were a substantial part of himself. He lived in them; he subordinated his method of existence to them; he studied nature to learn her secrets, and the birds and the small animals learned to know him as their familiar friend. At the same time he was equal to the impressions received from nature by the imagination of the poet. There are many passages in his different volumes, notably in "Concord and Merrimac Rivers," where he rises into the highest spiritual moods in writing of the outward world. He ceases to be a naturalist and becomes a seer. It is here that he is in sympathy with what is best and highest in Emerson. He touches the same range of ideas, but they come to him as swallow flights of recurring thoughts; they are hardly ever more than immediate impressions. The great charm of Thoreau's study of nature is its freshness, its simplicity, its directness. There is immense fondness for the woods, the landscape, the water and the sky, and the language in which they are described is that familiar speech which shows that the very color of things has been impressed upon the writer's mind and heart. Something of the same individuality of impression is found in the writings of Mr. Frank Bolles and Mr. Bradford Torrey. Neither of these men have the spiritual impressions of nature which are always cropping out in Thoreau's writings, but they are his equals in patient observation, in close and right seeing, in reporting things at first hand.

Another interesting feature of Thoreau's writings is the independence of his views. No person who is a strict conventionalist could take much satisfaction in his writing, but any one who thinks for himself and appreciates fresh points of view in others will find in his books, as we find in Emerson's, a freshness of view in matters of experience that is as attractive as it is bracing. Mr. William Ellery Channing, who wrote in 1873 a book, entitled,

"THOREAU, THE NATURALIST,"

confined the biography of his friend entirely to the reports of his moods, his whims and his ideas, but this was so entirely contrary to the usual method of writing biography, which commonly requires the mention of some of the material facts of a man's life, that his book never found much favor with the people. It did not even mention the date of his death, though it mentioned nearly everything else that belonged to his personality. Thoreau took the stand in dealing with the facts of life which was that of a come-outer. His friend Emerson understood him exactly, and valued this fine independence of conventions which confirmed his own view of the methods of enjoying life. He never voted, never married, never attended church, and had not a particle of respect for the opinions of any man or body of men, but his great object in life was to find out the truth for himself and experimentally. Most men take their knowledge of life on tradition, but he cared nothing for traditions and repudiated them whenever they came in his way. A man of such independent views may be right or wrong, but he is always interesting. One of the most delightful characters in French literature is Montaigne, who was one of the most independent of men, and who dared, as Thoreau dared, to live as he thought best. His confessions in regard to himself are those which only a brave and true man could write, and they make his writings immensely interesting. Dr. Sam Johnson is, perhaps, the most interesting personality in English literature, and this comes from the fact that he dared to strike out and say what he thought, and Boswell had the courage to write out what he heard Dr. Johnson say, and thus preserve it for all time. Thoreau had no Boswell to report him, but, like Montaigne, he reported himself. His writings are wonderfully rich in their dissent from the established opinion. They are not simply the one-sided opinions of a radical, but they express the habitual and well-grounded convictions of a man who has an order and a creed of his own, and whose life is regulated by it. It is this quality that gives a meaning to his utterances which other men do not express, and it imparts to his writings

A PERSONALITY THAT GROWS

with his fame.

It is not necessary to indorse his opinions in order to commend them. The value of the truth from his point of view consists in its honesty of statement and its sincerity and candor. Whatever Thoreau wrote about life and nature was sincere. He asked nobody to help him to understand the world in a natural or in a spiritual sense, and the truth which he arrived at was his own discovery. Here again he strikes the same note which Emerson strikes, although the latter was far more a conventional man than ever Thoreau was. You feel in reading Thoreau that you are in a world of fact and observation which is beyond the ordinary range of thought and experience. There is a sense of the wholeness of life, apart from its traditions, which you find in no other writer. It is as if a new world had been entered for a young person to take up the writings of Thoreau for study, but it is a world which every one ought to enter, and in which a true side of life is approached and studied by one who made himself the master of his thought before he gave it expression. One may demur at a great deal which Thoreau writes, but it will nearly always be found to be consistent with itself, if you grant his point of view. It is a notable thing to find such a consummate truth-seeker in literature. The world is full of books in which authors repeat the conventional and say nothing that is out of the ruts, but throughout these 10 volumes, in which Thoreau is always writing down his observations on nature and life, it is impossible to find a commonplace remark or a dull line. His inspiration is perpetual, and it always smacks of the soil. Thoreau lived in the natural world, communed with nature, with the birds and the animals who came near him, and gathered the secrets of life at first hand. He scorned to use information gathered out of books, and yet he was an omniverous reader of the best literature. No other man in American letters, except Emerson, was such an adept in using over again what he had read as a part of the expression of his own opinion. The result is that no other

AMERICAN, EXCEPT EMERSON

has written with the same freedom, the same sincerity and richness of expression, that Thoreau has employed in treating freely the higher side of our common life.

There can be no question whether his writings are destined to live. They are sure to be read by future generations. They owe nothing to the day or the hour. Their merits have a per-manent basis, like the sun, and they abide like the stars, forever and ever. Thoreau's style is individual, closely identi-fied to his thought, the expression of a man who never rests until he can put his thinking into fitting words. It is a part of himself, and it was a style that began with his thinking and was mature and characteristic from the first. It is the style of a sincere and earnest man whose mind and heart are deeply engaged in his subject, and it is in some respects the most unique and remarkable style ever employed by an American. Mr. F. B. Sanborn has written a biography of Thoreau for the "American Men of Letters" which is an adequate account of his career, giving all the facts which could be gathered about him and the environment of his life in Concord. It was such a book as Mr. Sanborn with his great fondness for detail was admirably prepared to write, and it is indispensable to the literary appreciation of Thoreau. The Riverside edition will be hereafter the one by which his writings will be best known, and a brief account of the different volumes is interesting as the conclusion of this notice. His letters are not now included among his works, but are reserved for separate and extended publication. They are numerous and characteristic, and they belong midway between a biography and his formal writings. The first volume in this new edition is "A Week on the Concord and Merrimac Rivers." It was written in March, 1847. It had hard luck in finding a publisher, but the late firm of James Monroe & Co., Boston, brought it out apparently in the summer of 1849.

RIPLEY AND LOWELL WROTE

kindly notices of it, but it did not sell at all. He was so confident of the success of this work that he borrowed money to pay the expense of publication himself, and was afterward obliged to take up the occupation of a surveyor in order to cancel his obligation. The time is coming when a copy of the first edition of this work will be as rare as the first edition of Hawthorne's "Scarlet Letter," and the late Mr. Alcott did not express himself too strongly when he wrote of this book: "It is purely American, fragrant with the life of New England woods and streams, and could have been written nowhere else. Especially am I touched by his sufficiency and soundness, his aboriginal vigor—as if a man had once more come into nature who knew what nature meant him to do with her: Virgil and White of Selborne, and Izaak Walton and Yankee settler all in one." This is the first, and perhaps the best, of all Thoreau's writings.

"Walden" was published in 1854, but the narrative covers two years that Thoreau lived in his Walden camp, 1845-47. It is a kind of charmed writing which it contains, and it is more consistent as a treatise by itself than any other of his writings. "The Maine Woods" is the next volume in this edition, though it was the second brought out after Thoreau's death. It is entirely occupied with sketches of travel in the forests of Maine. In this work Thoreau was one of the first Americans to explore these forests with the instincts and the spirit of a lover of nature and a literary man. "Cape Cod" was published in the same year with "The Maine Woods." It attempts to do for the Cape region of Massachusetts what he had already done for the forests of Maine. It is rather more a circumstantial book than that volume, but even here Thoreau breaks out in enthusiasm for the sea and the desert, and is original in his comments and reflections. One of his most delightful volumes, as presented in this edition, is the one entitled

"EXCURSIONS IN FIELD AND FOREST."

It was the first volume brought out after his death, and in its present form it includes a large number of miscellaneous papers, which contain his writings of a disconnected character on different aspects of nature. Here "A Yankee in Canada" is introduced, which completes his account of travels in the outer world, beyond Concord. Four volumes, "Summer," "Autumn," "Winter" and "Spring," are drawn directly from his journal, and express in every variety of form his comments on the changes of nature and of animal life, as he familiarly observed them. The final volume is entitled "Miscellanies," and gathers up his writings as they relate to men and affairs. It also includes his poetry to a limited extent, and translations from the Greek classical poets. It is necessary to a complete representation of his thought, and it is introduced by Emerson's biographical sketch of his friend, which is as just and as fair an account of this remarkable individual as has yet been written. Each of these volumes contains an index by itself, and this final volume has a general index similar in character to the one which has been recently added to the Riverside Emerson. By means of this Thoreau can be studied topically, and his views of all sorts of subjects can be ascertained in a moment. Such an index is simply invaluable in finding out where an author's best things are, and it is so minute and detailed that everything in those 10 volumes is rendered accessible to the student of his writings. Three different portraits of Thoreau are given, the only three extant, and in all the material aspects of good book work this edition is representative of the best productions of the Riverside Press. ["The Writings of Henry David Thoreau." With bibliographical introductions and full indexes. The Riverside edition. In 10 volumes. Boston: Houghton, Mifflin & Co.; crown 8 vo.]

Boston *Herald*, December 18, 1893.

"His

Week hardly sold at all, and his *Walden* was a long time in paying the expenses of its publication." This is true enough of the *Week* but hardly so of *Walden*. On the 18th of January, 1856, Thoreau made the following reply to an enquiry: "The *Week* had so poor a publisher that it is quite uncertain whether you will find it in any shop. (The fact being that there were seven hundred copies in his father's garret at that very moment!) I am not sure but authors must turn booksellers themselves. The price is $1.25. If you care enough for it to send me that sum by mail (stamps will do for change) I will forward you a copy by the same conveyance."

"The price is $1.25." At the Arnold sale, in December, 1900, a copy of the *Week*, "editio princeps," was sold for $52.50! Such are the ironies of Literature.

To the same correspondent, February 10th., 1856, Thoreau wrote: "I thank you heartily for the expression of your interest in *Walden*, and hope that you will not be disappointed by the *Week*. You ask how the former has been received. It has found an audience of excellent character, and quite numerous, some 2000 copies having been dispersed. I should consider it a greater success to interest one wise and earnest soul, than a million unwise and foolish." *Some Unpublished Letters of Henry D. and Sophia E. Thoreau*, pp. 27, 31.

Walden was published on the 9th of August, 1854, and at the time of Thoreau's writing the above cited letter had sold at the rate of one hundred copies a month. In the list of books published by Ticknor and Fields in that year *Walden* is advertised at one dollar, retail. The publishers should, then, have received something over $1,300 within eighteen months; so a book selling at the average rate of five copies a day could hardly have required "a long time" to pay for its publication.

"He was so confident of the success of his work that he borrowed money to pay for its publication." It is difficult to imagine Thoreau amongst the money-changers, indeed his journal affords ample evidence that he dealt directly with his "publisher falsely so called." "Nov. 28, 1853. Settled with J. Munroe & Co., and on a new account placed twelve of my books with him on sale. I have paid him directly out of pocket, since the book was published, two hundred and ninety dollars, and taken a receipt for it. This does not include postage, proof-sheets, etc. I have received from other quarters about fifteen dollars. This has been the pecuniary value of the book." *Autumn*, p. 339.

Apparently the book had cost Thoreau some twenty-nine cents or so a copy; the sum paid Munroe & Co. included his "old account" and doubtless that firm was his only creditor for the *Week*.

"Articles for which he could find no market while living." It cost so little to boil the pot for Thoreau that he had as little to do with the 'market,' and his dealings there were marked by his spirit of sturdy independence. Whilst serving as a tutor in William Emerson's family at Staten Island, in 1843, he coquetted briefly with the 'market.' His essay *The Landlord*, and his review of Etzler's book, *Paradise (to be) Regained*, are the outcome of that flirtation. Next, and not until 1847, Horace Greeley's friendly zeal secured a place for his paper on *Thomas Carlyle and his Works* in Graham's Magazine. In 1848 The Union Magazine published *Ktaadn and the Maine Woods*. This contribution occupied a place in five consecutive numbers—something quite noteworthy when one remembers the editor's dislike for the ominous words, "to be continued." It was five years later that Putnam's Magazine presented Thoreau's *Excursion to Canada*, which was abruptly discontinued after George William Curtis had taken the liberty (editorial) of tampering with Thoreau's text. He had written of an old soldier whom he had seen at drill in the garrison in Quebec, "I observed one older man among them, gray as a wharf-rat, and supple as the Devil, marching with the rest who would have to pay for that elastic gait." Curtis had substituted 'eel' for the other fellow: Thoreau promptly condemned the libelous confusion of personalities and refused any further "copy." In vain did Greeley write, "I am sorry that you and C. cannot agree so as to have your whole MS. printed. It will be worth nothing elsewhere after having partly appeared in Putnam's." But Thoreau was inexorable, and he stood bravely by the much maligned "eel (*Anguilla tenuostris*)"—as he would have respectfully written it.

In 1858 the *Atlantic Monthly* presented three parts of *Chesuncook*, and then the series suddenly ended. Thoreau had written, "It is the living spirit of the tree, not its spirit of turpentine, with which I sympathize, and which heals my cuts. It is as immortal as I am, and perchance will go to as high a heaven, there to tower above me still." This pantheistic avowal Lowell, then the editor, had stricken out

"O, what a breach was there, my countrymen!"

Lowell, the graceless Harvard under-graduate, who had been 'rusticated' and consigned to the spiritual refrigerator of the Rev. Barzillai Frost, of Concord, Mass., therein to calm the turbulent current of his hot young blood. Lowell, "Jim," his old-time under-classman, had elided a sentence from his glowing tribute to the lordly pine; had thrown down the very capstone that he had put in its place in the full fervor of his nature-worship. This Lowell had stricken out!

Thoreau was all aflame. This Lowell, even the "Jim" who parts his hair in the middle (!),—what can he know about heavenly things!

Lowell never mentioned the hurtling thunderbolt that came from Concord; it is equally true that he never forgave it. Emerson once said of him: "Lowell has a great deal of self-consciousness, and he never forgave Margaret Fuller and Thoreau for wounding it." *Talks with Emerson*, p. 69. English edition.

In the month immediately following Thoreau's death the genial and generous James T. Fields reopened the *Atlantic*'s pages, in pious expiation, and within two years five of Thoreau's posthumous essays appeared to appease his injured Shade.

The ripples of this rupture ruffled even the calm pages of Thoreau's journal. The offense was committed in July, yet on Nov. 16th, Thoreau wrote:

Preaching? lecturing? Who are ye that ask for these things? What do you want, you puling infants? A trumpet sound that would train you up to manhood! or a nurse's lullaby? The preachers and lecturers deal with men of straw, as they are men of straw themselves. Why, a free-spoken man, of sound lungs, cannot draw a long breath, without causing your rotten institutions to come toppling down, by the vacuum he makes. It would be a relief to breathe one's self occasionally, among men. Freedom of speech! It hath not entered into your hearts to conceive what those words mean. The church, the school, the magazine, think they are free! It is the freedom of a prison yard. What is it you tolerate, you church to-day? Not truth, but a lifelong hypocrisy. The voice that goes up from the 'monthly concerts' is not so brave and cheery as that which rises from the frog-ponds of the land. Look at your editors of popular magazines. I have dealt with two or three of the most liberal of them. They are afraid to print a whole sentence, a sound sentence, a free-spoken sentence. We want to get 30,000 subscribers, and will do anything to get them. They consult the D.D.'s and all the letters of the alphabet before they print a line.

Ubi doler, ibi digitus! True enough, but if the "articles" of such a man did not sell "while he was living," there is a reason: he was a "Poet-Naturalist"; he was not a dealer in pot-boilers.

APPENDIX

An Afternoon in the

University Library

"An Afternoon in the University Library" first appeared in the Inlander *1 (1891): 150–153 and was reprinted in Dr. Jones's Bibliography of Henry*

David Thoreau *(Cleveland: Rowfant Club, 1894), pp. 38–43. The final, bracketed note is, of course, Dr. Jones's.*

I AM the 'most thumbed book' in this library, as Willis said to Walter Savage Landor about the *Imaginary Conversations.*"

I looked around in surprise, for I was certain I was the only person in the alcoves on that sultry afternoon.

"Nor has any book here a more romantic history."

I jumped to my feet and sought the speaker.

"The manuscript of me lay neglected in the desks of caitiff publishers; it was despised and rejected when read by their 'tasters'; dealt out at last piecemeal in a dog's-meat of a journal; pirated into a book by a Yankee admirer—the more's the wonder—and two years later printed at home on the 'half profits' plan, which I compute generally to mean equal partition of the oyster *shells* and a net result of *zero.*"

That trick i' the voice I do well remember;
Is't not the King?

Shakespeare's lines leapt from my lips, and I involuntarily added:

"Carlyle!"

Was ever the like? Right by my side, on an alcove shelf, a well-worn copy of *Sartor Resartus*, as I am a living man, talking! Then from another alcove a different voice:

"You may be the 'most thumbed' book in this library; what of that? More people eat potatoes than *pates de foie gras*. I am not 'thumbed.' I find audience 'fit though few.' I claim, however, a more romantic history than yours. I am one of a thousand copies. The first of us to leave the publisher's shop was sent as a present to one of the gentlest souls that ever brake the bread of friendship. It went to Worcester, Mass. After some time, seventy-four of us were duly given away. In the course of two years two hundred and fifteen of us were slowly sold over the counter. We were often looked at, and as often put down again with a disgusted 'humph!' At the beginning of the third year, the remaining seven hundred and ten of us were piled up in the publisher's cellar. We were tied up in close packages of fifty, and had we not been immortal we had smothered. After two weary years we were taken forth and sent by express to Concord, Mass. There we were received by a rustic looking man who had the serenest face I ever saw, and he handled us with more tenderness than any that had yet touched us. On his own back he carried us, parcel after parcel, up to the garret of his father's house, and when he had piled us compactly, he wiped the sweat from his brow and then surveyed us with a look of quiet cheerfulness. I happened to be at the top corner of the package I was in, and also at the top of the pile, and the paper having been torn during our journey, I could easily look over his shoulder when he sat down at a plain pine desk and wrote in a book:

"For a year or two past my publisher, Munroe, has been writing from time to time to ask what disposition should be made of the copies of 'A Week on the Concord and Merrimac Rivers' still on hand, and at last suggesting that he had use for the room they occupied in his cellar. So I had them all sent to me here, and they have arrived to-day by express, filling the man's wagon, seven hundred and six copies out of an edition of one thousand, which I bought of Munroe four years ago and have ever since been paying for, and have not quite paid for yet. The wares are sent to me at last, and I have an opportunity to examine my purchase. They are something more substantial than fame, as my back knows, which has borne them up two flights of stairs to a place similar to that to which they trace their origin. Of the remaining two hundred ninety and odd, seventy-five were given away, the rest sold. I have now a library of nearly nine hundred volumes, over seven hundred of which I wrote myself. Is it not well that the author should behold the fruits of his labor? My works are piled up in my chamber half as high as my head, my *opera omnia*. This is authorship. These are the work of my brain. There was just one piece of good luck in the venture. The unbound copies were tied up by the printer four years ago in stout paper wrappers, and inscribed 'Henry D. Thoreau's Concord River, fifty copies.' So Munroe had only to cross out 'River,' and write 'Mass.,' and deliver them to the expressman at once. Nevertheless, in spite of this result, sitting beside the inert mass of my work (this made me wince), I take up my pen to-night to record what thought or experience I may have had with as much satisfaction as ever. Indeed, I believe that this result is more inspiring and better than if a thousand had bought my wares. It affects my privacy less, and leaves me freer." [Dr. Jones placed an asterisk at the beginning of this extract directing the reader to "Thoreau's Manuscript Diary, under the date Oct. 28, 1853. quoted in Higginson's *Short Studies of American Authors*, p. 31."]

"Day after day, for nine long years, we lay in that garret, and night after night I saw that man writing in his book at the desk. But of late he coughed a great deal, and night by night I saw that he wrote less. I often caught a look of deep longing in his eyes when he peered out of the garret window on the distant fields; but he did not seem sad, and I never heard from him a single sigh or one repining word.

"One day a solemn hymn floated through the window on the wings of a May breeze from the parlor of the house to our resting place, and then it ceased; and nevermore did I see that serene man writing at the pine desk.

"Some months later we were transported from that garret to the bindery of Ticknor & Fields, and thence to *The Old Corner Bookstore*, each of us having a new jacket on and wearing a new title page. The latter purported that each of us was published by Ticknor & Fields, Boston, 1862, when the actual truth is that we were at that date just fourteen years old—no sucklings, I assure you. But I laughed, for, you see, the binder had not bethought him to tear out a back leaf which announced to the reader that '*Walden, or Life in the Woods, by Henry D. Thoreau, will soon be published.*' Why, bless you, that identical book had been published by Ticknor & Fields nine years before!

"I am an '*editio princeps,*' despite my lying title page. I was born in my author's brain and I was borne on his back when I, too, was 'despised and rejected.''

"And do you say that when you came flouted back into yon garret your author received you as cheerily as you tell?" enquired *Sartor Resartus*.

"Even as I said," was the reply.

"Then," said *Sartor*, "I take back every vaporing word of mine an' will sit at your feet so long as books are read! I take great shame to myself for____"

*   *   *   *   *

"I beg your pardon, Mr. ____, but it's time to close the library."

It was the good Librarian. I had fallen asleep while endeavoring to digest an Ann Arbor boarding-house steak, and I owe it to the Librarian to tell what I dreamed.   *   *   *

[The writer begs leave to say that the essential facts regarding the "1862 edition" of *A Week on the Concord and Merrimac Rivers* are as stated in this fanciful paper. The copy of that book now in the University library is veritably one of those that were carried on Thoreau's back. Will the scholars that use it handle it tenderly for the sake of its history? Seven hundred and five of the unbound sheets were brought by James T. Fields from Thoreau's mother. This edition was exhausted inside of five years and a new one, from fresh type, issued in 1867.]

Index

Adams, Raymond, xi, xxv n
Agassiz, Louis, 133, 210
Alcott, Amos Bronson, 9, 10,
  45, 85–86, 93, 99, 102, 107,
  109, 128, 135, 155, 184–188,
  208, 221
Alcott, Louisa May, 186
Alger, W. R., 102
Allen, Grant, 141
Allen, Irving, 62–63, 117, 205–213
Angell, James B., xvi
Aristotle, 34, 68
Arnold, Matthew, 105, 111, 174
Atlantic Monthly, 38, 72, 85,
  87, 100, 203, 225, 226
Audubon, John James, 123
Augustine, St., 129

Bancroft, George, 215
Barnum, P. T., 101–102, 134
Bartlett, Dr. Josiah, 146
Bigelow, Mrs. Edwin, 145, 147–
  148
Blake, H. G. O., xviii, xxi, xxv,
  38, 39, 83, 86, 92, 103, 155, 159
Blake, William, 93
Bode, Carl, 47
Bolles, Frank, 218
Boston *Daily Advertiser*, xx,
  43, 70, 71, 77
Boswell, James, 4, 79, 134, 219
Briggs, C. F., 99, 101
Brook Farm, 9, 36
Brooks, Squire and Mrs., 147–
  148
Brown, Capt. John, xviii, 13, 66,
  70, 72, 80, 82, 85, 87, 127,
  131, 136, 157, 165, 166, 211
Brown, Dr. John, 77
Brown, Mrs. (Mrs. Emerson's
  sister), 7
Burns, Anthony, 10
Burns, Robert, 106, 174
Burroughs, John, 3, 12, 13, 86,
  133, 142
Butterick, Francis, 146

Carpenter, Edward, 163
Carlyle, Thomas, xiv, xvi, 8, 12,
  22, 108, 125, 155, 174, 175,
  225, 232
Channing, William Ellery, xii,
  xx, 38, 46, 49, 71, 75, 76, 85,
  91, 119, 123, 128, 135, 139,
  144, 155, 156, 160, 164, 169,
  218
Childs, Lydia Maria, 6–7
Coleridge, Samuel Taylor, 19,
  131, 176, 177
Conway, Moncure, 7, 16
Cooper, James Fenimore, 215
Cromwell, Oliver, 13
Curtis, George W., 66, 84, 135,
  210, 225

Dakin, Deacon, 196
Darwin, Charles, 7, 122, 138, 142
Dial, The, 82, 84, 111, 192
Diogenes, 54, 101, 138, 167, 170
Dircks, W. H., 117, 160–163
Duyckinck, Evert, 84